The
DUET

HAILEY GARDINER

Cover design by Yummy Book Covers

Editing by Heather Austin and Jenn Lockwood

www.haileygardiner.com

To my sisters. I'm incredibly proud of the music we made together and the amazing women you've become.

Goodnight, everybody.

Chapter 1

Ella Mae

What kinds of fools decide to get married *outdoors* in December?

Fools in love, I suppose.

Chloe Paulson and Hunter Ward are beautiful, perfectly paired souls. Watching the two of them meet at the end of the aisle makes my heart swell.

I try to keep my eyes on the soon-to-be wedded couple, but it's proving to be difficult. I lay the blame at the feet of another beautiful soul providing the music for said walk down the aisle.

Connor Cane.

Hunter and Chloe are good friends with country music's hottest new act, and somehow, he had the time and was willing to perform live at their intimate wedding ceremony. I'm sure his booking fee is astronomical at this point, but here we are, getting a private serenade of "Make Up," his latest single. This feels like a gift I don't deserve.

Girls across America would kill to be in my shoes right now.

I owe my front-row seat to my best friend and roommate, Lainey Helms, who introduced me to Chloe. She sniffles, glancing skyward before blinking rapidly to keep the tears at bay.

"I can't," she whispers, looking tortured.

"You must." I take her hand in mine and give it a squeeze. Noble of me, really. Comforting others in my own moment of emotional turmoil.

Lainey is engaged to Hunter's twin brother, Luke. They're set to be married next summer, which must be part of the reason she's getting all misty watching Chloe and Hunter tie the knot. She's up next. They're going to be sisters-in-law.

And I'm going to be homeless.

This is what happens when you're the last woman standing. The only one in our tight-knit group of friends who doesn't have marriage in her plans in the near future.

I'm far too busy chasing my dream of getting a *cut*.

Not, like, a haircut. The one all the girls are shelling out for these days. The one with the shag bangs?

I'm talking about *the* cut.

One of my songs getting cut by the right artist. And not just any artist—an artist like Connor Cane. One who could take my name and pull it from the slush pile of rejected country ballads and crossover pop tracks and turn me into a hitmaker.

I know I have the talent, persistence, and patience required to persevere in my line of work as a songwriter. What I'm lacking in...is luck. The twist of fate that results in so-and-so hearing a song you wrote and sending it on to so-and-so who then gets it into the hands of an artist who just so happens to need a song. Your song. *The* song.

My time will come. I know it will.

Despite facing heaps of rejection in the past, I haven't given up hope on making this dream a reality. It's still alive and well, dwelling in that little corner of my heart where all my closest-held desires collide. And although it might be a little awkward, I know exactly what I have to do to move one step closer to making this particular dream of mine come true.

As soon as this ceremony is over, I'm doing it.

I'm going to talk to Connor Cane.

It will be less of an act of bravery or an attempt at networking for my own gain, and more of a necessity. The reasons being as follows:

Reason Number One:

Connor Cane has IT. The evasive combination of charm, charisma, and raw talent required to be a performing artist. That front-of-stage, celebrity-status, stands-out-in-a-crowd presence that immediately draws you in and makes you want to buy whatever he is selling.

Reason Number Two:

There are, like, five people at this wedding. He's already seen me. There's no avoiding him even if I wanted to.

Which leads me to Reason Number Three:

This will be a reunion of sorts. Connor and I knew each other before he was famous. Back when he was just Connor—my older brother's best friend.

He and Trent have remained friends despite the fact that Trent lives in Washington. But Connor and I on the other hand? We haven't seen each other in several years. Not since his career started to take off and he became country music's blue-eyed beau. We don't exactly run in the same social circles in town.

Correction. Connor hasn't seen *me* in a while. But I see him all the time. Everywhere I go. Gracing the covers of magazines at my local grocery store. Interrupting my YouTube videos with ads featuring him brandishing protein powder, or suitcases, or whatever they're paying him to promote these days.

Occasionally, I've even seen clips of his music videos playing on the TVs in Target. The man gets around.

I didn't miss the widening of his electric-blue eyes and subtle tilt of his lips as he watched me take my seat before the ceremony started. I did the classy thing and waited for him to acknowledge me. I read somewhere that's what one does when in the presence of royalty.

Which he surely must be, now that he's riding the waves of his success. He'd mouthed something to me as we made eye contact, and I'd nodded and smiled back like I totally got the message. But the truth is, I can't for the life of me read lips. So hopefully he didn't say, "Get up here during the chorus and harmonize with me, would you?"

Because if so, the opportunity has passed. A travesty. Singing backup for Connor Cane would be a peak moment for me, especially since this crowd is made up of friends and family. I'd totally make an exception to my usual no-singing-outside-the-recording-booth policy.

I tune back into the sound of his voice, warming the cold winter air surrounding us. That voice carries a magic, something that puts us all in a trance when we hear it.

And that's the *main* reason I've harbored a crush on him for years.

There are several other reasons, such as the fact that he is insanely handsome. He's got a wave of surfer-boy golden hair and a smile that will make you dizzy. He's a genuinely nice guy. Plus, he writes killer songs. Songs that will make you forget any other man exists aside from him.

But I've mostly been crushing on his voice.

Mostly.

Connor delivers the last line of the song, the clarity of his tone passing into my ears and prickling across my skin. The intimacy of his performance nearly causes me to burst into rigorous applause.

Impressively, I refrain. Wedding etiquette, you see.

Connor takes a seat somewhere behind me, and Chloe and Hunter reclaim my attention as they exchange their vows. Heartwarming, inspiring lyric ideas are already meandering through my mind as my friends are declared husband and wife and share their first kiss.

Here's the truth about single songwriters like me...

More often than not, we don't have a love life to wax poetic about in our songs, so we have to borrow other people's love stories.

We're thieves, really. Clever little devils spinning tales from the woes of others' heartbreaks, and the fairytale happiness of moments like the one I'm witnessing now. We have to fictionalize the highs and lows of relationships because we're too busy writing and creating to make time to find love ourselves.

At this stage of my life, I'm not looking for a serious relationship. But I'd be lying if I said that watching Lainey, her older sister Ava, and now Chloe find their respective happily ever afters isn't making a tiny corner of my heart pinch in envy.

I'm happy for them. I am. And I'm grateful for the songs that their love stories inspire me to write.

But one day, once I'm settled and successful in my career, I do want to find my own happily ever after, too.

Today is not that day.

Today is for celebrating Chloe and Hunter.

And for some harmless flirting with Connor Cane because I'm an opportunist, and he's a first rate flirt.

The outdoor ceremony is taking place at Hunter's childhood home in Franklin, Tennessee, right in the middle of the sprawling backyard. Lainey's event-planning skills came out in full force for this one. Pine and glittering branches. Vibrant reds and shimmering silvers. Classic, timeless, and seasonally appropriate without being tacky.

"You did good, sister," I praise her as we stand to follow the bride and groom into the house for the reception.

"You think so?" She sighs. "They only gave me three weeks' notice."

"Terribly inconsiderate." I cluck.

"Terribly."

"And yet it suits them perfectly."

Lainey lights up as her fiancé, Luke, joins us.

"Hi," he says, his voice honey-sweet, wrapping an arm around her waist and kissing her cheek.

"Hi," she sighs.

They lose themselves in each other, and I drop back a pace. Watching them together is like watching kismet. They even move in sync, their leisurely steps landing in time.

A third greeting comes from behind my left shoulder.

"Well, if it isn't Stewie Two."

I turn to find him in an easy stance behind me, hands in his pockets. His blue eyes crease at the corners as he graces me with that half grin I've seen in the ads.

"Connor Cane," I say, a genuine smile climbing my lips.

"Bring it in," he says, motioning for me to embrace him as if we're teammates celebrating a win in our recreational basketball game.

"Bring what in?" I ask. He doesn't bother to answer my question. Instead I'm drawn into THE Connor Cane in a magnificently executed bear hug.

The sheer security I feel as my face smashes against the planes of his chest astounds me. I've never been safer in my life. If somebody were to strap us together and toss us out of an airplane without a parachute, we'd survive.

I take a deep drag of his scent and close my eyes—purely so I can try to recall every detail of this moment when I need creative inspiration.

Not because I'm going to lord the fact that I got a lingering hug from Connor Cane over anyone who mentions his name forever and ever, amen.

Oh, you saw him buying Tic Tacs at the gas station once? How quaint. When I last saw Connor, he enveloped my entire body with his in an intimate embrace. It was...transcendent.

"What are the chances we see each other here?" Connor asks, pulling away far too soon for my liking. "I've missed you."

He doesn't mean it. If he had missed me, we would talk more often. But I take his words and pocket them all the same.

"It's been a minute," I respond.

Connor studies me, and I have to keep a satisfied smile from rising on my lips. I wasn't expecting him to give me an appreciative once-over. I had anticipated, given my status as the best friend's little sister, a quick squint at my legs and then an appropriate amount of eye contact. But no. His gaze loitered, traveled over me with a slight tilt of his head, until his smiling eyes met mine again.

"Look at you," he says, gesturing to my body. "You look...well."

Not exactly the adjective that would add spice to my Connor-Cane-encounter story, but I'll take it.

"So do you," I say. "The picture of health."

He laughs.

"Connor, that song was…" I do a conjuring gesture with my hands as I search for the word to describe how his performance split my heart in two. "Really great."

"Thank you." He grins. "If I'd known you were going to be here, I would have had you join me."

"It's a good thing you didn't, then." I brush a strand of my blonde hair back behind my ear. "I would have sullied your nearly perfect performance."

"*Nearly* perfect?"

"Don't think I didn't see your chord slip on the second verse."

He smirks. "You must have been watching me pretty closely to notice."

I turn away, hiding my smile.

"What's new with you? Are you still writing?" he asks as we turn together to join the rest of the wedding party.

"I am," I say. "Been at it for a few years now."

"Good for you," he says with a nod, like he's truly proud of the creative genius I've become. "I always knew you had it in you."

His words send a spark of confidence through me. I glance at him sideways, wanting to ask him a million and one questions about music and writing and touring and what he's been up to since I saw him last.

I open my mouth and then close it again, not wanting this easy conversation to morph into an interrogation.

"Stewie sent me one of your cuts a while back," he says.

I press my lips together in response to hearing the nickname Connor gave my brother back when they were buddies in college. Our last name is Stewart. Trent loathes nicknames with the passion of a thousand suns, but somehow Connor gets away with *Stewie*.

I'm Trent's younger sister. Thus, I've been dubbed Stewie Two.

Then I register the fact that my traitor of a brother sent Connor one of *my* songs. Without my permission. One that was probably never meant to be heard by anyone other than members of my family.

Oh, dear. Things have taken a turn for Ella Mae Stewart.

Chapter 2

Connor

I had to do a double take when I first saw her.

The beautiful woman seated in the second row couldn't possibly have been the same girl I'd met back in college.

Ella Mae has always been pretty, but the past few years have been good to her.

Very good to her.

She's poised. More sure of herself. And she seems happy to see me. We're having a normal, casual conversation, just like we did back when she'd tag along with me and Trent. This feels oddly refreshing. Most people don't treat me quite like they did before my music started doing well. Back when I was *just Connor*.

"So..." Ella Mae says with a grimace. "Did you like it?"

"What, the song?"

"The song."

"Loved it."

She raises her eyebrows a fraction. "Did you really?"

"It was brilliant." I glance back up toward the house in an attempt to hide my grin. "I especially loved the line where you listed all those different varieties of fish."

She missteps, her heel dropping into a hole in the lawn. I grasp her upper arm to steady her. She's wearing a long-sleeved, fitted, silver dress that cinches on one hip. The top part of her thick, honey-blonde hair is swept back with a velvet bow. I've always thought that Ella Mae dresses like a lady. Bold colors, velvet, and silk. She's classy as ever.

"You okay?"

"Fine." She shifts her arm from my grasp and adjusts her dress. "Of all the songs he could have shared with you," she mumbles, "he sends you *that one*."

I snap my fingers, creating a beat to sing along to. "*Are you a trout or a minnow or an albacore tuna…*"

A pink flush colors her cheeks, and I'm swept back to when I'd give her a hard time about anything and everything. Teasing her again now feels as natural as hugging her did.

I finish singing the line with gusto.

"*Salmon, piranha, or a BARRACUDA, BABY.*"

She gets an adorable wrinkle in her nose. "I'm going to kill him."

"I thought it was masterful."

"I specifically told him it was for *his ears only*."

"An ode to fishing? You expect him to keep something so relatable all to himself?"

She lets her breath out in a huff.

"Don't hold it against him, Stewie Two. He knew I'd appreciate it as a fellow fish fanatic."

She eyes me as we near the back porch steps. "I promise I can write real songs."

"I never said you couldn't."

She seems satisfied by my response.

We enter the house, and Ella Mae introduces me to the caterers, Ava and her husband, Finn. Ava has a hard time not gawking at me, but Finn treats me like we've known each other for years.

"Please"—he gestures to the food—"enjoy yourselves."

"I plan to."

I follow Ella Mae's lead and start loading up my plate with all kinds of sweet things—things I'd normally avoid if I was on tour, but it's nearly Christmas, and I want to enjoy myself and this bubble of freedom I'm in for a few hours. The groom, Hunter, shoots nearly all my music videos, and I trusted him and his family enough to show up to this wedding alone. No security guard. No manager. Just me and my guitar.

"So," Ella Mae says, "what are you working on right now? Anything fun?"

"Just trying to finish up my second record."

Her eyes widen. "No way. That's exciting."

"Yeah, it is."

"Sounds like it," she deadpans, imitating my inflection.

"You want the truth?" I say, biting into a cake pop. "This second record is kicking my butt."

"Mmm." She nods, taking a bite of something chocolate. "I've heard the second record is much harder to write than the first."

"It's true. I can attest to that fact."

"Why do you think that is?"

"There's a lot more pressure," I say. "More people are depending on me. I don't want to let anybody down. I want the fans to like this music just as much as they liked the old stuff, even though it's different. And I'm different."

I'm rambling. I'm not a rambler. But I'm immediately comfortable with Ella Mae. It's easy to talk to her. It helps that she's not shaking and stammering in my presence like most women I meet do.

"Do you have enough songs?" she asks, covering her mouth with the back of her hand as she chews. "Or too many songs?"

"The former. Back Road hasn't given my track list the green light yet," I say. "They're, uh..." I squint off into the distance. "Not very excited about what I've written lately."

"That's stressful," she says. "I'm sorry."

We're silent for a beat, picking off our plates before she speaks again. "Are you feeling uninspired?"

I think back to the past few weeks that I've spent trying to write something that will make the executives at my record label happy. The countless writing sessions that leave me feeling spent and tired. Back Road is really pulling out all the stops, getting me into the room with some of the very best writers in town. I'd even spent a week in Los Angeles, hoping that another writer would help me craft the songs I'm missing from this record. Unfortunately, it doesn't work that way.

I spent my whole life writing my first record, and now I've got to come up with a whole new set of songs within a set timeframe. It's a completely different experience this time around.

"I think you'd understand this since you're a writer yourself. You can't force the songs to come, you know?" I say in an attempt to explain. "It's been a while since I've written something I'm really proud of."

"Hmm." She nods. "I get it. I sometimes have weeks or months where I can't write a good song to save my life." She gives me an amused smile. "And that's when things like 'The Fishing Song' emerge."

"No," I say skeptically. "That song is a stroke of genius."

Ella Mae rolls her pretty eyes at me. They're striking. Green and somehow gold around her pupils, like she's got the sun gleaming right there in her eyes.

"The songs will come, Connor," she says, giving my arm a squeeze—an act of familiarity that catches me off guard. Nobody touches me like that. At least, not when my security guard is around. "You've just gotta have faith."

"Or maybe I need to start recording other people's songs."

"No," she says incredulously. "Don't do that. Your songs are better."

"Better than yours?" I say, baiting her.

She snorts, tossing her hair back. "Certainly not."

Chloe and Hunter are making their way around the room and stop in front of us, cutting our conversation short.

"Hi, friends," Chloe says.

"Congratulations, guys," Ella Mae says, pulling Chloe to her in a hug. "You are so stunning. I couldn't be happier for you."

"Thank you for coming," Chloe says, giving me a hug, too. "It means a lot that you're both here."

"I see you're enjoying a cake pop," Hunter says, gesturing pointedly to the stick in my hand. "See, Chlo? I told you I wasn't the only man who would appreciate this superior treat."

Chloe is a tiny, sweet thing—clearly with a major soft spot for her best friend turned husband. "Alright, I concede."

"Maybe I can ask Finn to save a few for me," Hunter says, his brown eyes growing wide. "I can stuff them in my carry-on for the flight."

Ella Mae snorts.

"Where are you honeymooning?" I ask.

"Mexico," Hunter answers. "Chloe has never left Tennessee, so I'm taking it upon myself to introduce her to the wonders of the world—starting with churros on the beach."

I arch an eyebrow at him, lowering my voice. "And by that do you mean—"

Hunter nods. "Exactly." He winks at his wife, who blushes in response.

"How does it feel to finally be married?" Ella Mae asks.

"Well," Chloe sighs, "the first five minutes were wonderful, but then Hunter had to go and embarrass me, per usual. Now I'm regretting my choice."

Hunter pretends to be offended, taking my cake pop off my plate and helping himself to a bite.

"And there he goes again." Chloe grimaces. "Get your own cake pop, honey."

"Did you want the rest of this?" he asks, his mouth full.

"It's your wedding," I say to Hunter. "Treat yourself."

"Cheers." He polishes the thing off. "Do you realize, Connor, that if it weren't for your music video, we might not be standing before you as husband and wife today?"

I shake my head in disagreement. "I can't take any credit. I'm sure you two would have eventually gotten together."

"Doubtful," Hunter says, smiling at Chloe. "It was like pulling teeth to get her to act like she was into me, remember?"

"Whatever," Chloe says.

"Hey, she did a great job. It all worked out," I laugh.

"Whenever you're ready to settle down, Ella Mae," Hunter says with an impish grin, "I'll cast you in one of Connor Cane's videos."

Chloe squints up at her husband.

"What?" he says, looking to me for support. "It worked for us. It could totally work for our friends."

"I'm not worried about you one bit," Chloe says to Ella Mae. "Things will happen for you when the time is right."

"Wait." Hunter looks back and forth between Ella Mae and me. "How rude of me. Have you two been properly introduced?"

"We have," I say, looking to Ella Mae to elaborate. "When was it again?"

"Probably about five years ago. When Trent first moved out here for school."

"Who's Trent? Which school?" Hunter's palpable excitement makes me laugh.

"Her older brother is one of my really good buddies from college," I explain. "I knew Ella Mae back when she was just a wee thing."

"Well, *I*..."—Ella Mae presses a hand to her chest—"knew Connor before he started bleaching his hair."

I glare down at her, and she gives me a look that dares me to deny it.

"I *do not* bleach my hair," I insist, brushing a hand over my head. "These highlights are natural. From the sun."

"It's December, bro," Hunter says, placing my now-empty cake-pop stick back onto my plate. "Nice try."

"I was always told to watch out for guys who dye their hair," Ella Mae says, quirking an eyebrow. "They can be a little...high maintenance."

"Me?" I say innocently. "Come on, Chloe. Vouch for me here. You've done my hair a few times. Am I high maintenance?"

She bites back a smile.

"On second thought," I say, pointing a finger. "Don't answer that."

"I've actually been thinking about highlighting my hair," Hunter says. "Maybe you could send me the name of your stylist."

"There *is* no stylist, guys. Like I said, it's from the sun."

"Ahh. *The sun*," Ella Mae says as if the argument has been settled. But I know she still doesn't believe me.

"I'm having a thought here." Hunter raises his index finger against the tip of his nose.

"Congratulations," Ella Mae quips.

"Connor writes songs."

"I do."

"And Ella Mae...you also write songs."

"You're stunning us with your brilliance, Hunter. Really," she says around a bite of food.

"Here's an idea. Have you ever written a song...*together*?" He splays out his hands, leaving the suggestion hanging in the air like it's a prophecy.

I glance over at Ella Mae, immediately picking up on the sparkle dancing in her eyes. I've seen that same eagerness in other writers and artists when a golden opportunity is dangled in front of them.

She wants it.

She wants to write with me.

And why shouldn't she? A cut on one of my records would definitely help her out. She'd be in high demand if the song performed well.

"I don't think we have," I say with a tilt of my head. "We may just have to change that."

The shine in her eyes turns into a full-on glow, one that fills her whole face. I've always liked how unguarded Ella Mae is. It makes her easy to read.

"Really?"

"Why not?" I say.

"Even after the fishing song?"

"Especially after the fishing song," I laugh. "Give me your phone."

"I might still have your number," she says.

"I guarantee you it's changed," I grumble. I have to change it every so often nowadays for my own safety.

She fishes around in the clutch hanging from her wrist and hands me her cell phone. I put my number in her contacts as *Naturally Blond Connor.* My reasoning is two-fold. Not using my real name gives me some security if someone steals her phone. I also feel partially offended that she genuinely thinks I dye my hair. What kind of pansy does she take me for? I spend a week in the wilderness with her brother every year, for crying out loud.

I may whiten my teeth, occasionally get facials, and spend an inordinate amount of time styling my hair, but I do *not* highlight my hair.

"Good things are happening here," Hunter says with a wide, toothy smile. "I can feel it."

I glance down at Ella Mae, who's still lighting up the room at the prospect of writing a song with me. It's flattering, but it also reminds me of how I used to feel when I first started out in the business. It's refreshing to see that energy reflected in someone else.

"Yeah," I say. "Good things."

Chapter 3

Ella Mae

You know those people who are perpetually late? The ones you have to lie to and say the event starts an hour earlier than it actually does?

Shame on those people. Social disrupters. Annoyers of the prompt.

I am one of those people.

There's some part of my brain that doesn't compute time. I don't know if I'm always trying to squeeze in one too many tasks before leaving, or if I'm overconfident in my driving-speed capabilities. But either way, I'm typically late to things.

As an artist, this is to be expected. Musicians, especially, are notoriously late. Free spirits.

I'm hoping and praying that Connor Cane is also a free-spirited annoyer of the prompt, because I'm currently ten minutes late for our writing session.

Lainey always tells me I should *look up* the destination well in advance, then calculate what time I need to leave based on the estimated time it will take to get there, and add in a few additional minutes as a buffer in case there's an accident or unexpected traffic.

And to this, I say...

Where's the adventure in that?

Connor sent me the address for Back Road Studios in Nashville this morning. I'd guessed it wouldn't take me more than thirty minutes to get there.

My guesstimation turned out to be wrong, per usual, and now I'm screeching into the parking lot like a stunt driver on the set of an action movie.

I've heard it said that being late sends the message, *You are not worth my time.*

This is NOT the message I want to send to Connor Cane.

I haul Wanda, my beloved mint-green VW Bug, into a parking space and barely remember to cut off the engine before hurtling out the door and into the cold.

It's a few days before Christmas, and I'm hoping we get some snow. Not the kind of lingering snow that will overstay its welcome until January, just a little festive skiff.

I'm almost to the studio doors when my eye catches on a big white truck parked a few spaces away from the entrance.

My heart does a little dance in my chest at the sight.

Frank.

He still drives it.

A Ford F-150. White.

To this day, every time I see an F-150, I think of Connor. There have even been a few times I've sworn it was him sitting there in the driver's seat, hat turned backward over his blond hair, toned forearms that give way to his big hands gripping the steering wheel.

To see Frank, his beloved truck, here in the parking lot takes me right back to when I'd first moved to Nashville—when we first met.

There's something endearing about the fact that Connor could own several disgustingly expensive vehicles at this point in his career, and yet he still chooses to drive that truck. I'm sure he chose much more refined names for his new rides. Theodore the Tesla. Marguerite the Mercedes.

Amidst my reminiscing, I'm reminded that THE Connor Cane might be pacing in the studio right now, impatiently waiting for me to show up. Now is not the time to stop and snap photos of Frank for my own personal use. Scrapbooking, if you will.

I'll save that for when I'm leaving.

I give Frank a pointed look as I pass him. "You stay right there, you hear me? I'm coming back for you."

I enter the studio lobby, my guitar case swinging in one hand, a leather tote bag containing a notebook and a wide array of colorful pens in the other. You never know what color ink is going to strike your fancy during a writing session. Sometimes switching from a boring black pen to a neon-green one is just the thing that helps get the lyrics flowing.

A pretty brunette looks up at me from the desk in the center of the modern, sleek lobby.

"How can I help you?"

"Hi," I say. "I'm here for a writing session."

The girl clicks around on her computer screen. "With whom?" Her eyes flick back to my face.

"Connor Cane," I say, lowering my voice and leaning over the counter as I say his name. Gotta keep these sorts of engagements on the down-low.

"May I see your ID?"

I slide my driver's license across the desk so the girl can verify my appointment.

Am I beaming? I think I'm beaming. I take my smile down a few notches until it arrives at one that I hope appears more professional. No reason to be beaming this early in the game. Connor and I haven't even written a song yet.

This smiling-at-anything-to-do-with-Connor is becoming a regular thing now that he and I have been back in touch. He texted me about a week ago, asking if I was free over Christmas to meet up and try to write something.

Lainey and Ava had tried to help me divine further meaning from his first text, but it was ultimately decided that "writing session" was not code for something scandalous.

He was simply being a gentleman and keeping his word, doing a favor for his buddy Hunter.

I'd tried to prep for the session over the past few days, going back in my voice memos on my phone to find some ideas we could try to build off of. I'd also updated my running list of song titles in my notes, in case he's a title-writer.

Long before I started hearing his songs on the radio, he'd play songs he was working on for my brother and me. We'd sit in Connor's truck bed and take turns playing tunes. I'm very curious to see Connor in action today.

Our conversation this morning went as follows:

Connor: *fish emoji* Are you a trout or a minnow or an albacore tuna...
Ella Mae: *unamused emoji*
Connor: Been finding more obscure varieties of fish for us to lyricize in my next hit single.
Ella Mae: Such as...?
Connor: Vampire squid is at the top of my list.

Ella Mae: Said no one ever.

Ella Mae: I've been meaning to tell you...

Ella Mae: Picked up a bottle of lightening spray for my hair. Actively trying to get to that Connor level of blond...

Ella Mae: Naturally, of course.

Connor: *unamused emoji*

Connor: I'll see you at 2?

Ella Mae: *thumbs-up emoji*

I glance up at the clock hanging on the wall behind the reception desk. It is now 2:15. *Rats.*

"He's in Studio B." The girl at the desk hands me a little key card and a visitor sticker. "Through those doors, down the hall, and it will be on the right."

"Thanks!"

I plaster the sticker to my shirt and follow her directions. I wind up outside a solid black door without a window, labeled with a big silver *B*.

I take a deep breath and floof my hair up a little. Don't want to look dampened or distressed in Connor's presence.

I lay a knock on the door and only have to wait a moment before it swings open.

And there he is in all his glory.

Connor's a big dude. And I...am not a big dude. My eyes are level with his collarbone, so I first take in the neckline of his simple white t-shirt. The couple of necklaces he's wearing are doing great things for what I can see of his defined chest. I allow my eyes to wander up past his cut jawline, over his lips (have mercy), then onto his straight, masculine nose. My gaze finally lands on his eyes.

WOWZA. Never gets old. That shade of Bora-Bora blue pulls me in like the tide.

"Nice of you to finally show," he says, clearly feigning annoyance. The corner of his lips twitch, giving him away.

I drop into a quick curtsy. He's royalty, remember? I'm not a *heathen*. "Do forgive me."

He snickers and gives me a little appreciative half smile that would send most girls' hearts into a frenzy. But not mine. Ella Mae's heart is already frenzied from her frantic rush inside.

Connor swings the door open wide for me to come in. "Did you hit traffic?"

I debate lying and answering in the affirmative but decide telling the truth might amuse him and win me another one of those smiles.

"No, I didn't," I say with a squint as I enter the darkened room. "I'm naturally late to everything. It's a gift of mine."

I can see Connor's lips tilt up at my response. *Two points for me.*

In the years since I moved to Tennessee from my hometown in North Carolina, I've had writing sessions in all kinds of places. Greasy bars. Around campfires. In bedrooms, living rooms, and hotel rooms. And the occasional studio session for artists or writers with pockets big enough to afford renting one out.

Studio B has most certainly been misnomered. It should, at the very least, be called Studio BODACIOUS. Or perhaps it should get an upgrade to Studio A PLUS because it's glorious. As my eyes adjust to the moodiness, I take in the artfully placed framed vintage vinyl records and sconces on the walls. There's a massive mixing board that takes up half of the space, a plush velvet couch, and a few other seats making themselves at home around the perimeter of the room.

A man pushes his rolling chair away from the mixing board and stands.

"Ella Mae, this is Drew. He's the engineer I use on most of my stuff."

"Hey." Drew stretches out a hand, and I shuffle my belongings around so I can awkwardly grasp it.

"Nice to meet you."

Drew is giving me major Ryan Cabrera "On the Way Down" vibes, with his hair drawn up into wild spikes around his head. He's wearing choker necklaces and tight jeans. I like him already.

"Sorry to keep you guys waiting," I say, selecting a puffy leather armchair as my own. I place my bag down on the chair and lean my guitar case up against the wall beside it.

"No worries. We're glad you could make it," Drew says with an easy smile. He's a fellow late-at-heart. I can feel it. He probably got here a minute before I did.

Connor, on the other hand, takes a seat in a second rolling chair next to Drew's and claps his hands together. "Should we get started?"

Noted. No small talk. Just cut to the chase. Eager Beaver has definitely been here at least thirty minutes or more.

I jump into gear, popping the clasps of my guitar case open and pulling her out.

Yes, she is a *her*.

My favorite guitar to write with. A baby Taylor. Mahogany. I could drink the woodsy scent that accompanies this gal. It's that good. Makes me feel like I'm transported out to the middle of a forest every time I pick her up to play.

Connor reaches for his own guitar. A Martin. No surprises there. While I bought mine at a local music store back home in North Carolina, Connor's is definitely custom. He slings it onto his lap and starts picking at the strings absently.

Even his unintentional strumming sounds like a song. My little songwriter heart lifts, knowing that we're going to create something today that didn't exist before. That act of creation sparks more joy in my soul than anything else in the world.

"So," I say, clipping my tuner onto the end of my guitar. "Got any relationship updates or life drama you wanna tell me about before we get into it?"

He looks at me, amused. "Is this how you start every writing session?"

"Don't you? We've got to shoot the breeze for a bit first. Get to know each other."

"We already know each other."

"But it's been a while, Connor," I say, stating the obvious. "I don't even know who you're currently dating. Or whether you've recently gone through a terrible heartbreak. I mean, I could Google it, I guess, but where's the fun in that?"

Connor continues to stare at me, his fingers stilling on his guitar strings.

"You and Trent never talk about me?" He seems almost offended that I'm not up to date on all things Connor.

I settle back into my chair and scoff. "You really think Trent tells me anything? I can barely get two words out of the guy when he finally does answer my phone calls."

Connor nods. "Good man."

"Honorable man," I agree.

Drew looks back and forth between us.

"What a man." He shrugs. "Just thought I should contribute to praising this man...whomever he is."

"You know him, dude." Connor whacks Drew's shoulder with the back of his hand in a *hello-you-idiot* affectionate way. "Stewie."

Drew nods. "Oh, right. Stewie."

"Ella Mae is Stewie's younger sister." He flashes me a grin. "Also affectionately known to me as Stewie Two."

Drew sizes me up. "Seriously?"

"Why is this so hard to believe?" I ask.

"You and your brother look nothing alike."

"What a relief." I sigh. "If you'd told me I look like a flannel-clad mountain man, I'd be highly offended."

"You could pull off a flannel," Drew says decisively.

"Thank you."

"You're welcome."

"Anyway..." Connor resumes his absent strumming. "I'm a little concerned right now, Ella Mae."

PHEW. Hearing my real name on his lips in his subtle Southern accent just sent a rush of tingles down my spine. I'm a sucker for a gentleman, and Connor looks and sounds the part.

"Why is that?"

"If I didn't know better, I'd say you came here to write a love song with me today."

What I want to say is, 'WELL DUH, CONNOR CANE. How else do you expect the world to fall in love with you all over again? Your first record was full of love songs.'

But I refrain, looking at him expectantly.

"I brought you in for one reason and one reason only."

"And what might that reason be?"

"I need you to help me write..." Connor lets out a dramatic sigh. "...a *hunting* song. Drew, you've got to hear this song Ella Mae wrote about fishing..."

I sigh.

Chapter 4

Connor

Was I really expecting to write a bro-country song with Ella Mae in today's session? Of course not.

So why was I unprepared for her frank questions about my love life? Or lack thereof?

My pride might be slightly wounded knowing that she genuinely doesn't keep up with my personal life. It's my fault, I guess. I could talk to her myself. But I mean, doesn't she read the news?

I will admit, it's reassuring knowing that anything I decide to share with her brother stays between the two of us. Apparently, I made a wise choice in making Trent my best friend. He's a vault. Locked down.

I'm not particularly in a divulgatory mood. I don't want to talk about any of my past relationships or current failed attempts at dating while touring and recording an album. So there's only one way to handle this conversation.

Turn the spotlight on Ella Mae instead.

"What about you?" I ask casually, leaning back in my chair. "If you're so keen on writing a love song, why don't we sift through some of your stories instead of mine?"

She gives a derisive laugh. "As much as I'd love to regale you with tales of love won and lost, regrettably I've got nothing interesting to share."

Drew and I exchange a look. There's no way she's getting off that easy. A beautiful girl like Ella Mae has got to have some good stories.

"Nothing?" I counter. "I find that hard to believe."

She looks between Drew and me, clearly feeling cornered. "You guys know what it's like out here. Dating in Nashville is *dismal*."

Drew raises an invisible glass in concurrence. "Hear, hear."

I snort. Dating is hard for artists, maybe. But dismal?

"I disagree."

"Do you?" Ella Mae leans forward, resting her arms on top of her guitar. "I would think that you, of all people, would know what it's like being a musician trying to date other musicians. It's impossible. We're all self-absorbed and emotional."

I swallow. She clearly hasn't read the tabloids, or she'd probably know that she just summed up my previous relationship with Lauren Hunt, who is also a well-known country singer. Another relationship gone south because of our conflicting schedules and inability to prioritize both each other and our careers.

Maybe Ella Mae is onto something.

"Wow," I say flatly. "What a positive outlook you have on love."

She starts picking at her guitar strings. "It's not love we're talking about here. It's *dating*." The last word comes out like a curse.

"Okay, then." Drew laces his fingers together. "How about we each tell each other about the last date we went on? Maybe that will spark an idea."

I give Drew a cutting look. He knows about my last date, and it's not exactly something I'm eager to share about. It involved paparazzi interrupting our dinner and my date asking to leave before dessert.

And it had been six months ago.

"Orrrr..." he drags out, catching onto my loaded expression. "A recent date. In the more recent...past."

Ella Mae furrows her brow.

"You first, Ella Mae." I raise an eyebrow at her in challenge.

"Fine." She eyes me for a second. "My roommates and I had a competition going to see who could clock the most dates in each month, but now they've both found someone, and I'm..."—she clears her throat—"too busy to go on dates."

"Sure you are. Tell us about the last date you went on," I prod.

She sighs. "For a hot second, a few months ago, I was on a dating app."

Drew and I both gasp collectively.

"Ooooh," he says. "I like where this is going."

"The last date I went on was with Cole Madson."

"The tennis player?" I clarify.

"Nice." Drew nods appreciatively. Must be a fan.

"Listen." Ella Mae fiddles with her guitar. "You guys have to promise not to say a word about this. To anyone."

Both Drew and I lean in closer. Cole is a pretty high-profile guy. I'm dead curious to know how this date went.

"Go on."

"Okay," she says, shifting in her chair. "He took me to the aquarium."

I can't help but grin.

"What are you smirking about?" She narrows her eyes at me.

"The aquarium."

"Yes?"

"How fitting."

I can see her trying hard to not give me the satisfaction of smiling at my relentless teasing, or showing any sign that she likes it.

But I can see that smile working its way up her lips. And now I should probably stop staring at her lips, or even that general region of her face, because my throat starts to itch every time I do.

"Would you like me to continue, or not?"

"Please." I gesture toward her.

"So we met up at the aquarium, and as we were leaving—"

"Wait," I say. "You skipped the whole date."

She blinks. "Nothing else happened."

"Nothing?" I ask.

"Goodness, Connor. We walked around, admired the aquatic life, and chatted a bit. Now let me finish my story."

I raise my hands in surrender. "Fine, sorry."

"So as we're leaving the aquarium..." She pauses and looks pointedly at me with her eyebrows raised, waiting for me to interrupt. I pretend to zip my lips. "Cole suddenly gets sheepish and embarrassed. He starts blushing like a rose."

I snort. It's hard to picture that massive dude as bashful.

"He tells me he'd love to take me to dinner but asks if I wouldn't mind driving."

"Oh no," Drew says. "DUI?"

Ella Mae shakes her head. "Nope."

"Why did he want you to drive?" I'm surprised at the slight edge I can hear in my own voice. I'm feeling a protectiveness arise toward Ella Mae as she's recounting her date with a famous tennis player. Someone who could have easily taken advantage of her sweetness and...

"He'd run out of contact lenses and lost his glasses. The poor soul couldn't see a *thing*."

"No!" Drew cries.

"I guarantee you he couldn't make out a single fish in that aquarium," I laugh. "Or you, for that matter. Everything was a blur."

"He really tried, though," she says, pity in her voice. "He was very sweet."

I should hope so. If not, I'd be tempted to find out where he lives and...

Why am I feeling this sudden urge to rush to defend Ella Mae's honor? She's definitely the kind of girl who can handle herself. Must be because she's Trent's sister. It's what he would do.

"So did you take him?" Drew interrupts my train of thought.

"To dinner?" Ella Mae flips her hair back over her shoulder. "Of course I did. He did pay, which was nice. And then I drove him home."

I can't help but laugh in disbelief.

"Man," I say. "Now I get why you're so cynical."

"Did he get a second date?" Drew asks. I look at Ella Mae curiously, suddenly eager to know whether or not she was into the athletic, relentlessly driven type. Despite the obvious points against him for going into his date blind as a bat.

She gets that cute wrinkle in her nose again. "He did not. And I promptly deleted the dating app and haven't used it since."

I lean back in my chair as she runs a thumb over her guitar strings. Why does the knowledge that she's not currently dating anyone make me feel a little more confident in my choice to bring her here today? Ella Mae is a catch.

No fishing pun intended.

And knowing that she's single despite her insistence that she's *too busy to go on dates* intrigues me.

Her eyes lift to meet mine. "Your turn, Connor."

I run a hand through my hair. Why does this feel so vulnerable, telling her about my personal life? I know Ella Mae. And she knows me.

Maybe I'm overly cautious, but the more successful I become, the harder it is for me to trust people, to share things about my personal life.

"Uh..." I rub a hand over the back of my neck. "Well..."

She looks at me expectantly. But I can't bring myself to start talking. Something about her naturally honest demeanor puts me at ease. But I can't open up just yet.

Because I don't just *tell people things* anymore. I can't risk it. So much of my life is publicized, and bits and pieces are shared in the songs I write. If I want to keep anything to myself, I have to guard it closely.

"Look, Connor," she finally says gently. "You don't have to share anything personal with me. I was just trying to loosen you up so that we can try and write something good today. Something you can be proud of."

"That's why *you're* here, Ella Mae. You're going to help me save the record."

She gives me a curious look. "No, I'm not. I guarantee you your record is not in need of saving."

"You haven't heard any of the new songs. They could be terrible, for all you know."

"Impossible. Your first record was fantastic," she says. "Every song felt so genuine and true to who you are."

Our eyes lock for a moment, and her expression is open and honest. She likes my music. But she's not kissing up to me like some people do. She's telling the truth, and not just because it's what I want to hear. It's refreshing.

"I want whatever we write together today to feel like that," she says. "Honest and authentic. Something you could sing and really believe. That's the only way your fans are going to buy into it."

"I wasn't *fishing* for compliments, but thank you. That's very sweet of you to say."

Ella Mae lets out an exasperated sigh. "Is this fish thing going to haunt me every time I'm around you?"

"Yes."

She reaches into her bag and pulls out a notebook. "I'm determined to give you a new song to associate with me that has nothing to do with *fish*. Or water."

I laugh. "It won't work."

She looks at me with determination and flips open her notebook. "Oh, yes it will. How about we try building on an idea I've been working on?"

"Absolutely," I say. "Take it away, Stewie Two."

Drew turns around and scoots his chair up to the mixing board, setting up the Pro Tools session so we can record ideas as they come.

Ella Mae starts strumming away, humming to herself as she reviews her notes.

I have to stop myself from staring as I hear her sing again for the first time in a while.

I'd forgotten how nice her voice sounds. The past few years of constantly writing and recording have clearly been good to her. Her voice still has that unique, almost lilting, folk quality to it, but it's stronger. More refined. Fuller.

I shift in my seat and watch the chords she's playing with her left hand, matching them on my own.

"Okay..." She sits up and slaps a hand onto the sound hole of her guitar. "I've got something for you."

Chapter 5

Ella Mae

The first song idea I play for Connor is one I've been messing around with for a few days. I don't have the lyrics nailed down yet, but I do have the general idea of what it should sound like.

"And for the last part of the chorus," I say, flipping the page in my notebook so I can read the rough lyrics I'd scrawled out the other night. "I've got something like, 'How many hearts does it take until you find the one? How many rules do you break until the game is won?'"

"Hmm," Connor says, strumming out the chords I'd played for the chorus. "What if it was minor instead?" He changes the progression and plays it for me.

"I like that."

We jam around with the idea for about thirty minutes, but things aren't flowing. We both know what it feels like when you land on an idea and it just works, and this one isn't it.

"I don't know," Connor says, leaning back in his chair and setting his guitar down. "I'm feeling stuck."

"Me, too."

"Wanna try something else?"

"Yeah."

I flip through my notebook again, looking for something that I think might be a good fit for Connor Cane.

A slow smile spreads across my lips as I stumble upon a page that's got a title, one line, and a few chords written out at the top.

"How many happy songs do you have on the record?" I ask.

Connor tilts his head thoughtfully. "Probably not enough."

"I started writing something a while back," I say. "I think it might work for you."

"Let's hear it."

"Fair warning," I say. "It's sappy."

"I can do sappy." Connor grins.

"Good. The other day, I was thinking about my mom and stepdad, Mark," I say, settling back into my chair. "The way they talk about the moment they realized they wanted to be together."

"How did they meet?" Connor asks.

"At church. My mom always says that she'd seen him a hundred times before, but one day, she really *saw* him. And there was a very identifiable, clear moment where she knew he was the one she wanted."

Connor nods thoughtfully.

"The title I've got for it is 'Always You.' And the tag would be something like, 'There is nothing more true, it was always you.'"

"That's good," Drew says.

"Here," I say. "I'll play it for you."

I clip my capo onto my guitar over the third fret. The fingers on my left hand effortlessly find their home on the neck of my guitar while I pick out a pattern on the strings with my right hand.

Every songwriter uses a different method to create. Some write lyrics first and then fashion a melody to carry them. Others, like Connor and I, hum out melodies over chords and then find the right words to fit.

I'm one of those writers who believes that a good melody makes or breaks a song. If you've got a fantastic melody, listeners will latch onto that first. That's what every writer wants—to write something catchy enough to play on loop in someone's head.

Connor joins me on his guitar. We fall into a rhythm, playing in sync with our guitar parts complementing each other.

I close my eyes, listening to the chords and feeling the vibration from my guitar against my stomach. When I first start writing a new song, I ask myself, *what would this song sound like if it was already written?*

I pretend this song already exists and absently start humming, meandering through the chords I'm playing on my guitar, weaving a melody over the music Connor and I are creating.

I find a little melody that sticks, so I sing it on a *da da da*.

Connor nods, starting to hum it along with me. I open my eyes and watch him. He's concentrating, his lips in a flat line with his eyebrows drawn low.

He starts to sing some nonsensical lyrics, anything that comes into his mind. This is the intuitive part of songwriting that always thrills me. As you sing random words over the melody in your mind, sometimes a string of lyrics will flow out naturally, and you have to rush to write them down.

This is one of those moments.

"Like the morning sun on the rise," Connor says. We stop, and he repeats the line again.

"I didn't see you," I finish.

"Yeah, yeah." He nods. We repeat the line together, searching for the next lyric. I drop my guitar and pull my notebook onto my knee, jotting down the words.

"I always romanticize the church where they met. In my mind, it's filled with stained glass windows," I say.

"With a nice spotlight beaming down right on your stepdad?" Connor laughs.

"Naturally. She couldn't miss him." I smile.

The next line comes easily after that.

'Till the soft light opened my eyes, warming me right through.

Connor hums out a new melody for the pre-chorus, keeping the chords underneath the same. "We're telling this story from the future, right? Looking back on that moment they met."

He sings the pre-chorus line again, filling in some random words until he sings, *"I remember when you noticed me."*

We sing it again together.

"I remember when you noticed me."

I continue singing, making up the next line with the turn of the chords.

"For a moment then, I couldn't breathe."

I instinctively change the melody on the last word, lifting it as a lead-in to the chorus.

"I like that," Connor says. We sing through the whole first verse and pre-chorus together.

This is what it feels like when you land on the right idea. There's a flow, a rhythm you get into. Some of the best songs I've written come out in five minutes. It genuinely feels like the song already exists out in the ether, and I'm just the vessel through which the song comes into existence.

I can tell Connor is feeling this, too, the creative energy crackling between us and filling the room with something innate and emotional.

"You guys wanna lay that down?" Drew asks.

"We probably should," Connor agrees, turning to me. "Let's have you record some guitar first."

"You got it, boss."

Drew pulls a mic stand toward me and positions the microphone to capture my guitar. He hands me a pair of headphones, and I lift them over my hair, leaving my left ear uncovered so I can hear myself play.

"Go ahead and play a little bit," he instructs.

I mess around with a picking pattern as he adjusts the levels on the mic and in the Pro Tools session. A metronome click sounds in my right ear, steadily pulsing out a rhythm to keep me on beat as I record.

"That sound about right?" Drew asks.

I adjust my picking to match the speed of the metronome. "Hmmm...maybe a little bit faster."

He adjusts the BPM, and I continue to play along for a minute to get a feel for the speed of the song. "Yeah, that's good."

"Okay," he says, clicking around on the screen. "Ready to roll when you are. I'll give you four bars as lead in."

I nod, waiting for the click to start up and mentally counting the beats. When I reach the right spot, I begin to play, recording the four-chord guitar part on a loop, singing the melody in my head until I reach what I hope is the end of the pre-chorus.

"Is that good?" I ask, my fingers stilling.

"Sounds fantastic," Drew says. "Love the sound of that guitar."

"Thank you," I say. "She's my favorite."

Connor snorts.

"Let's double it," Drew says.

I record the exact same thing over again on top of the part I've already captured. Layering guitar parts over each other in recordings helps fill the song out.

"Let me throw something down, too," Connor says when I'm done.

Drew adjusts the mic to suit Connor, who then slides his own pair of headphones over his ears. I set my guitar aside and relax into my chair, watching him record.

He doesn't use a capo like I do, instead using bar chords to play in the same key. He plays a different picking pattern, complementary to mine but not exactly the same. He finds new notes, playing in harmony and occasionally letting some dissonant notes linger.

I keep my headphones on, listening to our guitar parts as they twine together.

"That's dope," Drew says once Connor is done. We remove our headphones, and Drew plays the guitar tracks together over the speakers, adjusting levels and roughly mixing as he goes.

"Can you pause that for a second?" Connor suddenly asks Drew. Then he tries out a couple different chord progressions that could stem off from the chorus. I strum along with his ideas, but after a few minutes, he sits back and shakes his head.

"Where do you think it should go, Stewie Two?"

"Honestly? I think it could just stay the same throughout the song. At least until we get to the bridge. Is that boring?"

"Not at all," Connor says. "Let's try it." Drew starts playing the song again on loop so we can write the chorus.

Things start to flow, and it takes us no time at all to write down the chorus using my original tag line I'd suggested at the end.

The second verse flows just as easily now that we know the melody line.

"I could see you ten years from now
Holding my hand tight
As we walked down this same winding road
Under the streetlights

I remember when you looked at me
For a moment then I couldn't breathe"

Things start to feel stagnant again once we reach the bridge.

"I hate writing bridges," Connor mumbles in frustration.

"Let's come back to it," Drew suggests. "I say we get the rest of the song down first."

"This feels good," Connor says. "I think we're onto something."

My chest warms at his words.

"Anyone wanna lay down a scratch vocal?" Drew asks.

"You do it," I say to Connor. "I can add some harmonies later."

He shrugs. "Okay."

I hand him my notebook with the lyrics we've written so he can reference them as he records.

The main recording space has a baby grand in one corner, a drum set in the other, and various mics set up to capture a live band together. Drew gets Connor situated in the padded vocal booth, which is accessed through the larger recording room.

We can see him from our position through a small window on one side of the booth.

Connor starts doing some vocal warmups, and I immediately hunt for my water bottle in my bag. Heaven knows I'm going to need something to cool me down once the man starts doing his thing. I already know his voice is going to melt me into this armchair until I become a part of it.

As soon as Connor's voice starts coming into the room through the studio speakers on either side of the mixing board, I involuntarily hold my breath.

Oh my.

Because it's just a scratch vocal, a placeholder for when he decides to record the real thing, Connor's not overthinking his performance. There's an openness to his tone. A sweet warmth in the low end of his voice as he sings through the verse and pre-chorus.

Then he reaches the chorus, his voice landing in its sweetest spot. That distinct, raspy, soulful thing he's got going for him that does funny things to my pulse.

"I knew then and I know now
You were all I wanted
Couldn't say it out loud
Didn't want to lose this
Gold light, your eyes
Summertime feeling
There is nothing more true
It was always you
It was always you"

I guzzle down my water, feeling heat rising in my face as he finishes the chorus. He fumbles up a lyric on the second verse and laughs into the mic.

"Let me try that again."

He nails it on the second try, easing into the second chorus with even more tenderness now that he's familiar with it. Drew stops recording as we reach the bridge.

"Wow," I breathe.

Drew presses the pedal at his feet so Connor can hear him in his headphones. "That was smooth, man."

"Sounds so good, Connor," I chime in.

"Thanks," he says. "I'll come back in so we can finish the bridge."

And we do, in no time at all, once Connor suggests we keep it simple. A single line that repeats and builds on itself.

When we're standing face to face
Everything falls into place

"I think you should get in the booth, Stewie Two," Connor says. "We need your voice on this."

I wave a hand dismissively. "No, you don't. But I'd love to add a little somethin'-somethin' if you want me to."

"Have at it."

Drew gets me situated in the vocal booth, adjusting the mic to a comfortable height.

"You ready?" he asks once he's seated back at the mixing board.

"Yes, sir."

I let Connor carry the first verse, then jump in on the chorus, singing the melody line an octave above him. Our voices climb and fall together in unison, and I lose myself in the song. My heart is swelling in my chest as I sing, feeling proud of this thing we're making together.

I'm so absorbed in the song that I don't realize I'm singing the second verse along with Connor until I reach the second pre-chorus.

"Shoot," I say into the mic, and Drew stops recording. "Sorry about that. Got a little carried away."

"All good," Drew says.

"Lay down that second verse for me," Connor says. "I like it."

"If you insist," I say.

"I'll back you up to the end of the chorus," Drew says.

This time, Connor's voice has been removed, so I'm free to sing the second verse and pre-chorus by myself.

I stop Drew once we reach the chorus. "Can we fly my first chorus to the second one?" I ask. I liked my first take well enough to copy-paste it and use it for the second chorus rather than re-recording it. "I'll add some harmonies, if that's okay."

"You got it."

I layer a higher harmony over the melody on the first pass, then double it.

"Let me add another part," I say. I'm in the zone now. I can hear all the harmonies in my head and just need a few minutes to get them out.

Connor and Drew let me play around, adding ad-libs and harmonies over Connor's voice throughout the song.

"Nice," I say once we reach the end. "I think I'm good. Thanks for letting me mess around. That was fun."

"Come on back," Drew says.

I slide my headphones off my head and push open the door to the vocal booth. As I return to the mixing room. Drew's playing the song back, finding where my harmonies and background vocals should sit in the mix.

Connor glances up at me, and the look on his face makes my heart squeeze in my chest. He's got his fingers steepled at his lips, an unguarded smile barely visible underneath.

He sits up and blinks, his expression becoming neutral again. But I tuck that little moment away, knowing that whether he meant for me to see it or not, I witnessed a moment of genuine appreciation.

Appreciation for me.

"Good work, team," I say, returning to my seat on the couch.

"Wanna listen back?" Drew asks.

He starts playing the song from the beginning. The smile on my face grows as we listen, feeling incredibly proud of what we've created together.

Connor holds my gaze for a moment as the song ends. He smiles.

"Thank you," he says.

And I know he means it.

Chapter 6

Ella Mae

"Take my money!" Lainey yells, flinging herself back onto the couch dramatically. "Take it all!"

I've just shown her the video Connor and I recorded at the end of our writing session. A live take of "Always You."

"Look, Ella Mae..." Lainey says, taking the phone from my hands. "See how he's looking at you right here?"

She rewinds the video, pauses it, and zooms in on Connor's face.

I'd had my eyes glued to my notebook, reading the lyrics. I hadn't realized that Connor had occasionally glanced over at me with a ready smile, waiting for me to respond and play back to him.

"He's a performer, Lainey," I insist. "This is what he does."

There's a reason I'm not pursuing a career as a country singer. You have to have that certain something. Charisma. The ability to capture a crowd and hold their attention.

Connor's got it. He's charming me even now through the video screen. And there I am, guitar on my lap, staring down at that notebook like it's about to burst into flames, instead of instinctively looking over at him and connecting as we sing together.

"I don't know," she says in a sing-song voice, returning my phone. "He sure checked you out a lot in that video."

"Too bad I didn't notice," I mutter, zooming in on his face again. "I would have enjoyed an excuse to look back."

We sigh together and sink back into the pillows on my couch. I'm still renting out the basement apartment of the townhome Lainey owns at Carriage Court. She's planning on moving into Luke's loft in downtown Franklin once they're married, but for now, I'm savoring the time I've still got with my best friend as my roommate.

I'm also in denial. In the very near future, I'm going to have to find somewhere else to live.

Alone.

"So what happens now?" she asks, giving my leg a pat. "Is he going to record the song?"

"Only if the label approves. And even if, by some miracle, it does end up on the record, I highly doubt it would be a duet."

"Dang it. And here I was hoping I could convince the two of you to sing this at my wedding."

I grin over at her. "The two of us? I thought you booked me as a solo act."

I'm not much of a performer, but when Lainey asked me to sing at her wedding, I couldn't say no. We haven't settled on a song yet, but I'm honored that she wants me to play a part in her big day, especially after witnessing Connor's performance at the Wards' wedding. The experience of hearing the perfect song played by the right person during a special moment like that is incredibly hard to put into words.

"Fine. I have an ulterior motive. If both you and Connor were supposed to sing together, maybe you'd actually show up on time."

I slap her playfully on the arm. "Stop it!"

"He'd hold you accountable!"

"I will *not* be late to your wedding!"

She appraises me with her hazel eyes. "Ella Mae, darling. Don't make promises you can't keep."

I give her a nice leisurely eye roll in response to *that*—something a high-and-mighty prompt person would say.

I pull myself up off the couch and take a seat at my desk. It's a humble setup, but it does the job. My laptop and monitor are connected to an interface and two microphones—one fitted with a pop filter to record vocals, the other positioned to record my guitar. I'm no pro at production, but I'm confident that I can capture my ideas live and in a professional enough way to pass on to those who can spit-shine them up.

"What happens if Connor doesn't use the song? Could another artist record it?" Lainey says from over my shoulder. "It's so good. It would be a shame if nobody ever got to hear it."

"That would be entirely Connor's decision. It belongs to him now." I wave my hand through the air. "I've released it into his tender loving care."

"Bet that isn't the only thing you'd like to release into his tender loving—"

"LAINEY." I whirl on her in my spinning chair like a queen on her office chair of a throne. "Don't do this to me. I can admire him. I can crush madly on his voice. I can be his friend. But nothing more than that."

She stands and places her hands on her hips. "And whyever not?" I know she won't bring it up, but she's got to remember the two very valid reasons why Connor and I could never exit the friend zone.

"You know why."

"Okay, but have you ever *asked* Trent if he'd be okay with you dating his best friend? How do you know if you haven't asked?"

"That's not the only reason."

"I know you've sworn off musicians, but Connor's not—"

I hold up my hand to cut her off. I don't want to go there—dredging up my heartbreak from several years ago when I was younger and naive about the way things work in this industry.

"And that rule still applies. Never again. No more musicians for me."

I spin back around to face my desk and open the last session I'd been working on. Yesterday I'd done a virtual co-write with an artist in LA and needed to get the demo sent over to his manager.

"Don't you have some packing to do, ma'am?" Lainey asks. We're taking the same flight home to North Carolina tomorrow to visit our families for the holidays.

"I'll finish up later."

"We've got an early flight, remember?"

"I know."

"Want me to pack for you?"

I turn around and gasp. "You'd do that?"

"I would. My suitcase is already zipped up. Ready and waiting by the front door."

How annoying.

"I mean, I wouldn't say no to you picking out a few outfits for me while I finish this up."

"You haven't even *started* packing?" Lainey tsks. "Ella Mae Stewart, I'll never understand you."

"You're better at all of the planning and organizing than I am," I concede. "I trust you on the packing front. Just don't forget my ugly Christmas sweater for your mom's party."

"I would never." Lainey hovers over my shoulder and brings my phone around, placing it in front of me. "Just in case you need proof that I'm right about these things."

She gives me a squeeze on the shoulder on her way to my room.

"Love you!" I say.

"SAVE IT!" she yells back from inside my bedroom. "FOR CONNOR."

I look down at my phone and see that she has the video paused on one of the moments when Connor was looking at me.

I tilt my head and force myself to look at it despite the fact that it makes me slightly uncomfortable.

Well, that's not *nothing*.

I might not be looking at a sign that he's utterly gone for me, but he sure ain't trying to hide that perfectly crooked smile of his...

I sigh and close out of the video, opening my photos.

As we were leaving the studio, Connor followed me out.

"Let's take a picture," he said. "For Trent."

So we stood in front of his beloved Frank and smiled for a selfie. He immediately texted it to my brother.

"Don't expect a prompt reply," I said dryly. "He's got a turnaround time of three to five business days. He blames it on the lack of service out there in the wilderness, but I think it's a cover. He just doesn't like talking to people."

Connor laughed. "Trust me. I know."

He hugged me again, and I secretly relished every second of it. Then we parted ways and wished each other a Merry Christmas.

He waved to me out of Frank's window as he pulled out of the parking lot, and I felt a little unexpected twist in my heart at the sight.

Seeing Connor driving that same truck brought me right back to my first few months here in Nashville. I had been starry eyed and over the moon to be pursuing my dream of being a songwriter. Trent had done his brotherly duty and showed me around, introducing me to his friends. He even gave me a place to stay before I found a cheap apartment to rent.

I can still remember the first time Connor and I met. Trent had invited me to come with them to find some peace and quiet after a long week of tests they'd had to take in school.

We drove down some back roads until we found an open field where we could look up and see pinpricks of starlight scattered overhead. Connor parked, pulled out a blanket, and spread it out in the truck bed. Memories of that night come back to me so viscerally. Sitting together in Frank's truck bed under the clear night sky. Taking turns playing songs and passing a guitar around. Laughing and teasing and joking together.

Those were happy times.

That was before I'd met *him*.

Before my innocent notions about love had been shattered to pieces—and my heart right along with them.

But now?

Seeing my best friends each find their person is shaking up my perspective all over again, turning some long-held beliefs about trust and love and marriage right back on their heads.

Ava and Finn. Luke and Lainey. Chloe and Hunter.

When I see each of them with their person, it's nearly impossible to imagine them without each other.

There's a part of my heart that has been closed off for years—windows barred, doors padlocked. But it's gradually starting to open up again. It's the part of me that used to believe in fate. In soul mates. In finding that true, lasting, forever kind of love.

He made me question whether there were good, lovely, honest men still left in this world. But I've met a few now. And they're real. They're each taking really good care of my best friends.

I tap on the selfie Connor and I had taken together. We look happy. *I* look happy.

Despite my lack of desire to jump back into the dating pool, I know that, at some point, I need to do it. If I'm not open to finding the kind of love that my friends have found, it's never going to come into my life.

I'm suddenly thankful for my writing session with Connor all over again. We had fun. Effortless fun. Throwing ideas back and forth. Singing together. Jamming playfully like we'd done when we first met. Even Drew has stolen a part of my heart that I'll never get back. I'd hang out with the two of them any day, if they'd have me.

The reality of my impending loneliness is starting to feel less intimidating. Yes, all my closest friends will be happily married, and I will still be single. I'm essentially being replaced in my role as the best friend, especially Lainey's. She's like a sister to me. I know things are going to have to change once she and Luke are married. They already have.

The start of a new year is just a couple weeks away. I can choose to be afraid of what's ahead, to feel like I'm being left behind while my friends continue to progress, or I can choose to be brave. To put myself out there again. To be open to new friendships. New relationships. Maybe even seek them out when the time is right.

"Please tell me you have some sort of occasion that warrants wearing this dress," Lainey says, stepping out of my room with an emerald-green dress from my closet held to her body. "Because if not, I'm immediately taking it into my possession."

"Take it!" I smile. "It's yours."

"I could never," Lainey says while twirling around with the dress.

"Consider it payment for your packing services."

"You've got yourself a deal." She beams at me.

"I know how much Luke loves you in a pretty dress." I grin back at her. Seeing my friend thriving in her relationship genuinely makes me happy.

I have to trust that, in time, I'll get to experience that same happiness myself.

One month later...

Connor: Stewie Two!
Connor: Do I have some exciting news for YOU.
Ella Mae: SPILL
Ella Mae: Did you land a role in a big action film?
Ella Mae: Go on a bad date you're dying to tell me about?
Ella Mae: I'm here for you. Whatever the news is, I'm ready to receive it.

Connor: haha

Connor: Thank you for your confidence in my acting and dating abilities.

Connor: Guess what?

Connor: Back Road wants your song on the record.

Ella Mae: WHAT?!

Ella Mae: Are you serious?! Connor!!!

Connor: They love it.

Connor: The fishing song. *fish emoji*

I shouldn't cackle, but I do.

Ella Mae: STOP IT.

Connor: JK.

Connor: Always You.

At this point in our conversation, I debate calling Connor on the phone. This isn't news to be shared over text, and I want to ask a thousand questions and scream with glee.

But then he sends me another text.

Connor: I'm in a meeting with the label execs right now. My manager will be sending you an email soon with all the details.

Ahh. Good thing I didn't jump the gun and bother him with a call.

Connor: Proud of you, Stewie Two. *thumbs-up emoji*

Ella Mae: Proud of US.

Connor: The album is officially saved.

Ella Mae: It never needed saving.

Connor: Maybe true.
Connor: But it definitely needed you.

Chapter 7

Connor

"Let's at least narrow it down to the top three," Drew says patiently, clicking on one of the many recordings we've been listening through for the past hour.

I huff out an impatient breath and sit back in my chair, rolling my neck from side to side.

"At this point, they are all starting to sound the same," I respond impatiently.

Drew hunches over the keyboard, scrolling down through the files Back Road sent over a couple weeks ago. "I'll start rolling them again from the top. You tell me if you hear something you like, and I'll save your favorites."

I lean forward, resting my elbows on my knees and rubbing my hands over my face.

After the busyness of the holidays passed, I sent over a handful of demos to the label executives, hoping that at least one of them would land well and my record would be finalized. I was shocked to learn that as soon as they heard "Always You," they gave me a call.

"This is it," they said. "This is the one."

A weight immediately lifted off my shoulders, and I couldn't wait to tell Ella Mae that she'd be getting a cut on my second record—something that could change the course of her career forever.

The sense of relief I felt at hearing this news was short-lived because the label then gave me a stipulation."We love the song, but we think it needs to be recorded as a duet."

Their plan was to have a bunch of Back Road female recording artists lay down vocals for the track to give me options to choose from. The recordings started coming in days later, unlabeled without names so I wouldn't be biased in my choice. Though I listened to them all as I received them, there wasn't a clear winner right off the bat.

It's been two weeks now, and the label execs and my manager, Mallory, are on my case. I'm here at the studio, listening through the recordings and trying to decide which singer I want as my duet partner for the final cut.

My deadline to turn in songs for the record is coming fast, but for some reason, I'm not feeling *any* of these versions of the song. The female voice on the current version we're listening to sounds way too intense. She's biting out the lyrics like they did something to offend her.

"Next, please," I say with a grimace. "It's too much. No subtlety."

I close my eyes, listening as the next girl comes in with some nice harmonies during the first chorus on her version. I nod along, trying to warm myself up to her vibe, the delivery of the lyrics Ella Mae and I had written. But something still feels off.

"This one's pretty good," I finally say. "Who is it?"

"Harper Jackson."

"Thought so."

"Top three?"

I nod reluctantly. "Yeah."

"She'd be a good fit," Drew says, dragging her version to a separate file. "Her stuff is doing really well on country radio right now."

We weed our way through the songs, whittling our list down to three versions I could live with. It's not that the vocalists aren't good—because they are. Professional. Polished. Perfect, even. Any one of them would sell the song.

"Can you email me the files? I'm gonna go for a drive and listen again. Hopefully that will help me make my decision."

Drew nods. "Good idea."

I leave him to continue his work, exiting the studio and making my way toward my truck.

Frank has been my trusty steed since my college days. I'm hoping he'll help me know what the right move should be for this song. He's seen me through it, good times and bad.

A man can always count on his truck.

I drive out of the parking lot and head east toward the Belfair high-rise apartment complex, where I'm temporarily renting a place before I take off on tour again. I crack my windows a bit, resolving to get a workout in at home before the night ends. It'll help me clear my head and my lungs. These days, I only get to enjoy time outdoors in bits and pieces, and it's starting to weigh on me. Living out of a tour bus isn't as glamorous as one might think. Most daylight hours are spent on the road or inside a venue.

I take a deep breath and steel myself before playing the top three duet options again.

Don't compare them. It's not fair.

It's entirely unfair, in fact, to compare these versions of the song to the original demo with Ella Mae's voice.

She wins in my book by a landslide.

I've had the idea brewing since that first day I listened back to our demo before sending it to the label.

Ella Mae and I sound amazing together.

I pull up our demo on my phone and push play, turning up the volume so I can listen to what I consider to be the original version of this song. To record this as a duet with anyone other than Ella Mae is going to feel forced, no matter which way I slice it.

Her voice comes through Frank's speakers, and I'm immediately settled. It feels as if she's right here in the passenger seat, singing to me with a soft smile on her lips.

I gradually feel my stress begin to ease as I listen to our voices rise and fall together. There's a kind of magic captured in a first recording that is difficult to replicate. Neither of us were trying too hard to be perfect. There's a purity in Ella Mae's voice that's missing in the other performances. They feel too well-rehearsed to me. Too punchy.

Her voice is captivating. Raw and somehow smooth at the same time. She invites you to lean in closer with her phrasing and her effortless delivery choices. She's not selling something when she sings, and yet I'm completely sold.

This is the version of the song I want the world to hear. Two acoustic guitars. First-take vocals. Sparse production with some added subtle ambient sounds in the background. But the essence of the song needs to stay the same.

I pull into my underground parking space when I reach the apartments, rolling up my windows and cutting the engine.

The choice is so obvious to me, but I doubt the label executives will see things the same way. They'll naturally want a Back Road artist on the track. Someone with a bigger presence and draw than an up-and-coming songwriter like Ella Mae Stewart.

How can I convince them that she's the one we should go with?

I pull up the video of us singing together on my phone and watch through a few seconds of it. This is candid, behind-the-scenes content. Just the sort of thing my PR team would approve of me sharing.

And that's when an idea hits me.

I've learned to give myself a few hours or days before posting things online to really ensure that it's something I want the world to see and for the media to dissect in the news. Typically, I don't act impulsively or share anything right away.

I head inside my apartment, throwing my guitar case on my bed before changing into some workout clothes. I've got a large spare room I've been using as a home gym.

I used to be able to go for a run or hike whenever I felt like it, but I started getting accosted on the trails by fans, and it put me on edge. You never know when someone is watching or following you when you're out by yourself, trying to do something normal. My ability to go out whenever I please is another small thing I've lost since my first record released two years ago.

After I wind down from a weight-lifting circuit and a quick run on my treadmill, I make myself a protein shake and sit down at my kitchen counter to revisit the song.

Despite the fact that I've given myself time to clear my head and think things over, Ella Mae's version is still my favorite.

I don't need days to mull over this decision. I know exactly what I'm going to do, and I'm confident it's going to work.

Chapter 8

Ella Mae

I'm in the middle of a co-write when my phone starts vibrating incessantly from inside my bag.

"Just give me one second," I say eventually, excusing myself from the room so I can see what all the fuss is about.

I've got three missed calls from Lainey, a bajillion Instagram notifications, and a missed call from none other than Connor Cane himself.

We've texted a few times since our writing session, but he's never called me before. Could he have caused some sort of public scandal? Am I the trustworthy friend that came first to his mind to post his bail or arrange a tow?

Or maybe he just wants to chat. Catch up. Recap our holidays.

Curiosity is *killing* me. Knife to my throat.

Sorry, Lainey and social media, you're going to have to wait. It's only right that I prioritize his royal highness. I scoot myself a ways down the hallway and return Connor's call.

He picks up after just a couple rings.

"Hey, Stewie Two."

A wash of goosebumps prickles down the back of my neck at the sound of his voice. It's sultry. Enticing. I highly doubt he intends to sound so sexy when he speaks, but heaven bless him, he does.

"Well, hello."

"How are you?"

I back into the wall behind me, wanting to twirl my hair and offer a sigh up to the heavens. Pretend he's my high school boyfriend. Giggle like a nervous schoolgirl.

But instead, I maintain my dignity and smile into the phone. "You butt-dialed me, didn't you?"

Connor laughs.

"No, I meant to call you."

He pauses for a beat, and I stay quiet. This is the big reveal. He doesn't sound like he's in a prison cell. *Rats*. I'm betting he's stuck on a lyric or something boring and wants to run his ideas by me.

"I'm honored. To what do I owe the pleasure?"

Connor clears his throat. "Did you see my post?"

"What post?"

"Check your Instagram."

I pull my phone away from my ear and put him on speaker phone, swiping to open my app.

"Oh dear," I say. "If this is another one of your sponsored posts, so help me. I better not start getting ads for whatever you're selling after I click on it."

Connor snorts. "Oh, come on now. You like the ads. You like all my posts."

I grimace. Out of the thousands of likes on his posts, he somehow *sees* mine?

I feel violated.

Note to self: You may look at Connor's posts, but DO NOT DOUBLE TAP.

"What am I looking for?"

"I tagged you, Grandma. It can't be that hard to find."

I click on his most recent post and am shocked to see that it's a video that features...me. Myself. *Moi*. Next to Connor, singing "Always You" in Studio B.

Ahh.

"Well." I swallow. "This certainly explains all the notifications."

Connor gives a low chuckle. The video already has over thirty thousand views. Hundreds of comments. I scroll through a few of them and am simply overwhelmed by the amount of fire and heart emojis the comments contain.

"Wow." I press the phone back to my ear. "You didn't need to do that, Connor Cane."

"Why do you always call me that?" I can hear the smile in his voice. "So formal."

"Do you have a middle name?"

"Yeah."

I stay silent, waiting for him to divulge it so I can call him by his full name henceforth and forever.

"Anyway," he hedges. "Remember how I told you "Always You" was going on the record as a duet?"

"Don't change the subject. Middle name. Let's have it."

He's quiet for a moment. If he thinks I'm going to let this one go, he clearly hasn't met my persistent side. She's a fighter.

"It's..." He sighs. "It's..." He drops his voice low. "Robin."

I bite back a smile. "As in...the bird?"

"The bird. And my dad's favorite uncle."

"Doubly lucky."

"You'd better not tell a soul, Ella Mae."

"Whatever you say, Connor *Sparrow*—"

"For the love."

I cover the phone and laugh to myself. *Robin*. Terribly unfortunate.

"Like I was saying," Connor says, taking control of the conversation again, "the label had a bunch of female artists record their own versions of the song. I'm supposed to choose my favorite."

"Do you need my help?" I ask. "Send them over, and I can have a listen."

"I would, but here's the problem…" Connor says. "I'm not in love with any of them."

"Really?" I say, unable to hide the surprise in my voice. "None of them tickled your fancy?"

"Tickled my…*what*?"

"Your fancy."

Connor is quiet for a beat. "You know, sometimes I wonder about you."

"Sometimes I wonder about you, too. How you could have gone your whole career without anyone doing an in-depth study on all the bird references contained in your records."

"Stop it."

I giggle then, feeling that same rush I always do when we tease each other. It's way more fun than it should be. I could do this all day.

But preferably in person so I can watch his blue eyes flash when he's about to hit me with a witty comeback.

"Ella Mae. This is important."

"Right. Sorry. I'll stop." He used my real name. This means business. I clear my throat professionally. "You were saying…"

"I don't like any of the potential duet partners the label has sent me. They're just not what I'm looking for."

"Hmm." I hum. "Do you want some fresh options? I could try to find a couple other artists to give it a go. But I doubt there's anyone else *I* know that *you* don't know who might be a good fit for the..."

"Ella Mae."

"Connor Hawk."

He sighs.

"I posted the video of you and me because..." his voice trails off, leaving me to try to fill in the rest of his sentence in my mind.

You melt my heart when you play your guitar like that.

I needed a pretty face on my feed to boost my numbers.

You complete me.

"I want *you* to be on the record."

I furrow my brow, unsure that I heard him correctly. "Wait, what?"

"I want to put our version of "Always You" on the record. As close as we can get to the demo we recorded the day we wrote the song."

My lips part again in shock. "Wait, hold on. You want *my* voice on the duet?"

"Yes," he says. "I need you, Ella Mae."

Ooooh. OOOOH. I like where this is going. "Connor!" I say with a gasp. "You're making me blush."

"I'm being serious," he says, and I can hear the earnest truth there in his voice. "I need you on the record. It has to be you."

I take a moment to absorb what he's saying. Me. Ella Mae Stewart. Best friend's little sister. Songwriter. Non-performer. Featured on a Connor Robin Cane Record? *Astounding.*

"Our version is the only version I want on the record. I wanted to prove to the label that my choice is the right one, so I posted the video of us singing together to get the fans on my side."

"And...?" I ask. "*Are* they on your side?"

"They love it."

"Naturally," I snort. "You're in it."

"No, Ella Mae. They love it because *you're* in it."

I swallow.

Getting a cut on Connor's record would have been enough for me. The leg up I've been dying for in my career. The fulfillment of a dream I've been chasing for years.

But having the opportunity to *sing* on the record? That's something entirely different.

"Connor, I'm not a singer," I say, finding my voice again. "I'm just a writer."

"That's bull."

"No, really. I don't sing outside of recording booths and writing sessions. You know this."

"That may be true, but that doesn't mean your voice shouldn't be heard, Ella Mae. You're perfect for this song. It has to be you."

I pinch the bridge of my nose and squint one eye. Any other girl trying to make it in Nashville would be absolutely clawing at the opportunity Connor is dangling in front of me right now.

But I'm not any girl. I'm a songwriter. Not a performer. Not an artist. I never wanted to pursue that path for many very valid reasons. Reasons that include my severe dislike of singing in front of large groups of people.

Connor would never understand that. He was blessed with the natural ability to bare his soul onstage to thousands of strangers. We're not cut from the same cloth in that regard.

Besides, I know what artists can become once they taste success. Selfish. Corrupted by greed and the glitter of fame. Somehow, Connor has evaded that corruption thus far, but he's still young in his career. It's only a matter of time before he becomes aloof and distant as his notoriety grows.

I would know. I've had my heart broken by an artist before.

"I'm honored that you thought of me, Connor. I really am," I say. "But we both know that I'm better off operating behind the scenes. Why don't you send me the options the label has given you, and I'll put in my two cents?"

"I don't need your two cents."

I scoff. "Rude. Turning down my widow's mite."

"Listen, I've already made my decision. I'm going to convince Back Road that your voice is the one for the song, and they can take it or leave it."

"Don't waste the song on me, Connor. Sing it with someone who knows what she's doing."

"You don't think you know what you're doing when you sing?" There it is. That tone he takes with me when he's flirting. "It's not just me. You get people in their feelings. If you don't believe me, you should read some of the comments on that video, Ella Mae. You're amazing, and you don't even know it."

I don't plan on reading any comments about myself on the internet—a general good rule of thumb. But he has also just told me that I'm amazing, and his words transform me into a lovestruck teenager. I'm involuntarily sliding down the wall until I'm seated on the floor with my knees up in front of me.

"You're too good to me, Connor."

"Not as good as I want to be."

I bite my lip. He sounds *serious* right now. Dead serious. He and I don't do serious.

Not as good as I want to be.

What am I supposed to say in response to a comment like that? The silence stretches between us as I fiddle with the hem of my jeans.

"Let me put our song on the record, Ella Mae. It can't be anyone else but you."

"You're very sweet."

"You'll think about it?"

I sigh, casting my eyes toward the ceiling. "Yeah. I'll think about it."

"Let me know by tomorrow."

"*Tomorrow?*"

"Things are going to move fast once this song gets approved. They're ready to finalize the track list once we get this song dialed in."

"The fate of the entirety of Connor Cane's second album rests on me." I sigh. "No pressure."

"Maybe we can meet up tomorrow sometime," Connor suggests. "Chat about it more."

I twist a thread on my jeans around my index finger, smiling to myself at the prospect of seeing Connor again. "That would be great."

"I'll have to double check my calendar, but I think I've got some free time in the morning. Would you want to come by the studio?"

"I can do that," I say, my heart speeding up. Who knew hearing a man like Connor Cane say the words *come by the studio* could make a girl feel some type of way?

"Alright, Stewie Two."

"Sounds like a plan, Connor Cane. I mean, Connor—"

"Don't do it."

"Parakeet."

I can practically see him shaking his head on the other end of the line. "I'll text you tonight, and we can make plans for tomorrow."

"Sounds good."

We say goodbye and hang up the phone. I drop my head back against the wall and blow a long breath out, buzzing my lips together.

Connor Cane wants me to sing on his record. But do *I* want to sing on his record? My immediate answer is no.

He's practically irresistible, but I must resist.

I tell Lainey about Connor's offer over dinner at home that night.

"You're crazy if you say no to this, Ella Mae," Lainey says once I've finished, flipping her long braid over her shoulder. "You *can't* say no!"

I knew she was the wrong person to ask for advice on this delicate matter. Of course theatrical, dramatic Lainey wouldn't hesitate if someone offered her an opportunity like this. She possesses a confidence that I don't have when it comes to performing.

"Lainey, I *can't*!" I exclaim. "It's doing the song a disservice to have my voice on it. Nobody will listen to it. Country radio won't play it. If someone else does it, it at least will have a fighting chance."

"Would you stop it?" Lainey says. "You've got to remember that Connor is the artist here. He's the one asking you to do this. He wants *you*, Ella Mae!"

I sigh dramatically. "Oh, how I wish that were true. Although, he did tell me he 'needed me' on the phone."

Lainey gasps. "How did he say it?"

"*I need you, Ella Mae*," I say in my best Connor Cane voice.

Lainey flings herself onto the counter, slapping her palms on its surface. "Goodness GRACIOUS!"

"I know."

"I'm calling it now." Lainey sniffs. "You're destined for each other."

I shake my head. "No, Lainey. We're not."

"*Why*?"

"BECAUSE!" I yell. "He's my Jesse McCartney."

Lainey turns fully toward me in her chair. "Elaborate."

"You know how it is when you have a crush on a celebrity. It's all in your head. Daydreams. Listening to 'Beautiful Soul' on repeat on your CD player and imagining Jesse McCartney singing it to *you*. It's a fairy tale. Not something real."

"But Connor Cane *is* real."

"So is Jesse McCartney. But I gave up on marrying him long ago."

My best friend's hazel eyes narrow. "Did I just hear you say the M word?"

I roll my eyes. "Don't read into it, honey. I was speaking metaphorically."

She tilts her head, her eyes calculating. "You've thought about marrying Connor Cane, haven't you?"

"Pshh."

"You have!"

"Fine. Yes, of course I have. Along with every other woman who has ever heard his songs—but only in the imaginary celebrity-crush kind of way. Plus he looked fantastic in his suit at Chloe and Hunter's wedding, okay?"

Lainey nods in agreement. "That he did."

I occupy myself by stabbing at the pasta on my plate and forking it into my mouth in an attempt to stop digging myself into this hole before it's too late.

"I'm a writer, Lainey. I want my name to be in the liner notes inside the CD case, not featured beside Connor's on a track," I say in a last-ditch effort to get her off my case.

"Nobody buys CDs anymore, Ella Mae," Lainey points out.

"Not true," I argue. "I do."

"No, you buy vinyls. Not the same thing."

I have amassed quite the collection of records in recent years. I love how it feels to carefully position a record on the turntable before dropping the needle and hearing it crackle as the record spins, listening to full albums from start to finish, as they were intended to be listened to.

Lainey and I eat in silence for a minute. When I finally risk looking over at her, she's got her eyes trained on me.

"You remember when we made our performing debut?" she says with a smile. "Third grade talent show?"

"How could I forget?"

"You were so nervous before we went onstage that I had to practically drag you out there with me."

"I tripped over my own feet," I laugh. "It's a wonder I recovered in time before the music kicked in."

"You didn't think you could do it, but I reminded you that you weren't alone. I'd be right there, singing and dancing along with you. The audience would be watching both of us, and if one of us made a mistake, it would be okay. Nobody would even notice."

I nodded, remembering the buzz of nerves I'd felt. "I couldn't have done it without you."

"This opportunity with Connor..." Lainey says, looking at me keenly, "it's the same. I get why you're nervous about it—he's a big deal. But you're not doing this alone. It's a duet. He's got your back."

I allow myself to meet her eyes, to let my fear show for a moment. I know she won't judge me for it. She never has.

"I know this scares you, but maybe Connor is scared, too."

"What could he possibly be scared about?" I scoff. "The man is fearless."

"Oh, I don't know," Lainey says sarcastically. "Maybe he's afraid that his second album is going to flop. Especially after the first one did so well."

Lainey's right. Connor has expressed this fear to me several times. I suddenly feel the weight of his request pressing into me with even more intensity.

"Maybe he needs someone to have his back for once," she says thoughtfully. "Maybe singing with you is enjoyable and easy for him. Maybe he needs that right now."

"I highly doubt that. The man's got everything he needs already," I say stubbornly, despite the thickness gathering in my throat. "And"—I stab another noodle with my fork—"what if his fans hate it?"

Lainey arches an eyebrow at me. "I read the comments on that video, Ella Mae."

My chewing slows. I swallow.

"They already love it. How could they not? Your voices together...it's magic."

Connor had essentially said the same thing.

"This is your decision to make, but remember that you're worthy of this. You know I'll always be your biggest fan."

I give her a sappy look. "What would I do without you, Lainey?"

She flips her hair back over her shoulder. "Have a lot less fun."

As we clean up the dishes, I feel an aching appreciation for my best friend. These moments spent with her are precious. Soon enough she'll be a married woman, and things will be different.

I mull over her advice as I retreat down to my basement studio, feeling grateful for her constant confidence in me.

Would I regret turning this opportunity down? Ten years down the road, would I hear "Always You" on some obscure heart-wrenching commercial and say to myself, *It should have been me*?

The answer comes more clearly to my mind and heart than I anticipated it would.

I sit down at my studio desk, picking up my phone to respond to a text from Connor.

Connor: I'm free right at 9 for about an hour.
Ella Mae: Wanna grab coffee?
Connor: I can't remember the last time I went out for a coffee haha
Connor: I could curate a museum collection featuring coffee cups with baristas' numbers written on them.

I smirk, envisioning Connor trying to politely pry a flirtatious barista off his person.

Ella Mae: Dreadful thing, being famous. Let the man order his coffee in peace!

Ella Mae: How about I pick it up and bring it to the studio instead?

Ella Mae: Send me a screenshot of your order.

Ella Mae: Heaven knows it's three paragraphs long.

Connor: *unamused emoji*

Ella Mae: Tell me I'm wrong. It would be on brand for you, knowing what I do about how you maintain that gorgeous hair color.

Connor: Double shot of espresso.

Ella Mae: ...that's it?

Ella Mae: I'm oddly disappointed.

Connor: Let me guess yours.

Connor: Grande Pumpkin Spice Latte with steamed almond milk.

Connor: Four pumps of white chocolate mocha syrup, topped with a hearty helping of whipped cream and a drizzle of salted caramel.

Connor: And a blueberry muffin to go.

Ella Mae: *cheers emoji* Make it two.

Chapter 9

Connor

When Ella Mae asked if she could meet me for coffee this morning, I almost agreed immediately.

But then the past two years came rushing back to me in a moment of clarity. I used to be able to go to a coffee shop without thinking twice about it. But now? I have to contemplate where I'm going and when. Whether or not it's worth getting stopped for pictures by those brave enough to come talk to me. Then there are the people who think they're being sneaky, snapping photos when they think I'm not looking.

I hate to break it to you, but I'm always looking.

As grateful as I am for my career and getting to do what I love every single day, part of me misses the simplicity of my life before. Being seen with Ella Mae could cause some speculation about our relationship status, and I would never wish the wrath of the media on her before I could properly prepare her for it.

Not that I'd be embarrassed at all to be seen with the enchanting Ella Mae Stewart. But I decide that it's probably best if we meet more discreetly to discuss the record.

Thankfully, she offered to pick up coffee and meet me at Studio B. I've been here for fifteen minutes already, waiting for her to turn up.

When she finally comes blustering through the door, her hair tied up in a navy-blue ribbon, dressed in a striped sweater tucked into high-waisted jeans, I have to stop myself from staring.

Worth the wait.

"Here you are, sir," she says with ceremony, presenting my coffee to me. She grabs her own drink, curling up on the couch with her legs tucked underneath her, looking as comfortable as if she were in her own living room. She occupies any space she's in with that same down-to-earth ease. A welcome contrast to most of the people I work with who are constantly trying to impress.

"Thanks for this," I say, raising my cup in her direction as I take a seat in the rolling chair in front of the mixing board. She raises her own in response.

"Sure thing, Connor Cane."

"What are you drinking this morning?"

She purses her lips. "White chocolate mocha."

"A-ha." I grin. "At least I got one part of your order right."

We drink in silence for a moment, and I become conscious of the fact that this is the first time that Ella Mae and I have ever been alone together. Just the two of us. I swallow at the realization, feeling that same tightening in my chest I'd felt when I saw her at the Wards' wedding back in December.

Being in her company is easy. I know her. I like being around her. Simple as that. There's nothing more to it.

"I texted Stewie this morning," I say, tugging my phone out of the pocket of my jeans. "Told him we were having coffee."

Ella Mae smiles. "What did my dearest brother have to say?"

"Not much." My eyes flick up to hers. "As expected."

Trent is a man of few words. Direct and quiet. To some, he comes off as rude, but our years of friendship have taught me that he's just observing. Thinking before speaking.

"He said..." I clear my throat, pulling open Trent's text. "That he wishes he could have joined us."

"He quit coffee. Did he tell you that?"

"He did?"

"One of the guys who works for him got him into growing his own herbs to make tea. He's a tea drinker. A proper gentleman."

I laugh, unable to picture Trent brewing tea from herbs he grows himself.

"I wouldn't be surprised if he takes up baking sourdough next."

"Or raising goats."

"Like a milkmaid," Ella Mae says dryly.

I nearly choke on my coffee, picturing burly Trent dressed in an apron, doing anything that requires finesse.

"Do you make it out to visit him often?" I ask.

Ella Mae shakes her head. "Usually only once a year. And I have to schedule my visit strategically. He prioritizes your summer man-camp over me every year."

"*Man camp?*"

"Why is it so exclusive?" she asks, ignoring my laughter. "I've waited for years to get the invite. I'll even volunteer as the camp cook."

I raise my eyebrows. "Now that is an enticing offer. We usually live off canned beans and jerky."

"Ugh." She wrinkles her nose. "You boys need me."

Trent and I spend a week out in the wilderness near Wildwood– a cluster of cabins he owns near Olympic National

Park in Washington every summer. Fishing, camping, hiking. With how busy my touring schedule is this summer, I doubt I'll be able to squeeze it in.

"I'm hoping he'll come to my show in Seattle in a couple months."

"Oooh..." She clicks her tongue. "That'll be a hard sell for our boy Trent. Big crowds. Loud music. Not really his thing."

"You don't think he'd do it? Not even for me?"

She shrugs.

"If *you* were playing the show with me, he'd for sure come. He'd do anything for you," I point out.

Easy to see why.

"True. He's a good one, that Trent."

I could listen to Ella Mae talk all day. She's got the sweetest Southern accent—a little Carolina mixed with some Tennessee. As much as I want to just shoot the breeze with her, I'm dying to know if she's down to be on the record or not.

"So I'm meeting with the label executives this afternoon."

"Lovely."

I give her a minute so she can tell me what she's thinking. Instead, she becomes very occupied with her coffee.

"What should I tell them about 'Always You'?"

She lets out a long exhale and meets my eyes. I'm unsure from her expression where she stands. I've already steeled myself for rejection. I've even got an email drafted to send to Harper Jackson in case Ella Mae decides she doesn't want to do this.

But then I see her lips lift into a smile, and that tell-tale shine rises in her eyes.

"I've given this a lot of thought," she says. "Last night, I talked to my friend Lainey about it, and she gave me some great advice."

"What did she say?"

"She asked if I would regret not taking this opportunity, even though it's completely out of my comfort zone."

"And?" I say after a lengthy pause. "Would you?"

She meets my eyes. "I think I would."

Her words make my pulse thrum.

"Does this mean you're in?"

"Yes, Connor Cane." She smiles. "I'm in."

I reach over, gripping her leg just above her knee in excitement. Her eyes flick down to my hand on her leg, and I quickly slide it away.

"I'd hoped you would be."

"Are you surprised?" she asks, taking another sip from her cup.

"I wasn't sure what you were going to say."

She uncrosses her legs and leans forward, elbows on her knees. "I thought about this all night long. Barely slept a wink."

For some reason, I like the thought of Ella Mae lying awake, tossing and turning, unable to sleep because she's too wrapped up in thoughts of me. I know it's not necessarily what she was saying, but I'm going to allow myself to enjoy my interpretation.

"You feel good about it?" I ask. "You're sure?"

She turns contemplative, her eyes growing distant. "I don't want to regret anything."

I feel a smile tugging up on one side of my face. "You won't."

"So what happens next?"

I set my coffee cup down on the mixing board desk. "I'm going to pitch this idea to the execs today, and if they like it, Drew and I will tighten up the final production on the song."

"You don't want to re-record anything?" she says with a frown.

"Only if I absolutely have to," I say. "I love it as is."

"I do, too. It has that same authenticity of your first record."

I nod. "I thought so, too."

"Just so you know, I'm fine with it being track thirteen. Or a bonus track."

"I think the song could provide a nice break somewhere in the middle of the record, actually."

"Really?" she says, her eyes growing wide. "Wow."

My phone buzzes, and I look down to see it's a text from my manager, Mallory. "If this gets approved, they'll probably want you back here soon to sign off on everything. My manager is working on the paperwork right now."

Her eyebrows raise. "Already? That seems a little premature."

"I'm an optimist, Ella Mae." I flash a smile her way. "Plus, they won't be able to turn this song down when I show them the numbers from the video I posted. The fans love it already. They're asking for a studio version."

A pink flush colors her cheeks. *Dang, she's pretty.*

"You've got nice people, Connor Cane."

"For the most part." I grin, taking a sip of my coffee. "You haven't met any diehard fans yet."

She gets a mischievous look in her eyes. "How do you know I'm not one of them? Recording our conversations as we speak. Posting our text messages to seedy online forums..."

I frown. "You wouldn't do that...would you?"

She laughs, settling back onto the couch. "I could have posters of you plastered all over my bedroom walls for all you know."

Now it's my turn to look pleased.

"Posters, huh? Which posters are you talking about exactly?" I tilt my head. "I had a feature in *People* magazine a few months back. I think one of the photos was printed in poster size."

"Let me clarify, dearest Connor." She rolls her eyes, but I see the pink of her cheeks deepen in color. "I am *not* a diehard fan. I didn't even know your middle name. A true fan would know that."

"Not true. Nobody knows my middle name."

"I'm an admirer of your songwriting craft. Not a fan."

"I don't know that I believe you, Ella Mae."

Her eyes meet mine, and I feel something spark between us. I register how shamelessly I'm flirting with her right now. I don't know what comes over me when I'm in Ella Mae's presence. I can't help myself. I like her. I like talking to her. It's playful. Harmless. I know none of it holds any weight, and it's been a while since I've been able to be myself around somebody.

If she didn't make it so dang easy to flirt with her, maybe I'd have the desire to stop.

"I think I've got a copy of that magazine laying around here somewhere..." I joke. "Tell you what. Since you're such a big fan of mine, I'll even sign it for you."

She steels me with those green eyes. "Perfect. Then I can sell it on my private Connor Cane fan site and make a killing."

I shake my head, grinning. "Careful, Ella Mae. I'll make a fan of you yet."

She pushes her phone toward me. "Could you say my name again, one more time? So I can use it as my ringtone?"

I bark out a laugh. If someone else was in the room, this conversation would not be happening. But it's like we wind each other up. Bring out the ridiculous banter. I don't have to think before I speak with Ella Mae. She can handle the relentless teasing and dishes it right back.

My phone starts ringing. I reluctantly pick it up to see who's calling, slightly bummed about being interrupted.

Stewie.

I turn my phone around, showing Ella Mae the ridiculous photo I've got of her brother that pops up when he calls. A photo we'd taken together back in college, our long hair flipping out from under matching trucker hats we'd bought together at the mall.

"The dynamic duo." Ella Mae laughs. "Look at that *hair*." She tilts her head, looking closer at the picture. "Decidedly *less* blond than it is now."

I glare at her, answering the call.

"What up, Stewie?"

"Hey, man," Trent's deep voice comes through the phone. "You get my text?"

"I did."

He sniffs into the phone, waiting for me to elaborate. When I don't respond, he finally asks, "How was my sister?"

"Why don't you ask her yourself? She's right here," I say. Ella Mae narrows her eyes at me.

"Talking about me behind my back?" She motions for me to give her the phone. "Hand it over."

I reluctantly pass my phone to Ella Mae. She gives me a saccharine smile as she puts it on speaker.

Here we go.

"Hi, Trent," she says. "Connor was just telling me how much fun he had stripping down to his skivvies for a magazine shoot."

I can practically see Trent's judgmental glare. He would give me so much crap if he saw pretty much any professional photo of me. Hair styled. Nose powdered. Face clean-shaven.

"His...what?" Trent says.

"Aren't you so proud to know that your best friend's shirtless photo is now hanging inside every teenage girl's locker in America?"

Trent lets out a low rumble that resembles a laugh.

"Stewie," I say in a warning tone. "Don't you judge me, Stewie."

"Is the music not going well for you?" Trent asks. "I didn't know you'd resorted to selling photos of yourself in your—what did you say, Ella Mae?"

"Skivvies."

"Enough about me and my skivvies," I say defensively.

"We miss you, Trent. Wish you could be here with us right now, sipping your peppermint tea dressed with heaps and heaps of honey," Ella Mae says. "I'm glad you called. I've been wanting to catch up with you. Tell me about the latest happenings at Wildwood. Come across any strange varieties of scat in the woods lately? Bigfoot prints?"

I settle back into my chair, listening as Trent answers with a reluctant laugh. I find myself smiling behind my hand at the comments Ella Mae made about that *People* magazine photoshoot.

Then something registers in my mind that almost makes me laugh out loud. She most definitely *had* seen the feature and was playing coy.

Her tell? I hadn't said a word about the fact that I'd worn nothing but a pair of briefs in those photos. And yet, somehow, she knew that.

Chapter 10

Ella Mae

"We'll have you sign here..."

Claire, a lady from Back Road Records' legal team, points a manicured nail to a line on the page. I scribble my signature where she's indicating.

"And here..."

Good gracious.

Who knew singing on a song with Connor Cane would require me to sign my life away? His pretty blue eyes are pleading with me to patiently acquiesce and keep my mouth shut.

And so I will refrain from commenting on the length of these proceedings and practice perfecting my signature over and over again. I'll be well prepared for the distant day when people ask me for autographs.

Which never would have been a real possibility until now. All joking aside, the probability of people recognizing me is rising due to the video Connor posted. And I'm not just saying this to talk myself up. I experienced it firsthand this afternoon.

I was in the drive-through, treating myself to chicken tenders, fries and lemonade, which the employee nearly tossed onto my lap in some sort of fit.

"Oh my GOSH!" she screeched. "Are you the girl from 'Always You'?"

I tried to hide my discomfort at her outburst and gave her my best smile. "Yes, yes, that's me..." I squinted at her nametag. "Martha. Nice to meet you."

I had my first encounter with a Martha, a name which I shall now use synonymously with *diehard Connor Cane fan.* She crumbled into a blithering mess, muttering things about Connor and his inhuman beauty in a pitiful confession that made me incredibly uncomfortable. I couldn't understand half of what she said in her high-pitched outburst.

Now, I may be crushing on my co-writer (along with any woman who possesses the gifts of sight and hearing), but I most certainly am not eligible to be included in the Connor Cane fandom. Miss ma'am at the drive-through thankfully made that very clear.

What a relief.

After our coffee meet-up the other morning, I'd been writing songs.

And by writing songs, I mean *writing songs*.

Songs inspired by a certain man whose company I've been enjoying lately.

Not intentionally. But somehow his face is the one I see in my mind when I'm writing. If I'm writing about eyes, they're Connor blue. If I'm needing some inspiration for a storyline or hook, I'm bringing the moments I've spent with Connor into it somehow.

He's becoming my creative inspiration. Something I would never confess to him.

Unless he promised me a tender kiss on the cheek (captured in a photo, of course) or several minutes of uninterrupted eye contact to make it worthwhile.

I glance back up at Connor in between contract scribbles and see him smiling over at me, looking stupidly handsome in his checkered flannel and trucker hat turned backward on his head.

Take my secrets. Take them all.

"Do you have any representation?" Claire asks. "Who should we put down as your point of contact?"

My workload and schedule have always been manageable, so the need for a manager has never arisen. I've made most of my own contacts over the years, answered all my own emails, and built up a network by writing with anyone and everyone I could.

"Like I told Mallory over the phone, I used to have a deal with a small publishing company," I say, "but my contract ended last year. And I don't have a manager."

"Well, if you'd ever like one, I'll go ahead and throw my name in the hat now," Mallory says with a smile.

"Thank you." I raise my pen in a salute in her direction.

I'd happily work with anyone Connor keeps on his team. I can tell that he's picky about who is in his inner circle. I look over at Connor for approval. He's watching me with an intensity that I wasn't expecting.

"One thing at a time," he says, flashing a smile at everyone at the table in turn. "Let's not overwhelm my duet partner. We don't want her running for the hills."

"You might want to consider getting management," Mallory says to me. "Once this album drops, you're going to be in high demand, my dear."

I shake my head. "Oh, you're very kind, but I don't know about that."

"As you know, Connor has very dedicated fans," she says, tucking her dark hair behind her ear. "Once they hear this duet, they'll be searching for anything else you've got available."

"Do you have any other music you're working on?" Clark, one of the Back Road executives asks me. "A solo project?"

"Oh, no. I don't record my own stuff," I explain. "I'm just a writer."

"Hmm," Clark says. "Well, at the very least, we'd be interested in setting up more sessions for you to write with Back Road artists."

I can't help but smile at that prospect. "That would be amazing."

"But if you ever change your mind about pursuing your own path as an artist," Clark says, "we'd love to have that conversation with you."

I'm genuinely grateful for the interest, but I know myself. My dreams never included being center stage. I belong behind the scenes, helping artists articulate their feelings through lyrics, crafting the perfect melody to dance over the chords they've pieced together. True artists are much better equipped to stand up and deliver the songs I help create.

"Thank you," I say softly. "I appreciate it. 'Always You' is definitely the exception to my rule."

Connor meets my eyes, and his lips quirk up into a smile. The meeting adjourns a few minutes later, and I find myself being escorted out to the parking lot by Connor.

"How are you holding up?" he asks. "Is this too much for you?"

I'm touched by his genuine concern for me. "Not at all. Don't you worry your pretty little head about me."

Once we reach Wanda, surprisingly Connor doesn't immediately say goodbye. Instead, he shoves his hands into his pockets, leaving his flannel-clad muscled arms front and center for me to admire briefly before I depart.

"They didn't scare you off?" he asks.

"It would take far more than an obscenely long contract and a few label executives to frighten me, Connor Cane."

He eyes me thoughtfully. "Does anything scare you, Ella Mae?"

"Yes."

He waits for me to elaborate.

"Oscar the Grouch."

He gives me a judgmental stare. "As in...*Sesame Street*?"

"The very same."

He raises his eyebrows, clearly amused. "Anything else?"

I fish for my keys in my bag. "Singing in front of big crowds."

"Understandable," he says. "That used to scare me, too."

I tilt my head up to meet his eyes. They're the same shade of blue as the cloudless January sky stretched out above us. "Seriously?"

"I still get a little nervous. Every time."

"You're lying."

"It's true."

"Ahh!" I say as my fingers close over my keys. "There they are." I sling my bag over my shoulder and unlock my car. "It's refreshing to know you're human like the rest of us. You've got us all fooled. You make performing look easy."

"I do enjoy it now," he says. "But it's taken years of practice. I try to pretend I'm singing to just one person instead of thousands of people."

"Does that work?"

"Sometimes."

"I'll have to try it next time I play a writer's round," I say. "It takes me almost the whole show to start to feel comfortable, and by the time I do, we're usually on the last song."

"That's how it always goes."

"Unless you're Connor Crow Cane, of course."

He laughs, dropping his eyes in a rare moment of bashfulness. He shifts from side to side and clears his throat.

He's unsettled by something, and I intend to find out what it is. In typical, Ella Mae fashion, my mouth moves faster than my mind.

"What's up with you?" I say, flipping my hair back over my shoulder. "You're suddenly nervous as a cat."

His eyes flit up to mine. "What? No—"

"You are!"

He laughs, smiling off into the distance like I'm being ridiculous. "I'm not. I'm just—"

"What is it?" I say, drawing the words out. I place a hand on my hip and arch an eyebrow at him. "Out with it. You'll feel better if you just tell me."

Connor stills. Then his gaze locks on mine.

Uh-oh.

I wasn't prepared for him to hold me down with a look like that, all golden and glowing gorgeousness. I swear a halo of light appears around his entire being, and I force myself to hold my head high and not reveal just how much he unnerves me.

"I'm doing a listening party," he finally says. "We partnered with a local radio station to put on an event for a group of contest winners. I'm playing songs from the record. An acoustic set."

"Cool."

Would you—" He pauses, and I see a flicker of something I can't quite name pass over his face. "Would you want to come?"

If this were a movie, I'd coyly look up at him, fluttering my lashes. A breeze would play through my hair, the light from the setting sun casting me in a flattering glow.

But this is real life. And I'm me.

And he's...

Well, he's Connor Cane.

"I figured since you're officially on the record, you might want to hear more of it," he says, laying a palm over his chest. "Or is that presumptuous of me?"

"Not at all," I say. "I'd love to come. When is the show?"

"Next month. I can have Mallory get you the details."

Did I really just receive a personal invitation to spend an evening listening to Connor Cane play unreleased songs live? I feel my heart do a little strut in my chest.

"Name the day," I say with a smile. "I'm not missing out on a chance to be in a room filled to the brim with Marthas."

His eyebrows draw together. "Marthas?"

"It's the name I've given your fans," I explain. "Inspired by an encounter I had with a girl at the drive-through today. She recognized me from your video and then promptly asked me to propose to you on her behalf."

Connor laughs attractively. How can a laugh be attractive? They're supposed to be awkward and snorty. Too loud or too subdued. Not Connor's. He's got a lovely laugh.

"Marthas, huh? I like it."

"It was only a matter of time before I encountered one."

"They're harmless."

I tilt my head in skepticism. "That's what they want you to think, Connor. But you weren't there. Martha's marriage proposal was pretty desperate."

"Was it?"

"Absolutely wretched."

He laughs again. "I'd love to hear it."

"Hear what?"

"Her proposal. What did she say?"

I squint up at him. "Things I'd rather not repeat out loud."

He crosses his arms over his broad chest. "Let's hear it. Come on now. It's not like an offer of marriage comes my way every day."

"I read the comments on your posts, Connor. It's only a matter of choosing which devoted Martha you'd like to marry."

"Tell me what she said."

"I don't think I will."

"It's the least you can do for me, Ella Mae." There it is again. My name on his lips. It shouldn't send a prickle of nerves through my chest cavity, but it does. "I'm practically an old bachelor. Well past my prime."

I look at him incredulously. "You are the *definition* of prime."

He blinks a couple of times. "What's that supposed to mean?"

We stare at each other for a beat.

"Can I have my proposal now?"

"I wouldn't do it justice, you see. I'm not a Martha."

He throws me a cheeky grin. "Well, that's too bad. I might have accepted your offer."

GLORY BE.

"As flattered as I am to know that you'd readily consider a marriage proposal from me, you forget, Connor, that it wasn't *my* offer. It was Martha's," I say. "Besides, I have a rule when it comes to musicians."

Connor rocks back on his heels a bit in response to what I'd hoped would ring out as my closing argument. *Case closed.*

But he doesn't let it go.

"Oh, really?" he says, drawing out his words sarcastically. "Tell me about this rule of yours."

I only mentioned my rule about musicians as an attempt to get him off my case, but I can see a glint in his eyes now—the one he gets when he's about to attempt to even the score. I'm not eager to delve into a recounting of my past heartbreak and what led me to establish my rule, but I can't back down from him now.

Best to just tell the truth and be done with it.

I lift my chin, attempting to look confident. "I don't date musicians. And I'll *never* marry one."

Connor whistles. "Ouch. So this is what it feels like to be rejected by Ella Mae Stewart."

I roll my eyes. "Come on now, Connor. You and I would never suit. You're a musician. And I'm not your type."

He laughs, glancing away before meeting my gaze again. "Tell me," he says with a lift of his chin. "What is my type?"

"Let's see," I say, reaching for Wanda's car door handle behind my back. I need something to hold onto with him looking at me like that. I feel boxed in, trapped, even though there's marked distance between us. "I'd wager you're into the exotic brunette variety. Darling accent. Hollywood smile. Someone who'd look good next to you on the red carpet or on the cover of a magazine."

"Hmm." He tilts his head, assessing me with his eyes. "I'd say you check almost all of those boxes." The way his eyelashes dip down and back up just about does me in. "If it weren't for your blonde hair, I'd snatch you up right now."

"I know," I sigh dramatically. "But unfortunately, even if you wanted to, as you put it, *snatch me up*, my policy on dating men like you won't allow it. Let's be honest. It's best that I simply admire you from afar."

"And kiss my poster you've got hanging on your wall good-night?"

"Yes, exact—" I stop speaking as soon as I realize what he's accusing me of.

Martha-level devotion.

I'm not about to tell him that I do have a small shrine dedicated to Jesse McCartney gracing my desk where I work. The centerpiece is a photo my friend from middle school gave me after she met him at one of his concerts. She'd cut out my face from a different picture and pasted it over her own. A national treasure, she was.

I scoff. "I've already told you, I don't own a single poster of *you*."

"But you've seen one." He grins. "You knew what I was wearing—or should I say *not* wearing—in the *People* magazine shoot."

I lean back against my car door, aghast at his ridiculous accusation, which is most certainly not true.

Except for the fact that it *is* true.

"I told you I'll happily sign it for you, Ella Mae. All you need to do is ask."

I've got nothing to say. And so instead, I purse my lips and raise my eyebrows in challenge.

"See you at the listening party, Connor *Finch* Cane."

"It's a date," he says with a crooked grin. "You're already making an exception for me, Ella Mae. I'm touched."

"Don't flatter yourself, sweetheart. That is one rule I will never break." I give him an appreciative once-over. "Though I will admit I was sorely tempted after seeing that poster of you in your skivvies."

He throws his head back and laughs, and it fills me with the purest form of delight. I'm pleased to see his shoulders still shaking with laughter as I pull Wanda out of the Back Road Records parking lot.

Chapter 11

Ella Mae

"That's the one," I say with conviction.

Lainey pulls at the skirt of the dress she's trying on, a line forming between her brows as she inspects herself in the mirror.

"You think so?"

She's unconvinced.

Ava stands, circling around Lainey with her lips pursed. "I'm not sold on the skirt. It's kind of—"

"Unique," Chloe says.

"HUGE," Lainey sighs. "I'll hardly be able to walk down the aisle in this behemoth."

I cross my arms. "Lainey, it's *magnificent*. You could hide fifteen tiny ballerinas under there like Mother Ginger in *The Nutcracker*."

Lainey tosses her head back and laughs. Even Ava smiles at my joke, even though she's been taking this wedding dress business more seriously than any of us.

"That's it. Get this thing off me!" Lainey says, heaving herself toward the dressing room.

Chloe and I grin at each other. We're having way too much fun helping Lainey find her wedding dress this afternoon at a boutique in downtown Franklin. Lainey's been on the hunt for the perfect dress for months now, but she's running out of time as her end-of-May wedding draws closer.

She recruited all of us to accompany her this weekend in the hopes that we'll be able to help her make a final decision. This has been an all-day affair, kicked off with a yoga class and a stop at our favorite juice bar, keeping up our weekly tradition we started last year. Chloe gave up her Saturday Bud's Biscuits brunch ritual with her husband so she could join us. The shop we're currently in is our third and final stop of the day.

"So how does it feel?" I ask Ava. "Marrying off your beloved baby sister?"

Ava flops back onto the couch next to me. "I feel old."

"Good news. You're *not* old."

"Think about it, Ella Mae," she says, her brown eyes wide. "We're on the downhill slope of life now."

"You're right," I say dryly. "We're practically on our deathbeds."

Chloe has been quiet for most of the afternoon, but she smiles sweetly at the both of us. "I'd like to think things just get better from here."

"Amen," I say.

"I know it does," Ava says. "And I'm happy for Lainey. Being married is the *best*."

"So I've heard," I say. "Chloe? You're our resident newly-wed. What do you have to say on the subject?"

She smiles, lighting up from the inside. You can see in her expression how truly loved she is by her husband. It's written all over her face.

"Ava's right. It's even better than I thought it would be," she says.

I cross one leg over the other and lock my hands together over my knee. "Despite your rave reviews, I'm still not entirely sold on the idea of *matrimony*."

"Oh, Ella Mae. Why so cynical?" Ava asks with a raised brow. "What can we say to convince you to hitch yourself to a nice, fine husband?"

"Nothing," I say. "I like my solitude. And my space."

"So do I," Chloe chimes in. "But Hunter and I still give each other space to do our own thing, even though we're together basically all the time."

I narrow my eyes at her. "You're not helping my argument, Chloe."

She shrugs. "Y'all know I can't lie."

Lainey emerges a few minutes later, and all three of us gasp together at the sight of her.

"*Lainey*!"

"Oh my WORD."

She's a knockout in anything, but Lainey in this dress is a fairytale character brought to life. The dress has a tight lace bodice and delicate straps that drape down around her shoulders. The silk skirt shifts elegantly around her legs as she steps up onto the box in front of the mirror and takes a deep breath.

"You look..." Ava says with a sniff. "Beautiful."

Lainey beams as she turns around to face us. She gives us a nod, hands on her hips. "I think I've found it."

We stand, circling around Lainey and admiring the details of her dress. I can see the relief in her smile, the happiness she feels now that she's found something she truly loves and feels beautiful in.

Lainey reaches for my hand. "What do you think?"

I smile at her reflection. "I think Luke is going to die at the sight of you."

She smiles, her cheeks growing pink. "I can't believe this is happening." She squeezes my hand. "That this day is finally here."

Something twists in my stomach as I'm reminded that Lainey has a new best friend now. A forever best friend. My eyes are drawn to the rings each of my friends wear on their left hands, the outward sign of their commitment to the men they've chosen to marry.

"I'm so happy for you," I say. And I mean it. I am.

"You should wear your hair up to show off this neckline," Chloe says, helping Lainey sweep her hair back to give her an idea of what an updo would look like.

"Can you FaceTime Mom?" Lainey asks Ava.

Lainey and her mom had gone dress shopping back in North Carolina when we'd gone home for Christmas, but their efforts had been in vain.

"Oh, my darling girl," Linda says over FaceTime. "I wish more than anything that I was there with you right now!"

After tears are shed by all three women in the Helms family, Lainey then spends some time speaking to the shop owner, discussing alterations and finalizing the details for her purchase.

I can't keep the smile off my face, watching Lainey getting to experience this rite of passage with her best friends by her side. But I simultaneously feel a new ache in my chest that hasn't been there before.

Despite my jokes and cynicism, and my dedication to my career, I have to be honest with myself.

Deep down, I want what my friends have.

Someday, I want my face to look as shiny as Chloe's does when someone asks me about my person. I want to have a turn trying on dresses in a shop just like this one. I want to experience this level of commitment with someone who complements me like their men do.

"Are you convinced yet?" Chloe says, linking her arm with mine as we exit the shop.

I sigh. "You're an excellent saleswoman."

We fall into step together, walking in a group down the sidewalk. It's only mid-February, but today is unusually warm. Tennessee is teasing us with some real spring weather. I turn my face to the sun, feeling the light tingle on the surface of my skin.

"Have you all chosen your dresses?" Lainey asks.

Ava and Chloe nod. I grimace.

"Not yet," I say. "But I will. Soon."

"How soon, Ella Mae?" she replies. "My wedding is only a few months away."

"Says the girl who just barely committed to a wedding dress not five minutes ago." I link my other arm through hers and tug her closer. "Don't you fret, Lainey. The dress will find me when it's ready."

"Can we stop here?" Ava asks, pointing out an antique store on our left. "Finn refuses to shop at thrift stores with me. The clutter stresses him out."

"Ha!" Lainey laughs. "Luke is the same way!"

"What about Hunter?" I ask Chloe.

She shudders. "He's actually the one who brings the most crap home and tries to convince me we need it."

We laugh together as we enter the store, separating to explore on our own. I'm sifting through a cabinet of knick-knacks when I come across something that makes me smile.

It's a dainty little painting encased in a vintage gold frame. Birds. A whole flock of them. There's even a robin sitting there on a branch. I pick up the painting and pull out my camera to take a picture.

"Shopping for home decor?" Lainey asks from behind me.

I tilt the painting toward her so she can behold it in its tacky glory. "No, this just reminded me of Connor."

Her lips press together, and though she doesn't say a word, I know exactly what she's implying with her pointed expression.

"What I'm about to tell you," I say in a serious tone, "must go with you to the grave."

Lainey gives me a somber nod. "You have my word."

I lean closer and whisper in her ear, "His middle name is Robin."

She gasps. "*It is not.*"

"Sadly, it is," I laugh. "I always razz him about it. Fill in whatever bird name comes to mind. He hates it."

Lainey gets a mischievous look on her face. "Then you need to buy this. Give it to him as a gag gift."

"I can't do that," I say, flipping the painting over to see the price sticker. "It's so overpriced."

"Worth every penny."

We stare at each other.

"You're right."

A few minutes later, I walk out of the store with my painting in hand.

Ava's got a haul of two massive bags of random treasures, smiling and ready to face the wrath of her minimalist husband.

We stop in a few more shops before ending up in front of the L.M. Ward office building, the investment firm the Ward family owns, where Lainey also works as an event planner.

I lift a hand over my eyes to shade them from the sun, glancing up across the street at the loft Luke owns.

"Is the mister home?" I ask.

"He's actually at the office," Lainey says.

"On a Saturday?" Chloe asks.

"He told me one of his clients wanted to meet in private while the office was empty."

"Who is it?" I ask.

"He wouldn't tell me," Lainey says with a pout. "Something about client confidentiality."

"It's gotta be someone famous," Ava says.

"Shall we pay him a visit?" I ask. "Find out who it is?"

"Absolutely," Ava says, her dark eyes glittering. "It's the least he could do for us, really. Introduce us to his celebrity friends."

Lainey grins. "A wonderful idea." She pulls open the door before leading the way through the office lobby toward the elevator.

"Are you sure about this?" Chloe asks from the back of the pack. "Won't his client get mad if he sees us?"

"We'll be sneaky," Lainey says, pressing the button for the elevator. When the doors open, we crowd inside, giggling like children.

"Shh!" Lainey says. "Pipe down, you three!"

Ava and I look at each other and try not to laugh as we ascend up to the second floor where the firm's offices are.

"Listen," Lainey says in a loud whisper. "I'll go first and make sure the coast is clear. When I give you the signal, you follow after me."

"What's the signal?" I hiss.

There's a ding, and the elevator doors open.

"...if that's something you're interested in," Luke is saying to someone on his right—a tall, handsome, blond man who makes my insides quiver when his blue eyes lock with mine. Connor Cane. Looking as delighted to see me as I am to see him.

Chapter 12

Conor

What are the chances that the doors of the elevator open to reveal a group of women that just so happens to include the lovely Ella Mae Stewart?

I swear I'm on a lucky streak.

I first met Luke Ward at his twin brother, Hunter's, wedding. He owns an investment firm and came highly recommended from a couple other artists I know. We'd agreed to meet privately on a Saturday so he could help me diversify my investment portfolio. I'm trying to be smart with my money from the get-go. I've heard too many horror stories of successful people who lose everything, and I don't want to join that club.

Before the elevator doors can close again, Luke puts out a hand to stop it.

"Hey, love," he says to Lainey, his smile tight.

"Hi." She's got a guilty expression on her face as she slides out of the elevator, followed by her sister, Ava, Chloe, and finally Ella Mae.

"What are you girls doing here?" Luke asks. I can hear the edge in his voice as he turns to me. "I'm sorry about this. I swear I didn't tell anyone you and I were meeting today."

"Don't worry about it, man," I say, clapping a hand on his shoulder. "We're all friends, right?"

I can't help but smile at my fortune as my eyes land on my duet partner. She looks lovely, as usual.

"Ella Mae."

"Connor Cane."

She looks up at me slyly, her green eyes glistening.

"Can I talk to you for a second?" Luke takes Lainey by the elbow and guides her away from the group. They immediately become engaged in an intense, whispered conversation.

"What are y'all up to?" I ask.

"Just doing a little shopping," Chloe says.

My eyes drop down to the two bags Ava has got in her hands. She blushes as our eyes meet and gives me a shy smile.

I've seen this look before. It's how all the—what did Ella Mae call them again?—the *Marthas* look at me.

"Looks like it was a successful trip," I say.

Ella Mae lets out a snorty laugh, then promptly tries to cover it up with a cough. I raise my eyebrows at her, noticing that she's also got a bag she's trying to keep hidden behind her back.

"What were *you* shopping for?" I ask her.

She's smiling like she's got a secret.

"I can't even tell you how thrilled I am that we ran into you," she says, ignoring my question. "For several reasons."

"Such as?"

But before Ella Mae can elaborate, Luke and Lainey join us once again. Luke's still got a frustrated look on his face, a deep line between his eyebrows.

"Go ahead," he says, prodding Lainey toward me.

"Connor," Lainey says in a very repentant voice. "We're terribly sorry for intruding on your business meeting with my dear fiancé. It was very unprofessional of us."

"Seriously, don't worry about it," I say with a smile. "I know you."

"To apologize for our interruption," she says, looking pointedly at Ella Mae. "We would like to extend a token of friendship."

Ella Mae stands up straighter. "Oh! Right..."

She brings the bag she's holding around to the front of her body and reaches inside. "Connor Cane, this is for you. I wasn't looking, really, but this called to me, and I just couldn't leave it behind."

She pulls a little frame out of the bag, quickly peeling off the price tag before handing it to me.

"What is this?" I take the frame from her hands.

"Just a little something that reminded me of you."

I flip it over and can't help but laugh as I take in the painting of a variety of colorful birds. Ella Mae leans in closer, pointing to a red-bellied bird perched on a branch.

"There you are," she whispers.

"Ella Mae," I scold. "You shouldn't have."

I flip the painting around and display it to the rest of the group. "Thank you. I will treasure this always."

I'm grinning at the ridiculous playfulness of this surprise, but also feel a heat building in my chest—one that I'm sure Ella Mae didn't intend to ignite.

She was in a random store, saw this bird painting, and she thought of me. And then she did something about it. If we hadn't run into each other here, she would have had to find a way to give it to me.

I was on her mind.

"We'd also like to make things up to you by inviting you to join Luke and me for dinner." Lainey turns to Ella Mae. "Along with you."

"Me?" Ella Mae says, arching an eyebrow. "Why just me?"

"Because that's what we had planned, remember?" Lainey says, widening her eyes.

Ella Mae tilts her head, questioning. Ava grabs Chloe by the arm, and they take a step back toward the elevator.

"Don't worry about us," Ava says. "We've got plans. Right, Chloe?"

"Right," Chloe says. "Hunter and I are busy. Very busy. In fact, we should get going, shouldn't we, Ava?"

"Yes, we should. Thank you for the fun afternoon, ladies," Ava says with a little finger wave. "We'll see y'all later."

It's painfully obvious what these girls are trying to do right now. Corralling Ella Mae and me into a corner. But am I bothered by it?

Not one bit.

I look over at Ella Mae. Her eyes are wide, like she's trying to communicate with Lainey telepathically. Lainey's not having it, and for that I'm thankful.

"Are you free tonight, Connor?" Lainey asks.

"You know what? This almost never happens, but I actually am."

"Great!" she says, clapping her hands together. "We're going to order takeout and eat at Luke's place if you'd care to join us."

"I just live across the street," Luke explains.

"Oh, nice," I say, shuffling closer to the elevator as the doors open once again. "I'd love to."

Ella Mae's arm brushes mine as we cram into the elevator, and I'm surprised at the jolt our brief moment of contact sends through my whole body. I glance over at her, wondering if she felt it too, but she keeps her eyes trained on the back of the elevator doors as they close.

I instinctively tug my hat down and hunch my shoulders over, keeping my eyes on the white lines of the crosswalk as we move across the street to Luke's loft apartment. I try my best to keep myself hidden behind a hat and sunglasses when I'm out, as cliche as it sounds. Long gone are my days of being able to hold my head high and walk around in public without being stopped and stared at by strangers.

Ella Mae walks half a step ahead of me, angling her body almost protectively as we move briskly down the busy street. Though we haven't exchanged words about the stress I'm feeling right now, somehow she caught on and is instinctively creating a barrier between me and the people around us.

It's comforting in a way.

I stay quiet and focus on following Luke and Lainey without making eye contact with anyone around me, unable to totally relax until we're safely inside.

Ella Mae holds the door open, allowing me to enter the apartment before she does. As she closes the door behind her, I pull my sunglasses off and meet her eyes.

I expect her to tease me about my intensity, the paranoia she clearly picked up on as we made our way from the office to Luke's place. But she doesn't say a word. She simply places a warm hand on my arm as she walks by, giving me a gentle smile of understanding.

She gets it. She gets me. I appreciate that small gesture more than she knows.

I put my sunglasses in the pocket of my jacket, taking in the bright sunlight streaming in through the floor-to-ceiling windows that make up the far wall of the loft. Luke's got a nice view of the L.M. Ward office on the other side of the street.

"Nice place," I say appreciatively.

Luke grins. "Thanks, man."

"Not as nice as it will be once I move in," Lainey says, placing her purse down on the kitchen island.

"Where do you live now?" I ask Lainey.

"Ella Mae and I are roommates. We live in my townhome in Carriage Court, not too far from here," Lainey says. "But once Luke and I are married, I'll be moving in and taking over Luke's bachelor pad."

"And where will you go?" I ask Ella Mae.

"That's the question of the hour," she says with a smile. But for the briefest of moments, a shadow crosses over her expression.

"I've been wanting to ask you about that, actually," Luke says. "I've got this place in Belfair that's going to be available soon. I could take you over to look at it if you'd like."

She raises her eyebrows. "Belfair? Sounds far too elegant for the likes of me."

"I'm renting an apartment in Belfair right now, actually," I say, nudging Ella Mae with my shoulder. "We could be neighbors."

She snorts. "If folks like him"—she jerks a thumb in my direction—"live in those fancy apartments, there's no way I'll be able to afford it. I'm a peasant."

"A *peasant*?" I laugh.

"You're so dramatic," Lainey says, rolling her eyes.

"It's true!" Ella Mae insists. "Ask me what I ate for breakfast."

"Cereal," I guess.

"Gruel," she says. "And a crust of bread."

"And by that she means an egg-white omelet with sourdough toast," Lainey says pointedly. "That I lovingly made for her."

"Killjoy," Ella Mae grumbles.

I grin. "Just wait until your royalty checks hit your account," I say. "No more gruel for you."

Ella Mae sighs. "Won't that be nice."

"Speaking of food, where should we get dinner?" Lainey asks, scrolling on her phone. "Anything sound particularly good?"

I slide into a seat at the kitchen island next to Ella Mae as she chimes in with suggestions.

I can't remember the last time I hung out with friends. I spend most of my time with my bandmates and people from Back Road Records. I try to see my family in Knoxville when I can, but my world has gotten significantly smaller. It's nice to feel normal and included. To be around people who want to be in my company because they like *me*, not just what I do for a living.

"Pizza?" Lainey says. "Does that sound good to you, Connor?"

"Pizza is always good."

Ella Mae points at me. "Correct answer."

Luke hands us drinks from the fridge while Lainey orders the pizza.

"Ella Mae played us the song you two wrote together," Luke says. "It's really great."

"Thank you," I say, glancing over at Ella Mae. "That song pretty much saved my record."

"He's being paid to say that," she quips.

"When does the album come out?" Luke asks.

"End of May."

"What day?" Luke asks.

"The 28th."

"Same day as their wedding," Ella Mae says.

"No way."

Luke nods. "That's the big day. Did Ella Mae tell you she'll be gracing us with a song?"

"Really?" I say. She avoids my eyes. "She didn't mention that."

Luke nods. "We want her to play during our first dance."

"No pressure," Ella Mae coughs. "The most romantic moment of the entire evening hinges on *my* performance."

I remember what Ella Mae told me when I asked her what she was most afraid of: Oscar the Grouch...and singing in front of people.

To willingly sing at her best friend's wedding in front of all their guests? That's a big move for her. A sign of her love for Luke and Lainey.

"What did I miss?" Lainey says, placing her phone down on the counter.

"We were just talking about how Ella Mae is singing at our wedding," Luke says, slipping his arm around Lainey's waist.

"I've been meaning to tell you," Lainey says. "I think you should sing 'Always You.'"

"Without my dearest duet partner?" Ella Mae leans toward me, her warm hand landing on my arm, head briefly resting against my shoulder. I'm caught off guard by the gentleness of her touch, the smell of her hair. It all happens so quickly, but I'm frozen to the spot, my heart pounding in my ears even after she pulls away.

"I could never carry that song as a solo," she says with a sigh. "You're not busy that day, right?" She squints up at me, a cheeky grin on her face.

"Not at all."

I shift in my seat and cross my arms, placing my elbows on the counter, still trying to get my bearings after Ella Mae's touch. I've hugged her many times before. But it's hard to deny the fact that when she touches me now, it doesn't feel sisterly. It feels like something else.

She's an attractive woman. Any man would feel the way I do if they had her attention.

"Connor's album comes out on our wedding day," Luke explains to Lainey.

"Well, if that doesn't sound like a good omen for both of us," Lainey says, "I don't know what does."

The conversation shifts into wedding talk. The three of them are all smiles as they discuss the wedding dress that had been found earlier that day. Luke can't take his eyes off his fiancée, and Lainey's shining like a star in the night sky.

I'm watching Ella Mae closely as I sip my drink. She's happy for them, I can tell. But a flicker of emotion occasionally crosses over her expression in moments where they're not looking directly at her.

But I notice it. I recognize that same look in myself from time to time.

Loneliness.

It would appear that we've got more than just a love for music in common. Becoming successful in our industry sometimes comes at a cost, and it would seem that Ella Mae and I are paying a similar price.

When the pizza arrives, we settle into enjoying our meal together. I'm on my second slice when my phone starts buzzing in my pocket.

It's my manager, Mallory, calling at seven p.m. on a Saturday. The music industry never sleeps.

"I'm sorry," I say, sliding out of my seat. "I've gotta take this."

Mallory's got a Back Road executive with her, wanting to talk through a few details around the final mixing and mastering of the record. I realize after a couple of minutes of getting grilled by the exec that this call is going to be much longer than just a brief check-in.

"Hey, Mal," I say when I can finally get a word in. "I'm out right now. Can I call you guys back in five minutes?"

We hang up, and I return to the kitchen. They all look up at me expectantly.

"Everything okay?" Ella Mae asks.

"Yeah," I say, feeling bummed that I'm going to have to cut my evening with her short. "It was my manager. I'd better head out."

"Take some pizza to go!" Lainey insists, making me a plate.

"Then you can eat it for breakfast tomorrow," Ella Mae says. "Straight out of the fridge."

Why does it not surprise me that Ella Mae is the type of girl who would eat cold pizza for breakfast?

I say goodbye to Luke and Lainey, thanking them for hosting me.

"I'll walk you out," Ella Mae says, sliding off her seat.

She follows me into the hallway, leaving the door ajar behind her. "Want me to walk you back to your car?" she asks quietly, her eyes softened with concern.

I look down at her, my chest feeling tight at her thoughtfulness. As feisty as she is, this five-foot-something blonde girl couldn't do a thing to stop a wild fan from coming at me.

"I'll be fine," I say, holding up my plate of pizza. "I'll use this as a weapon if necessary."

She grins. "Death by pizza." She stretches her arms out to embrace me. "Thanks for hanging out with us."

I wrap my non-pizza-bearing hand around her shoulders, pulling her tight to my body. Her hands circle my waist, and she squeezes me back. I like the way her body feels, all pressed up against mine—probably a lot more than I should, considering the fact that she is Trent's younger sister.

I reluctantly pull away. "See you soon, Stewie Two."

Chapter 13

Ella Mae

I'm only three minutes late to Connor's listening party at Back Road Studios. I count that as a win.

After parking and dashing inside the building, I'm directed to a room clearly designed for these types of events. There's a small stage set up at the far end of the room, furnished with two stools, several microphones, and an empty guitar stand. A massive wall hanging takes up the entire space behind the stage—a larger-than-life print of Connor's self-titled second album cover. The photo the label has chosen to feature on the record is a masterpiece—a sepia-toned close-up of Connor's face. I can see the freckles scattered across the bridge of his nose and the length of his eyelashes from here. If that photo alone doesn't make this record a chart-topper, I'll be shocked.

Just as I'd anticipated, the room is full of Marthas. Chattering excitedly. Weeping. I can feel their nervous energy and start to absorb some of it, too. Even though I know Connor personally, I can't help but feel a little Martha-ish as I stand awkwardly at the back of the room, scanning for an empty seat I may be able to take before he comes out onstage.

"Ella Mae!" Connor's manager, Mallory, says as she approaches me. "Glad you could make it!"

"Thanks for having me," I say.

"Connor saved you a seat up front," Mallory says, taking my arm. "Come with me."

"Up front?" I squeak, digging in my heels and pulling Mallory to a halt. "Oh, no. I couldn't possibly take a front-row seat."

Mallory stops mid-stride. "Why not?"

Surely the Martha's will sniff me out as a fake and murder me on the spot.

"I'll just find a seat back here."

She looks a little frustrated with me, but I really don't want to hustle up to the front row in front of everyone and draw attention to myself. "He specifically requested that you sit—"

Before she can force me into a seat on the front row, the lights go down, and a man steps out onto the stage. I recognize him as Dan Taylor, a local country radio host. The house music lowers in volume as he steps up to the microphone.

Mallory quickly leads me to an empty chair on the far end of the last row.

"Thank you," I hiss. She nods and then disappears into a darkened corner at the back of the room.

"Well, hello there," Dan says into his microphone.

There's some hollerin' in response to his greeting from a few particularly ardent Marthas in the crowd.

"We are so glad you're here," Dan says. "Thank you for being here tonight to help us celebrate the release of Connor's upcoming album. We can't wait to have him come out and play a few songs for y'all."

The rest of the Marthas lose it at the mention of Connor's name. I settle down into my seat, unable to keep the smile from crawling across my face. I'm going to give him so much crap about these unruly fans of his.

Dan explains the format of the show. Connor will be playing a few songs, some old, and some from the album. Between each song, Dan will come back onstage to ask some questions. At the end of the show, they'll open up the floor for a brief Q&A.

"Now that we've gotten that business over with," he says with a smile. "What do you think? Should we bring Connor Cane out here?"

The room explodes. The Martha next to me bounds to her feet, whacking her hands together in the most passionate display of applause I have ever witnessed. Her palms will surely suffer for it.

The ear-piercing screams intensify as a door opens at the front of the room. I catch a glimpse of the top of Connor's blond head as he is led to the stage by a burly security guard.

He climbs up the stairs and slings his guitar over his shoulders, shakes Dan's hand, and takes a seat on the stool on the right side of the stage.

I'm involuntarily brought to my feet, not wanting to be the only person in the crowd still seated. This man deserves a standing ovation, and he hasn't even sung a word yet.

I may be Martha material after all.

"Good evening."

The sound of his smooth voice over that sound system sends a rush of chills down the back of my neck. Where's my *Marry Me Connor* sign when I need it?

"Thank y'all for coming out," he says, looking out bashfully at the crowd. "When Dan approached me about doing this event, I told him I didn't think anybody would show up. But man, did you guys show up."

Connor's eyes scan down the front row, and I suddenly regret not sitting where he'd wanted me to sit. I hope he doesn't think I bailed on him or forgot about tonight.

Oh well. I'll simply have to take in his beauty from the safety of the back row where he won't be able to see me staring.

"Is it alright if I play a few songs for y'all?"

Cue the screams and '*I love you, Connor!*' declarations.

"This first song," he says, picking at his guitar strings, "came out last summer."

He pauses for a moment.

"This one is called 'Cry Baby.'"

He leans back on his stool, playing the intricate riff at the start of the song.

Even from the back of the room, I can see his strong hands, his long fingers striking the strings of his guitar. I feel my heartrate pick up as I watch him do his thing, feeling nearly breathless as he fills the room with the sound of his instrument.

Then he starts singing...and I'm gone. Emotionally destroyed. Blown to smithereens. I'm mesmerized, feeling the vibration of his voice reverberating through my ribs. He sings so effortlessly, his pitch and delivery on point. *Phew.* And to think he's only on the first song.

Once the first chorus kicks in, the Marthas around me start singing along. I, too, know every word. Pretty sure I cranked it up to full blast every time it came on the radio last summer.

I can't help but let my voice join in with all the girls around me, remembering how it felt to sing with Connor, to meld our voices in unison and then split off into harmony.

He finishes "Cry Baby," and the crowd cheers him on for a good while, only dying down once Connor places his guitar back on its stand. Dan comes back onstage and resumes his spot on his stool.

"Connor Cane," he says, shaking his head. "Such a great song, man."

"Thanks, Dan."

"How does it feel to have people singing lyrics you've written back to you?"

Connor's lips lift into a smile. "It's surreal, honestly. I can't believe it."

"This must be a dream come true for you," Dan says. "Getting to release your second album. Tell us a little bit about your journey and how you got to where you are now."

"Well, I've been singing and writing songs since I was about twelve years old, right around the time I experienced my first heartbreak."

Connor grins out at the crowd, and a Martha yells out, "I'D NEVER BREAK YOUR HEART, CONNOR."

"Thank you." He presses a hand to his chest. Endearing.

"Your first heartbreak at twelve?" Dan says. "That's way too young. What happened?"

"It was tragic. I wrote her a note in class that said, 'I like you. Do you like me too?' and then put two check boxes, one with 'yes' and one with 'no.' When she passed that note back to me, there was a big check mark next to the 'no' box. And so that day, I went home, and I wrote my first song."

We all laugh along with Dan at Connor's tale of young love spurned.

"Do you still remember it? That first song you wrote?"

Connor clears his throat and starts to sing. "*I gave you my heart and my mind and my soul, and all I got in return was a check next to 'no'...*"

Laughter ripples through the crowd again. As Connor answers a few more questions about his back story, it's clear that he's got every person in this room eating out of the palm of his hand. He's likable, humble, and relatable. Then there's the matter of his songs...forget about it. Truly the whole package.

He touches on writing songs in college while he was getting his business degree. "I'm very involved in the business side of my career. My degree prepared me so that I'd be able to manage my catalog and my assets—"

"*I'd* like to manage his assets," someone says from down the row, loud enough for me to hear. I snort, deciding to shelve that comment away to share with him later.

"I like to be involved in every aspect of my work. Not just the music. I think that sets me apart from a lot of other artists."

"I agree," Dan says. "How has writing this second album compared to writing the first?"

Connor lets out a little laugh. "You know how they say you spend your whole life writing your first record? It's true. Writing this second album has been a lot harder." He sits up in his stool. "But it's in a good place now. I'm really proud of these songs, and I can't wait for y'all to hear them."

"Can you tell us a bit about this next song you're going to play?" Dan asks.

"Well..." One side of Connor's mouth lifts. "It's a new one."

The titters and screeches abound.

"This was one of the first songs I wrote for the record. You guys are going to be the first to hear it. Hope you like it."

Oh, we like it, Connor. We LOVE IT.

I lean back in my chair, listening intently as he performs the song. I don't know why some people are blessed with an outward ease when it comes to performing, while others (like me) would rather sing when we're alone in a quiet stairwell where no one can hear us but the birds in the rafters. But I'm grateful I get to witness Connor in this intimate setting. It's clearly what he was meant to do.

Connor plays through a couple more songs off the new record, and I already can't wait to listen to them on repeat when the album comes out. Maybe I can bribe Connor to send me the songs early. Dan comes back out onstage in between, and they chat about everything from Connor's songwriting process to how involved he is in the production of his music videos.

Connor plays his hit single from last fall, "Make Up," and then Dan opens up the floor to questions from the audience.

I'm enthralled. Eager to hear what sort of deep dive we're about to take into Connor Cane at the helm of this group of dedicated fans.

Dan moves through the crowd, randomly handing people the mic and letting them ask Connor their burning questions.

"If you could be any mythological creature, what would you be and why?" a girl from the left side of the room asks.

Brilliant. Something I've always wondered myself.

"Hmm..." Connor sits back in his stool, staring up at the lights for a moment. "I think I'd want to be a merman."

Everyone around me laughs, but I simply gasp, stuck in a very vivid fantasy of Connor Robin Cane with a scaly, shimmering blue tail that sets off the shade of his eyes, washed ashore for me to stumble upon and admire—and frisk for injuries. Thoroughly.

"Because I love the ocean."

"Well said," Dan laughs.

One of the Marthas seated in the row in front of me is whipped into a frenzy when Dan comes by, practically yanking the microphone out of his hand.

"Hi, Connor. First of all, I love you…"

Connor smiles from the stage.

"I'd love to know if you have a favorite song on the new album."

"That's a great question," Connor says. "There are a few I'm really excited to play live with the band on tour. But I think my favorite song off the record right now is actually the last one I wrote for it, not too long ago."

My heart starts sputtering in my chest. Unless I'm mistaken and Connor wrote another song after ours, he's talking about our song.

"It's called 'Always You.'"

My cheeks warm as the Marthas scream in response.

Really? Out of all the songs on that record, which is sure to be incredible, that's his favorite?

"I wrote it with a good friend of mine, who's actually supposed to be here tonight."

Glory be.

My eyes grow wide, and I slink down into my seat as the whispers start rippling through the crowd.

Don't do it, Connor. Don't you dare—

"Ella Mae?" He puts his hand over his eyes to block out the spotlight, scanning the room. "Are you out there?"

What's a girl supposed to do when a man like Connor Cane calls you out in a crowded room? Cower in fear? Make a dramatic exit?

The only thing one *can* do.

I raise my hand slowly into the air, and Connor's eyes find mine from the stage. He smiles that gorgeous smile of his, and I feel like he's the hunter and I'm the prey.

Or if we're staying on theme, the fisherman and the...fish.

Caught.

Chapter 14

Connor

"Can we get the house lights up a little bit?" I say into my mic. The lights-and-sound tech in his booth obliges, and now Ella Mae comes into full focus from her seat at the back row.

I'd had a pit in my stomach for most of this event, staring at that empty seat at the end of the first row, thinking she hadn't shown up.

But at some point during the last song, I thought I saw her—all blonde hair and smiles at the back of the room. Good thing my eyes hadn't deceived me.

"There she is, ladies and gentlemen. Ella Mae Stewart."

I swear the entire crowd collectively turns around to see who I'm introducing by name.

She's smiling, but I can see the discomfort in her posture, like she's trying to shrink down in her chair. It's clear that she doesn't like being the center of attention. I'm sure she's going to make me pay for this later.

But she can't be too upset with me for telling the truth. I'm proud of our song, and I want everyone to know it.

"Ella Mae and I wrote this song together a few months back," I say, feeling a smile growing on my face as I look directly at her. She arches an eyebrow at me, questioning. "Maybe you guys have seen the video I posted—"

At the mention of the video, there's some whooping in the affirmative. "Cool. A few of you have seen it. Anyway, this song kind of completed the record, and I can't wait for you to hear the studio version. We recorded it as a duet, and we're both really proud of it."

Ella Mae crosses one leg over the other and gives me a close-lipped smile, as if to say, *You can shut up now.*

"Sing it!" someone calls out from the audience. "Sing the song!"

"Uh…" I say with a laugh. "I did not prepare Ella Mae for a performance tonight. I'm sure she's comfortable right where she is."

"Sing it!" someone else yells, and the chanting begins.

"Sing it! Sing it!"

I feel a knot building in my throat, knowing that Ella Mae would not be comfortable doing an impromptu performance, especially in front of all these fans.

She's shaking her head, and I can see her speaking to the chanters around her in an attempt to calm the storm I've unintentionally started. Mallory appears next to Ella Mae, and she makes eye contact with me, a question in her gaze.

This is on me now. Can I ask Ella Mae to do this for me?

I wouldn't say no to singing our duet together, but is this all too much for her? I guess it wouldn't hurt to ask. Worst-case scenario, she turns me down, and I sing it by myself.

"Ella Mae?" I say into the mic. "Do you wanna come up here and sing with me? You can say no."

Ella Mae meets my eyes, and it's like she's standing right in front of me. Like there's nobody else here in the room.

She shakes her head and smirks, like I'm getting a scolding. Then the corner of her mouth turns up, and she gives me a tiny nod.

No way. She's up for it.

"Come on up here, then."

Mallory and Ella Mae link arms, and together they make their way to the stage.

My security guard, Paul, helps Ella Mae up the steps. I can't keep the smile off my face as she walks toward me. She's stunning in a long white dress, the toes of a pair of white cowboy boots peeking out from underneath. She's got her hair down, all flowing and golden. She's angelic.

I swallow.

Maybe this wasn't such a good idea after all.

Dan leads Ella Mae to his stool, and they shake hands. She takes the mic and flips her hair back over her shoulders, then looks my way.

I'm just sitting here, staring. Smiling at her like a fool.

"Well, Connor," she says into the mic, "you've got me up here. Are we gonna sing somethin', or just sit here and look at each other?"

I let out a quiet laugh, coming back to the present moment.

Right. People are watching. The show must go on.

I look back out at the audience and am shocked to see that most people's faces are covered by their phones. We're being filmed. They're excited about this song. If we give them a good performance, they'll post about it and help build up the hype for the record, just like Back Road hoped.

Just like Ella Mae and I hoped.

"You wanna sing with me?" I ask Ella Mae, tilting my head to the right so I can see her.

"Let's do it," she says, taking a deep breath. "Quick. Start playing before I change my mind and pull somebody up here to take my place."

The crowd laughs. She's got them captivated already.

"Let's give her a warm welcome, shall we?" I say. "This is a rare occurrence. She doesn't like to do this kind of thing."

"I'll do it for you, Connor," she says.

I smile then, leaning back in my stool to find the first chord of the song with my left hand, letting the fingers of my right hand land on the strings.

"You ready?"

Ella Mae nods. I cover the microphone with my palm so it won't pick up my voice.

"You've got this," I say quietly, leaning toward her. "Pretend it's just you and me singing in the studio."

She nods again. I take that as a cue that she's ready to sing.

I play through the introduction of the song, picking out a pattern on my guitar strings. She starts to sway back and forth to the rhythm of the music with her eyes closed. I lean into the mic, letting the words flow out.

I glance over at her a couple times during the first verse, but she keeps her head down, eyes closed.

When we reach the pre-chorus, she lifts her mic and adds her voice to mine. Her harmony dances above my melody line, slightly different from the part she'd recorded. I like it. She's ad-libbing. This time, when I look over at her, she's got her face turned my way. Our eyes meet, our mouths moving at the same time, and something happens to me that makes me nearly choke on the first line of the chorus.

A chill runs over the back of my neck. Then down my entire spine. Something stirs in the deepest part of my stomach as I sing.

I'm no longer singing *with* Ella Mae.

I'm singing *to* her.

This room is packed full of people, but somehow it feels like she's it. An audience of one. I feel vulnerable. Like this is a confession. Like I'm baring my heart to her through this song.

She lowers the microphone and smiles gently at me at the end of the chorus. One of my strings buzzes under my left hand.

Dang it. I'm getting sloppy. I drop my gaze down to my guitar, forced to focus on the chord progression so I play it correctly. She's throwing me off my game.

Ella Mae lifts her mic to her lips and starts to sing her verse, and the room goes quiet as they listen intently. Everyone has to be feeling some version of what I'm feeling right now. I'm paying attention to every inflection of her voice. Her style choices and how she uses vibrato. How long she holds out notes and where she places certain words in her throat and on her lips.

She moves me. She's moving all of us, holding us captive with her voice.

I join back in with her at the second chorus, and our voices rise and fall together throughout the rest of the song. As we near the last line, I'm lost in the song. Lost in the sound of our voices together. I let my gut tell me how to deliver the last few words, and somehow, her instincts are the same. Where I go, she follows. Where she moves, I move. This isn't rehearsed. It's felt.

We hold out the last note together, looking at each other to know when to trail off. We pull back from our microphones, and I force myself to smile at her even though my pulse is doing funny things in my chest.

The crowd comes back to life, applauding and whistling.

Ella Mae lifts her microphone up to her mouth. "Can I go now, Connor Cane?"

I laugh, bringing my hands together to join in the audience's applause for her. "Ella Mae Stewart, everybody," I say.

I get up off my stool and set my guitar down on its stand. She stands, too, and before she can dart off the stage, I wrap my arms around her, pulling her close to me.

She's still got her microphone in her right hand, but she wraps her left hand around my shoulders. I feel her fingers digging into my back, her breath catching in my ear.

"Thank you," I say into her hair. "That was amazing."

"You are eternally in my debt."

I snicker, releasing her. "Feel free to call in a favor from me anytime."

As she steps back away from me, there's a second where I see something pass through her green eyes, the tilt of her smile. Something that looks a lot like what I'm feeling on the inside.

She turns to the audience and gives them a little dip of a curtsy. "Thank you!" she says before exiting off side stage.

I see that Paul is already there, waiting to escort Ella Mae out the same door I'd entered through. I'm glad we're on the same wavelength. I don't want her wandering around unprotected tonight after that performance. She'll get mobbed if we send her back into the audience.

Dan comes back out onstage, beaming like it's Christmas morning.

"Wow, man," he says as he returns to his stool. "That might be my new favorite song of yours."

I know I already said it was my favorite song, too, but now it may be for entirely different reasons.

Ella Mae is stirring up things inside me I've never felt before. It's more than just attraction. It's connection. I could sing with her all day, every day and never get tired of it. I'm going to be chasing the feeling I've got right now, this high I'm riding.

"Connor, we'd like to thank you for being here tonight." Dan turns to the crowd. "And for all of you who turned up to support Connor's album. Release day is when?"

"May 28th."

"Mark your calendars. Don't forget to grab your signed poster and t-shirt from the merch table before you leave."

Dan thanks the radio station and the sponsors, then I stand and wave to the audience before heading offstage. Ella Mae is there, waiting for me with Paul, and together we make our exit.

Paul follows behind us as we walk briskly down the hall to my green room.

I glance over at Ella Mae. "Hey," I say.

"Hey."

"You okay to stay for a bit?"

I hold open the door to the green room, and she steps inside.

"You're not giving me much of a choice, Connor," she says with a cheeky smile. "I feel like I'm being kidnapped."

Paul gives me a nod and remains stationed outside, letting the door close us in.

"Held against your will?"

She eyes me. "I never said that."

I set my guitar down on a stand near the lone couch in the room, then turn to face Ella Mae.

"Those were some pretty good songs you sang tonight," she says.

I drag a hand through my hair. Between the post-show high I'm feeling and the sparks that were flying while we sang together, I'm not sure I should be trusted to be alone in this room with her right now.

"Thank you for being here," I say. "It means a lot to me."

"Sure thing, Connor..." She smiles to herself. "*Heron*." She wanders over to a table filled with snacks and pulls some grapes out of a bowl, popping them in her mouth.

"For a minute there, I thought you stood me up," I say, coming to stand beside her. I reach across her body for the grapes. My hand skims against her arm, the sensation making my fingertips buzz.

"For a minute there, I regretted not taking your front-row VIP seat, but then I got to witness the mayhem you caused from my spot in the back." She chews on her grape. "You had everybody in that room all hot and bothered from the second you set foot on that stage."

I raise my eyebrows, my cheek twitching as I hold back a smile. "Everybody?"

Her chewing slows, and then she swallows. "So." She reaches for a water bottle and unscrews the cap, handing it to me in a clear effort to ignore my pointed question.

"Thank you," I say.

"What do you usually do after your shows?"

"Well, when I'm on tour, I've got the band with me. We go back to the bus and wind down before we head out to the next show."

She takes a swig of her water, not breaking eye contact. "What do you do after shows like this one when you don't have your bandmates to hang out with?"

I shrug, fiddling with the cap on my water bottle. "I don't know. Grab something to eat on the way home."

"By yourself?"

My silence is all the answer she needs.

"I think"—she pauses—"a show like the one you just played deserves to be celebrated. We should go get ice cream or see a movie."

I let my eyes roam over her pretty face, watching as her cheeks turn pink under my gaze.

"Ella Mae Stewart," I say. "Are you asking me out on a date?"

She levels me with a heated stare.

"No, Connor. This is *not* a date."

Her words hang in the air, feeling like a bold-faced lie.

I shake my head, feigning disappointment. "That's twice you've turned me down, Ella Mae. I don't know how much more rejection I can take. You're breaking my heart."

She eyes me with a tilt of her head. "Guess you're going to have to start writing songs about me, then."

A smile breaks out across my face. "Guess so."

Chapter 15

Ella Mae

"I've never been escorted by a security guard before," I say. "That felt like a rite of passage." I'm currently riding shotgun in Frank. "Paul seems very nice."

"He's a good guy," Connor says, adjusting his grip on the steering wheel. My eyes dart to his big, strong hands, then travel up his muscled arms.

Maybe agreeing to a celebratory outing with Connor wasn't the best idea I've ever had. I'm still a little shaken up over that song we performed together. The chemistry between us had been tangible, sparking in the air. I doubt those Marthas fully understood what they had just witnessed. Or maybe they did, and I've earned myself a nice target on my back. Maybe that's why Connor hasn't let me out of his sight.

Death by Martha.

"Are you hungry?" he asks.

"Of course," I answer. "I'm always hungry."

He looks over at me, amused. "What'll it be, then? Dessert?"

"Hmmm..." I say. "What's still open at this hour?"

Connor gestures to my favorite drive-through chicken place up ahead. "Does that sound good to you?"

"Always."

He grins over at me. "That's my girl."

My heart twists at his words. I'm not actually *his girl*, I know. But the possibility settles over me, and I like how it feels.

We pull into the drive-through, and Connor rolls down his window. He peruses the menu, rubbing a hand over his mouth.

"Order whenever you're ready," a voice says through the speaker.

"Do you know what you want?" he asks me.

"A number three combo with a lemonade. And a cookie."

He raises his eyebrows. "That was decisive."

"I come here twice a week," I admit. "If we were driving my car, they'd most likely recognize me and would already have my order in."

Connor laughs. He places his order and mine, then pulls forward to the next window.

"That'll be twenty-seven—" The young girl at the window turns to look at Connor, and her voice drops off. Jaw slacks. "Oh. My. Gosh."

Connor reaches for his credit card in his wallet, but I'm prepared to intervene. I lean over his body, practically laying on his lap so I can hand my card to her out the truck window.

"Here," I say, my voice strained from extending my body to its limits.

"What are you *doing*?" Connor says into my ear. I feel his hand wrap around my waist, and he tries to tug me away from the window. "Get off me. I'm buying."

"No, sir," I say. "Not today."

Luckily, the employee is still stunned and snags my card from my hand after I wave it wildly out the window. She swipes my card and hands it back. I slide back into my seat, triumphant after successfully asserting my independence by buying our late-night fast-food dinner.

Connor stares at me for a second.

"You're ridiculous."

"You like it."

He eyes me like he's unsure of how to respond. Instead, we both turn to the girl at the window, but she's still mute.

"I'll just..." Connor gestures ahead. "I'll just pull forward, then."

She gives him a slow, reverent nod, and he starts to ease the truck forward.

"Can I get a picture?" she blurts out in desperation. Connor abruptly stops the truck, nearly giving me whiplash.

"Sure," he says with a tight smile, glancing over at me. "You okay to take a picture?"

"She doesn't want *me* in the—"

"Yes, I do!" the girl says.

She pulls out her phone, puts it on selfie mode and turns around. Connor leans out the window, and I peer around his shoulder, both smiling for the photo.

"Thank you." Connor gives her a wave, which she returns practically in slow motion. Connor glances over at me as he pulls the truck to the next window, looking apologetic.

"Thank you for dinner," he says. "I'm buying next time."

"Deal." I smile at the prospect of there being a *next time*. "Is this what happens every time you go through the drive-through?"

"Not every time."

"It must get tiring," I joke. "Having women fawn over you at every turn. How often do you get free food? Maybe I should start inviting you to lunch with me so I can capitalize on their generosity."

I look over at Connor, and I'm surprised to see he's no longer smiling. He rubs a hand over his face and blinks at me.

"It *is* tiring, actually," he says quietly.

The second window opens, and Connor promptly puts that smile of his right back on and politely thanks the employee as he hands us our food.

He shuffles the bags over to my lap, and I sit in silence, feeling badly about giving him a hard time.

Connor pulls out onto the main road, keeping his gaze straight ahead as he drives.

I swallow and hesitantly place my fingertips on his upper arm. He glances down at my hand on his arm briefly before his eyes return to the road.

"Hey," I say softly. "I'm sorry for teasing you."

He shrugs. I pull my hand away. "All good."

We're both quiet as he drives, the shadows and the street-lights shifting outside my window.

"Mind if we go somewhere quiet?"

"Not at all." I open one of the bags on my lap. "Want a fry?"

"I'm good right now."

"You sure? It'll make you feel better," I say in a sing-song voice.

I see his lip twitch, and he holds out a hand. I place a fry in his palm and then pull one out for myself. We chew in silence.

"My life has changed a lot since I last saw you," he finally says. "Can I have another fry?"

"Yes, sir." I accommodate his request with a flourish. "Has it been hard for you?"

"What?"

"Getting recognized more often."

Another shrug. "Yeah, it has. I can't go anywhere without getting stopped."

"Darn," I say, clicking my tongue. "I was hoping to take you to the aquarium sometime. Guess that's out of the question."

Connor smiles over at me then, and I feel a sense of relief, knowing he's not angry with me.

"We could make it work," he says definitively. Like it's a thing. Like we're actually going to go together. "I've gotta help you redeem the aquarium after your date with Cole."

I laugh, leaning my head back against the headrest.

"Things might change for you, too, you know," he says.

"How so?"

"Didn't you tell me you got recognized the other day?"

I wave a hand through the air. "That was just a one-time thing."

"Hmm."

We drive in silence for a few minutes, and the streetlights start to disappear as Connor takes us out of the suburbs and into dark, open space. Back roads and farmland.

"Does this look familiar?" he says, taking a right turn onto a dirt road. "I think you came out here with Trent and me a couple times."

I peer out the window at the street sign. *Mooreville Road*. Stars dot the sky over shadowy hills in the distance.

I smile out the window. "That's right. I remember."

Little does he know just how *much* I remember. The glint of his white smile in the dark, the way his voice carried in the open air, the warmth of his guitar as he played us new songs he'd written.

He pulls over to the side of the road, cutting Frank's engine.

"Wanna eat in the truck bed?"

I nod, gathering our food and hopping out of the truck. We meet at the back, and Connor lowers the tailgate, hopping up to a seat and patting the spot next to him.

I pull myself up beside him, and we divide up our food. The night air is chilly, but the sky is clear.

"The stars are really putting on a show for us tonight," I say, tilting my head up toward the heavens.

"I like to come out here when I need some space," Connor says. "It helps me put things in perspective, you know?"

I glance over at him as he ducks his head, taking a bite of his chicken sandwich. A little bit of something clings to his bottom lip, and without thinking, I reach out, brushing it away with my thumb.

His chewing slows, and he looks over at me, his eyebrows drawn down over his bright eyes.

"Here," I say, handing him a napkin in an attempt to cover up my breach of his personal bubble—specifically the part that floats around his lovely lips.

He takes it from me, swiping it over his mouth, staring me down.

"You did great tonight," he says after he swallows. "Despite me putting you on the spot."

"It wasn't as bad as I thought it was going to be." I take a bite of a French fry. "Only you could have gotten me up there, Connor Cane."

His lips quirk up into a crooked smile. "Does that mean you'd sing with me again?"

"If it means I get chicken strips out of it? Absolutely."

"That's all it's gonna take?"

"I'm a simple girl."

He looks at me thoughtfully. "I like that about you."

My heart does a little dance at his words. We share a lingering look before I turn away, trying to hide my smile of pleasure.

"I took your advice when I was singing tonight," I say. "I tried to pretend I was singing to just one person."

"Yeah?" Connor says. "Who was it?"

"My person?"

The air feels charged as the implication of his question hangs between us in the air.

"There was a sweet Martha in the second row who had tears in her eyes throughout the whole song," I say, hoping my attempt at a lie is convincing.

Connor nods, jutting out his chin with a smile. "I saw her."

I don't bother asking him who he was singing to tonight. If it wasn't me, I'd rather not know.

When we're done eating, we crumple up our wrappers and napkins and stuff them into the paper bag the food came in.

"What do you usually do when you come out here?" I ask him, turning my head up to the sky.

"Sometimes I write. Sometimes I just sit and think. It's one of the only places I can go and truly relax," Connor says. "Somewhere I don't have to be *on* anymore."

"The side of fame nobody talks about, huh?"

Connor nods. "Yeah."

He leans forward, settling his elbows on his knees. He looks tired. All I want to do is reach out, to lay a hand right there in that tight space between his shoulder blades. Help him unwind.

But I'm not about to make contact with any other part of Connor again after that lip brush I'd initiated a few minutes ago.

"Is that why you don't want to be an artist?" he asks, turning his head to look at me. "You want to be able to get your fast food in peace?"

"I guess that's part of it," I say, smiling. "But it's mostly because I don't like being the center of attention. I'm not at home onstage like you are." My hand moves of its own accord, reaching out to squeeze his leg.

Whoops. I quickly pull my hand away, trying desperately not to dwell on how firm his thigh had been underneath my fingers.

"You could do it, you know," he says. "You're good enough, Ella Mae."

I shake my head. "Thank you, but I think I'll stick to writing. Leave the swoon-inducing performances to you."

He smiles, letting out a little laugh from his nose. We sit in comfortable silence for a moment, both taking in the sprinkle of stars above us. I'm painfully aware of how close our knees are to touching. How easy it would be to let myself relax and lean into him.

"Do you like hearing me sing?" he finally asks. His words are measured, his voice low.

My heart practically stops mid-beat in my chest. I'm burning, my face catching flame as he looks at me intently, a half smile working its way up his cheek.

I swallow, tilting my head back up to the sky.

"Of course I do," I say softly. "Along with the rest of America."

I know he's still got his eyes trained on me, but I'm blushing too hard to meet his gaze. He leans closer, much closer. Warmth prickles across my ear where the tip of his nose brushes. His knee finally meets mine, and I feel a humming sensation spread through my leg in a rush.

"What else do you like?"

Oh, good glory. All it would take is a slight turn of my head, a miniscule tilt of my neck to bring my face to his. To meet his eyes and let myself fall, fall, fall.

But I can't do it. I keep my gaze straight ahead, pressing my tongue against the back of my teeth and taking a breath to steady myself before I meet his eyes. He's grinning, teasing. Our knees are still connected, making me feel a little dizzy.

Connor Cane is too much. All charm, kindness, and flirtatious fun.

But he's also a musician. *Strike one.* And my brother's best friend. *Strike two.*

Two facts I'm not going to allow myself to forget just because he smells like summer and makes me feel like I've just jumped off a ledge and am in the middle of a freefall.

I clear my throat, twisting around to open up the bag of food again and sliding my leg away from his.

"You know what I like, Connor Cane?" I say slowly, pulling my cookie out from the bag. "Cookies."

He grins, leaning back on his hands again.

"Want some?"

Connor holds my gaze for a moment. "Sure."

I split the cookie and hand him half, bumping my piece against his. "Cheers."

"Cheers, Stewie Two."

And just like that, the line has been drawn. I'm back to being Stewie Two. Not the girl whose stomach is loaded with butterflies in his presence, wondering if it's possible he feels them, too. We eat in silence, and with the passing of another moment of connection with Connor Cane, I'm left shivering in the early spring air.

"Let's get you home," he says.

When we pull up to the townhome at Carriage Court, my car is already sitting there in the driveway. Paul and Mallory insisted that it wasn't a problem for them to drive my car back to my house so I could hang out with Connor.

They're all in cahoots, I tell you. Trying to get me to fall for Connor Cane.

And as I lean into another one of Connor's hugs on the porch before I head inside, I think their plan might be working.

Chapter 16

Connor

I'm defrosting a breakfast burrito in the microwave while trying to keep my mind from dwelling on the fact that I almost kissed Stewie's little sister last night.

It scares me how badly I wanted to take Ella Mae's face between my hands. To show her just how much our duet had affected me by brushing my lips across hers. But she held her ground, and I didn't take things any further than our usual flirtatious banter.

But I'd be lying if I said I hadn't wanted to.

It's been a while since I've had a full night's sleep. Typically, I'd blame it on stress, but last night, thoughts of Ella Mae magnified my insomnia. She unknowingly kept me awake despite every effort I made to drift back off.

I've learned that, after a rough night, I can do a few simple things to help set my world back to rights. I've already gotten my workout in, showered, had a cup of coffee, and now I'm devouring my burrito with one hand while scrolling on my phone with the other.

But even my fail-proof routine hasn't relieved me of constant thoughts of Ella Mae. I try to distract myself by opening up my Instagram, wondering if last night's show was as memorable for anyone in the audience as it was for me. I've been tagged in a bunch of videos and photos from the album listening party. I scroll through a few posts, responding with brief comments and reposting a couple mentions to my story.

A thumbnail catches my eye of Ella Mae and me onstage together. I've never clicked on anything so fast.

I turn up the volume, listening to our voices as they blend together. I find myself smiling as I listen. I'm not one to talk myself up, but we sound good. I wasn't lying when I told Ella Mae she could do this for a living. She's even better live than she is on a recording.

I scroll down to read the comments. The first few are complimentary, filled with an excess of emojis. Then as I continue to scroll, the comments start to take a turn.

Gold digger.

Who's does this girl think she is? Teribble.

Really? If you're going to throw shade at somebody online, you should at least spell-check your comment before posting it.

What a try-hard.

Wow hahaha. She thinks she can sing.

No, Connor. Just no.

An uncomfortable knot settles into my stomach. For every positive comment, there are several mean ones. Nasty. Unwarranted. Full of words I would never in a million years want Ella Mae to read. I finish my burrito, hot anger stirring in my chest.

I can handle people saying rude things about me. I'm used to the trolls, the criticism, and the critiques from complete strangers who pretend to know me.

But coming after Ella Mae? I won't tolerate that.

I close out of my Instagram app and immediately call Mallory.

"Morning, sunshine."

"Hey, Mal."

"You ready to sign vinyls until your hand falls off?"

"Yeah, I'll be there soon," I say, grabbing my keys and heading out to my truck. "Hey, did you happen to see any of those posts from last night?"

"Of course," she says. "I've been perusing them all morning."

"I was reading the comments on a video someone posted of me and Ella Mae," I say. "They were—"

"Terrible. With a double b."

I snort. "Yeah."

Mallory's quiet for a minute. "Does she know?"

"I don't think so. She's not very active on social media."

"Correct me if I'm wrong, but the hateful comments weren't about the song, right?" she says.

"No," I growl. "They were directed entirely at *her*."

Mallory sighs. "I'm sorry, Connor. It's ridiculous. You guys killed it last night, but you know how it is. This kind of crap comes with the territory."

I climb into the driver's seat of my truck, tossing my hat onto the passenger seat. Even just glancing over that direction reminds me of Ella Mae. How she looked last night with her long hair flowing down over her shoulders. The adorable upturn of the end of her nose. Her smile and shining eyes when I'd say something to make her laugh.

She's too sweet for her own good. Undeserving of this kind of internet cruelty. If only these rude people knew her in real life, they would never say such mean things.

"Plus, your fans can be particularly possessive."

"I know," I say. "There's nothing we can do about it? You know, to protect her?"

"I'm afraid not," she says with a sigh.

"That's not the answer I was hoping for," I grumble.

Mallory clears her throat as I'm backing out of the driveway.

"Be straight with me, Connor," she says. "How invested are you in this girl?"

"What do you mean?"

"Like, are you a supportive friend and collaborator? Or are you *invested*?"

I exhale slowly as I pull out onto the road. "I don't know yet."

"How well do you know her?" she asks. "She's going to need pretty thick skin to be unaffected by things like this. Also, I stumbled across something else this morning," Mallory says. "An article."

"About what?"

"Just a sleazy tabloid making claims that you and Ella Mae are an item."

I swear under my breath. I know there's a lot of hype around the album, but I didn't think the media would drag Ella Mae into things so soon. Our duet hasn't even officially released yet.

"*Are* you an item?" Mallory asks directly.

"No." I'm surprised at the disappointment I hear in my own voice as I say it. "Just good friends."

"Well, I'd say if you want to protect Ella Mae from the social media sharks, you need to give her some space. Let her get back to her songwriting. Don't post anything else with her in it. Then hopefully the rumors and comments will die down a bit before the record comes out."

"I honestly didn't think this would happen. I thought people would love her," I say. "Or at least love the song."

"The right people will," Mallory says gently. "You've got to remember, there are two sides to this coin."

"I know."

"And if at some point you and Ella Mae *were* to become an item..."

"Mal, stop."

"I'm just saying," she laughs. "I'm here to help you. You need to be very upfront with her. She has to know what she's getting into. From what I've gathered, she's not interested in being the girl onstage with you, Connor. It was nice of her to do it last night, but you have to realize that it makes her vulnerable."

I know Mallory is right, but it's still hard to hear it. I guess it had been selfish of me, inviting Ella Mae up to sing that song. It was out of her comfort zone, something she didn't volunteer for.

But she'd done it for me.

I can't ask anything else of her right now. It wouldn't be right.

With the album release approaching, it should be easy for me to stay busy. I've worked too hard on this record to not give it my all. Written countless songs, played endless shows. There's been so much buildup to the release of this record and the tour that will follow. I feel the need to prove that I'm here to stay. I'm capable of writing a great second record. Hopefully even better than the first.

I can give Ella Mae her space. It won't be easy, by any means. I'd gone to bed with a smile on my face last night. Spent a good amount of time thinking of non-date ways I could convince her to spend some more time with me.

But I'm going to have to put first things first and prioritize my career, just like I had to do with Lauren. Once things die down sometime in the future, I'll be free to date. To find somebody who's willing to put up with the crap that comes along with fame.

I should be happy right now, headed to Back Road to sign vinyls and copies of my record that fans had pre-ordered. I'm doing an acoustic set at a radio station this afternoon to promote the record and then meeting with Hunter Ward to discuss the concept for my next music video.

I'm grateful for these opportunities. And it does makes me happy, doing what I love.

But not quite the same way that Ella Mae does.

"Are these up for grabs?"

Hunter's got his hand hovering over a bowl of mints sitting on a side table in Studio B.

"Go for it, man," Drew says from his chair at the mixing console.

He's exporting stems to send to a pop artist I'm doing a collaboration with. My first crossover record. It won't be out until late summer, but I spent some time this afternoon helping him comp the vocals so we could get them sent off.

"So," Hunter says, popping a mint into his mouth. "I listened to the song on repeat last night."

Hunter and I have worked together on several of my music videos, including the video for "Make Up," which he starred in with his now wife, Chloe. He's good at his job, and I trust him to take my ideas and bring them to life on the screen.

"And?"

He sits down on the couch, leaning toward me with his eyebrows furrowed.

"I wondered if you could tell me about what inspired 'Ghost of Me,'" he says. "It's not a love song. And not as cut and dry as some of your others."

"Yeah, sure," I say with a shrug.

"He's embracing his inner sad boy," Drew says, his back to us.

I snort.

"Ah, yes," Hunter agrees. "The angst is there."

"I'm not, nor will I ever be, a sad boy," I laugh. "I think what I was trying to capture was the difficult side of my experience becoming a successful artist. I've had to make trade-offs. I've lost some things that I used to take for granted."

"Like what?"

"Like..." I pause, searching for examples. "Like not being able to take much time off. Going to the store. Going for a run or going to the gym. Dating—at least in a more traditional sense."

Hunter nods. "That makes more sense now. The lyrics felt metaphorical, so I wasn't sure if you were talking about a specific relationship or not."

"No, I didn't write it about a girl or a breakup, if that's what you mean. It's more of a reflection. Looking back on my life when things were simple."

"There's a line in the song," Hunter says, pulling out his phone and tapping his notes app open. "Where you said, 'Quiet hallways, empty chairs, I'm the ghost of myself when no one's there.'"

"Yeah," I say, shifting in my chair, a little uncomfortable with the deep dive we're doing into the thought process behind these somber lyrics.

"That line makes me think that we should shoot this video in a big empty room. You seated in a chair, right in the center. Simple, natural light." Hunter pauses. "I like the song. It feels very honest."

"That's what I was hoping for. Something more reflective than some of the other songs on the record."

We discuss more about the song and video, and Hunter compiles a document with all our ideas that he's going to send over to the Back Road execs to get their approval.

"What's the timeline with this one again?" he asks.

"I think we're supposed to shoot a couple days before I leave on tour."

Hunter sits back on the couch. "That's right. Are you excited to get back out on the road?"

I'm a little shocked at the immediate answer that comes to my mind.

No. No, I'm not.

Because going back on tour means leaving Ella Mae behind. For real. Once I'm gone, I'm gone. All day, every day is booked out. And even when I do have days off, they're usually spent traveling to the next show.

Maybe Mallory is right. This line of work I'm in is not really conducive to serious relationships—or relationships at all, really. My social circle is shrinking every time I reach a milestone in my career.

That's really what "Ghost of Me" is about. The loneliness I'm battling. Even though I'm surrounded by thousands of people who come to my shows, at the end of the day, it's just me.

I look up at Hunter, realizing my silence has stretched out longer than I meant for it to.

He has a knowing look in his eyes. "Right."

I let out a long breath. "Don't get me wrong, I love playing shows. But sometimes I feel homeless. Even when I come back to Tennessee, I'm usually living somewhere temporarily until I'm off on tour again."

Hunter nods. "It must be hard to be away that much."

"Yeah."

"You know what?" Hunter says. "I've learned that home doesn't necessarily have to be a physical place. Chloe and I got married in my childhood home, but my mom sold it right after the wedding. It was hard for me to lose the place that held all my memories of my dad."

"I'm sorry," I say simply.

"It's alright. It sucked at first," Hunter says. "But since Chloe and I got married, I've realized that anywhere we are can feel like home as long as we're together. She's my home now."

"Wow, man," Drew chimes in. "You'd make a great song-writer."

"Right?" Hunter says. "That's what I keep telling my wife. But every time I try to sing along to anything, she tells me to shut up.'"

I snort. I've heard Hunter attempt to sing a few times on my shoots, and he's entirely tone deaf.

———————

Two weeks later...

I've kept my promise to myself to leave Ella Mae alone. Granted, it's only been a couple weeks, and I've thrown myself into work to cope, but still. I've done it. I haven't shared anything else about "Always You," hoping that she'll get some respite from the media attention. But I've listened to it at least once a day, just so I can hear her voice.

It's my way of staying connected to her when I can't seem to get her out of my head.

Despite the fact that we haven't seen each other, we've still managed to text every few days. I look forward to our casual conversations, both work-related and not.

As I'm about to hit the hay after a long day of virtual and in-person interviews to promote the record, my phone buzzes with a text message from Ella Mae.

Ella Mae: I'd like to cash in on that favor you owe me.

A smile spreads across my face as I type out my reply. I'm intrigued.

Connor: What kind of trouble have you gotten yourself into, Ella Mae?
Ella Mae: Why do you automatically assume I'm in trouble?
Connor: Your middle name is trouble.

Ella Mae: And yours is a tender tribute to an uncle...as well as a beloved bird.

Ella Mae: Did you know robins are one of the only types of birds who still flit around during the dead of winter?

Connor: Fascinating.

Connor: Tell me about this favor.

A minute later, an invitation comes through. *Music Row Songwriter Soiree.* A party taking place at an event center near midtown next weekend.

Ella Mae: I got invited to this songwriter party, and I'd planned on taking Lainey as my plus-one, but she and Luke are celebrating his mom's birthday that night.

Connor: Are you asking me out?

Slooooow down there, sonny.

My fingers are typing faster than my brain can process.

The smile on my face slides a bit as I realize what I've done. After all the effort I've made to give Ella Mae some space, I'm about to agree to see her again. I don't even care what this event is. She wants me there? I'll be there.

Ella Mae: All my other songwriter friends are going and have found dates. I don't want to be the odd man out.

Connor: So it is a date.

Ella Mae: Not a date.

Connor: You even said the word DATE.

Ella Mae: MOTHER TERESA.

Ella Mae: Will you come with me as my SONGWRITER FRIEND?

I hesitate a moment, giving myself a second to think this through.

It couldn't hurt, could it? To accompany Ella Mae to a party and enjoy her company before I dive back into album-release stuff and prepping for tour?

It could hurt, you idiot. It could hurt a lot.

The thought of her being alone at this party, or even taking some other guy, makes it very easy to make my decision. One more night with Ella Mae, and then I'll get my head back in the game.

Connor: I'd love to go with you.
Ella Mae: I'll even drive if you want.
Ella Mae: And buy you dinner.

A smile tugs at one side of my lips.

Connor: I am not Cole Madson, Ella Mae.
Connor: If I'm going to be your date, I'm doing it right.
Ella Mae: Pick you up at six.
Connor: Nice try.
Connor: Frank will happily provide our transportation. And dinner is on me.

Chapter 17

Ella Mae

The night of the songwriter soiree arrives, and in true Ella Mae fashion, I still don't know what I'm going to wear. Lainey has had me try on fifteen different outfits. At this point, I've probably sweated off most of my makeup and will have to touch it up before I leave for the songwriter soiree.

"What time is he picking you up for dinner?"

"Six," I say, turning to appraise the blue dress I'm currently trying on in the mirror. "This one's way too tight."

Lainey arches an eyebrow. "I'd say that's a selling point, not a deal breaker."

"Nope." I shake my head, trying to shrug out of the dress as I re-enter my walk-in closet. "It makes me waddle like a penguin."

"The cutest penguin I ever did see!"

I sigh, running my hands over the remaining options left in my closet.

"What about the dress you wore to Chloe's wedding?" Lainey calls out from her seat on my bed.

I pull the shimmery silver dress out and run my hand over the fabric. "I love this one. But Connor's already seen me in it."

"Lucky him."

I slip into the dress and do a twirl for Lainey as I step out of my closet. The fitted long sleeves, gathering at one hip, and slit up my leg do wonders for my figure.

Her jaw drops. "YES. That's the one, Ella Mae."

I tilt my head, taking in my reflection in the mirror. "I *do* love this one. But I've already worn it with him!"

"Who cares?" Lainey says. "If you feel confident and comfortable in it, that's all that matters."

"You're right."

"You're a babe." Lainey stands, crossing her arms. "He's not going to be able to keep his hands off you tonight."

The thought of Connor Cane's hands anywhere near my person sends my stomach into a flurry. In quiet moments, my mind loves to conjure up memories of the last time I saw him. When we sat side by side on the tailgate, closer than we'd ever been before. The breathless seconds where he put his mouth to my ear, making my skin heat and my nerves prickle.

"I appreciate your confidence in my abilities to capture Connor Cane, but we're just going as friends tonight. I've made that perfectly clear."

Lainey turns me around by my shoulders. "You're crazy, do you know that?"

"And that's why you love me."

"You know what I say?"

"Don't bother lecturing me, Lainey."

"I say let the man love on you if he wants to, for goodness' sake!" She gives me a little shake by my shoulders. "Snatch him up before somebody else does!"

"Are you quite finished?" I say with a smirk. "I've got a party to get to, and I'd hate to be late."

"You're impossible." She exhales dramatically and then pulls me into a hug. "Have fun tonight, okay? Live a little."

"I'll try. For your sake."

She goes back upstairs to get ready for dinner with Luke and her soon-to-be mother-in-law.

I touch up my makeup, add an extra spritz of hairspray to the loose curls I put in my hair earlier, and grab my clutch and phone. I strap on a pair of heels and climb upstairs to wait for my ride.

It's truly a miracle. Five minutes to six, and I'm not scrambling, frantically applying lipstick or trying to find a missing shoe. I have Lainey to thank for my promptness. She practically babysat me to ensure I'd be ready on time.

True friends like Lainey are one in a million.

My phone then buzzes with a text from Ava.

Ava: Go get 'em, Tiger.
Ava: *kissy-face emoji*

Why do my friends think tonight is some sort of conquest? That I'm going to bat my eyes at Connor Cane and come off conqueror?

It's simply a night out with a friend.

A very handsome, sweet, famous friend.

A knock sounds at the door, making my heart skip around in my chest.

He's here.

I check my teeth in the mirror for lipstick stains before walking to the door and swinging it open.

As my eyes take in the sight of Connor Cane in a well-cut black suit, his hair styled to perfection, his smile bright and

warm, my resolve to keep him at arm's length already begins
to disintegrate.

"Hey," he says, and I feel my insides dripping like a popsicle
onto the pavement in muggy summer heat.

"Hey, yourself," I say. "Don't you clean up nice."

Understatement of the century. Connor Cane was born to
attend events like this one. Shake hands, kiss babies. He's ooz-
ing charm, and Southern sweetness, and everything any good
woman would want in a man.

"So do you." He shakes his head and grins.

"What?" I say, suddenly self-conscious.

"Ella Mae." His eyes do a slow drag down my body before
flicking up to mine again. "I'm afraid I can't take you anywhere
tonight."

I feel my smile falter. "Did something come up? You could
have called me."

"No, nothing came up," he says. "But I can't take you out
looking like that."

"Like *what*?"

Am I indecent? Oh, good gracious, is my dress tucked into
my panties somewhere? I do a quick scan of my body, and I
can't see anything wrong with my outfit.

I lift my eyes back up to meet Connor's, and he tilts his head
in response. "You're beautiful."

I swallow thickly as my brain absorbs his words, coupled
with the intensity in his eyes.

He didn't say, "You *look* beautiful, Ella Mae." He said I *am*
beautiful. Not just a surface-level observation. I feel vulnerable
under his gaze, like he's truly *seeing* me. My soul and my desires
and my mind.

And he finds me beautiful.

He's my Jesse McCartney. He wants me and my beautiful soul.
Now all I need is a serenade of "Beautiful Soul" from his lips
to satisfy my twelve-year-old self.

There's something sparking in the air between us, something charged and tangible.

Truth.

It's the truth.

He's *this close* to seeing through all my jokes, my teasing. All
the mechanisms I've used to keep him from getting too close. I
haven't wanted to acknowledge this swirling in my chest that's
grown into a tornado since I last saw him, certain that doing
so will only lead to heartache.

The truth is, my feelings for Connor are starting to run
deeper than a surface-level celebrity crush, admire-from-afar
status. This is more than a harmless flirt fest, a working friendship. I can admit it to myself now that he's here standing on
my front porch.

I've missed him.

I've gotten to know the real Connor both in person and in
our text conversations these past few months. My whole soul
feels warm and sunny and bright when I'm with him. He lights
me up with his kindness and sense of humor. His passion for
his craft and ability to create. His work ethic, and voice, and
everything else that makes him who he is.

I want more of him.

And I can see his truth written all over his face right now on
my front porch.

He wants more of me, too.

This realization sends a jolt of adrenaline through my veins,
emboldening me, making me stand a little taller. I could tilt

up on my tiptoes right now, angle my head a little, and kiss Connor Cane right on the mouth.

But I'm no dummy. This isn't something one just impulsively does, although I'm sorely tempted right now, under the influence of his intent gaze and delicious cologne.

Suddenly worried that he may be able to read these very personal thoughts in my expression, I drop my eyes, breaking our electric connection.

"Why, thank you, Connor Cane," I say. I take a step forward, and he shifts to the side, allowing me to pass by him on the steps. My shoulder brushes his chest, and I feel his fingertips graze my lower back for a moment as he follows behind me. Chill bumps break out across my skin at his touch.

If that's the way my body reacts from a literal brush from his fingertips, I would combust, becoming a flaming inferno like Jack-Jack from *The Incredibles,* if he had done anything more.

Good call, Ella Mae, darling. A kiss from Connor Cane would have ended with you buried next to Great Granny Jo back in the family plot.

I whistle as I walk around to the passenger door. "Frank! Don't you look dapper this evening. All washed up and shiny."

I give Frank's door a little pat, then reach for the handle. Before I can pull it open, Connor's hand covers my own. It's another brief moment of contact, but it does wild things to my heart rate. I quickly pull my hand out from underneath his. I can feel the warmth of his body at my back as he pulls the door open.

"Had to have Frank in tip-top shape for you." He's not saying anything remotely sensual, but my neck tingles as he speaks. Like he's whispering sweet nothings into my ear, not discussing truck hygiene.

Connor rests a hand on the side of the truck as he pulls the door open, waiting for me to climb inside. He's still got a little flick of a smile on his lips. That gleam in his eyes that invites me to get closer, to let things sink in a little deeper.

I can't do it tonight. I really can't. There's only so much a woman can take. I'm only human, after all. I'm going to have to really make an effort to keep my hands to myself and my eyes from betraying how he makes me feel.

I allow him to help me up into the truck, his hand on my elbow. Then I occupy myself by fiddling with the seatbelt to give myself a break before he gets inside.

It's only once he hops up into the driver's seat and closes the door that I realize I've made a massive mistake in inviting him to this party. I'm a goldfish trapped in a little glass bowl. Nowhere to go. Nowhere to look. Not able to breathe without having to acknowledge the man driving this truck.

What have I done?

"I see you vacuumed in here, too," I say lamely, gesturing to the interior of the truck cabin. "It's very...tidy."

Connor smirks. "Thank you for noticing." He puts his hand over the back of my seat, turning to reverse the truck out of my driveway.

I force myself to look out my window so I don't get caught staring at the angles of his face, the light stubble on his jaw. The way the golden evening light brings out the blue of his eyes and the white of his smile.

"Why me?" Connor says as he pulls out of my neighborhood.

"Huh?" I say, not at all sounding like myself. Nice. We haven't even made it to the party yet, and I'm already losing my cool.

"Out of all the people you know, why'd you ask me to come with you tonight?" he asks. "Don't get me wrong, I'm glad you did."

"If you're having second thoughts, you can make a U-turn here. Take me right back home."

He flashes me a smile. "No second thoughts. Just curious."

I pull one shoulder up to my ear. "I asked myself, 'Which one of my friends is going to be sitting at home alone this weekend and could use a night out?' And you immediately came to mind."

Connor scoffs. "You make me sound so pathetic."

"You're not pathetic," I insist. "Just anti-social."

He laughs. "I am not."

I look at him skeptically. "When was the last time you did something fun on a Friday night? And I'm not talking about anything work-related. I know that's your idea of a good time."

"Last month," he says without hesitation. "When you and I hung out after the listening party."

Oh, heaven bless him.

"Connor, I'm going to ask you a question. And you have to answer me honestly."

"Okay."

"Am I your only friend?"

He snorts. "No, Ella Mae. I have other friends."

"But am I your *favorite* friend?" I say. "I promise not to tell Trent if you say yes."

He glances over at me, and the look on his face makes my lungs constrict.

"Yes, Ella Mae. You're my favorite."

I settle back into my seat as my heart races wildly in my ribcage. His hand is right there on the console, fingertips

drumming out a beat. How easy it would be to lace my fingertips through his, to twine our hands together while we drive.

I sigh.

This is going to be much, much harder than I thought.

Especially now that I know *I'm his favorite*.

Chapter 18

Ella Mae

There may be a few perks to dining with a celebrity. Like the fact that we didn't have to wait more than a few minutes to be seated at the fanciest Italian place downtown. Not only were we escorted inside through a back door, we were given a table in a private room where nobody would bother Connor.

Our conversation flowed easily. The food was top notch. And I found myself relaxing into that comfortable ease that Connor and I share when we're together.

I did try to make good on my promise to buy dinner, but Connor had already taken care of it with the restaurant beforehand.

A *put-it-on-my-tab* kind of situation.

By the time we roll up to the songwriter soiree, we're already having a good ol' time. Being in each other's company brings out the best in us, and I have a perma-smile living on my face.

Paul's black SUV pulls into the adjoining parking space beside Connor's truck.

"I didn't realize we needed a chaperone tonight," I say as Paul hops out of the SUV.

"Connor's a real party animal," Paul quips.

"Don't listen to a word this man says." Connor shakes Paul's hand. "Paul here insisted on tagging along."

"I'll keep my distance," Paul says. "You won't even know I'm here."

And he's right. We have to scan a QR code to gain entrance into the party, and somehow, Paul has his own invitation on his phone ready to go. Once inside, he disappears into the shadows, but I'm sure he'll have his eyes carefully trained on Connor and me throughout the night.

The event is posh, to say the least. Strategically lit to create a mood, but not too dark to where I can't see the faces of those around us. Music is pumping through the space at a volume just loud enough to where I need to lean in closer to hear Connor speak.

I feel Connor's hand land at the small of my back again. It's barely there, subtle, yet impossible to ignore.

"Make your rounds," Connor says. "I'll follow your lead."

I scan the room for a familiar face. Shannon, a writer I frequently work with, waves to me from my right.

"Ella Mae!" she calls out.

As we make our way toward Shannon, her eyes widen. Connor has been spotted. Though the man needs no introduction, I'm going to introduce him anyway.

"Shannon, this is Connor," I say.

"So nice to meet you," she says, awe evident in her voice as she shakes his hand. "I saw the video of the song you two wrote together. It was amazing."

Connor modestly ducks his head, giving her a smile that's sure to make any woman weak in the knees. "That's very kind of you. It was all Ella Mae."

I wave my hand dismissively. "Not true. He's a diva to work with, as you'd expect, but we did our best with what we had."

Connor smirks at me and then turns back attentively as Shannon peppers him with questions. He's gracious and kind, despite her obvious admiration. I feel a sudden twinge of concern, worried that Connor might get overwhelmed by the attention people may give him tonight. He's the hottest thing in Nashville right now, and this room full of songwriters, producers, executives, and managers may all want a piece of him for themselves. I hadn't really considered this when I invited him to come with me, and now I'm feeling guilty for it.

When she finally stops to take a breath, I turn the conversation back on Shannon so she won't monopolize him.

After a minute more, I gently prod Connor's elbow. "Should we go get a drink?"

"Yeah, that would be great."

"It was good to see you, Shannon."

She shakes Connor's hand again and gives me a quick hug before we turn away.

"This way," Connor says, pointing to a bar set up on the other side of the room.

"Sorry about that," I say once we're out of earshot. "She went all Martha on you."

He snorts. "That was nothing," he says, nonplussed. "Are you worried about me?"

"Naturally."

He arches an eyebrow. "Afraid I'm going to misbehave? I won't make you look bad, I promise."

"It's not that," I say, noticing all the people looking our way. "I think we may encounter more fans of yours tonight. I'm sorry for not considering how uncomfortable that might be for you. If it gets to be too much, we can leave."

Connor glances behind him before lowering his lips to my ear again. "I want you to have a good time. Don't worry about me, Stewie Two."

We pass a few more industry friends on our way to the bar, stopping to chat and catch up. I'm unwittingly subjecting him to unabashed staring and lots of handshaking, and he's taking it all like a champ.

After about half an hour of mingling, we head toward the bar. We're nearly there when I spot a dark figure to my right with a tall blonde woman on his arm. The man turns his head, whispering something in the blonde's ear, and my heart goes cold. I recognize his cocky smirk. His moody gray eyes.

Mitch Allen.

Songwriter turned country artist.

He's sporting a few new tattoos, longer hair, and flashy stud earrings. The current reigning bad boy of country music.

And my ex-boyfriend.

"What do you want?" Connor asks. When I don't answer immediately, he turns toward me, blocking my view of Mitch and his vivacious lady friend clinging to his arm.

Connor's smile falters as he reads my expression.

"You okay?" he asks, concerned.

I swallow. "Yeah."

I must not be convincing in my answer because Connor's eyes darken. "What's wrong?"

I sigh. Might as well tell him the truth since we may end up having to speak to that wretched man at some point tonight. Mitch never misses a chance to kiss up to successful people, and I'm sure Connor Cane is someone he'd love to schmooze if given the chance.

"Hey." Connor squeezes my arm, encouraging me to meet his eyes. "Tell me what's going on."

"My ex is here." I grimace.

Connor's eyebrows raise a fraction, his frown deepening. "Who?"

"Don't make it obvious. If he recognizes you, he's going to make a beeline for us, and then I'll have to talk to the son of a gun."

"Where is he?" Connor's tone sends a jolt through me. His voice holds something I've never heard before. Anger. Protectiveness. He's practically growling, a scowl darkening his features.

"He's behind you," I say as quietly as I can. "Mitch Allen."

Connor doesn't even turn around to look for Mitch. He simply stares at me incredulously.

"*You* dated Mitch Allen?"

"I did."

"*Why?*"

"I ask myself that quite often, actually."

"Ella Mae," Connor says with a frustrated shake of his head, his nostrils flaring. "He's an as—"

"I know," I say. "Trust me, I know."

"If you don't want him to see you, we can leave. Paul can get us out of here right now."

I peer around Connor and find Mitch still there at the bar. He turns again, confound it all, and happens to glance my way. Our eyes lock, and I feel my stomach sink into my toes. He's talking to Barbie still, but he keeps his gaze on me, cool and unaffected.

"It's too late. He's seen me."

Connor shifts his body to block my view of Mitch. I feel my heart sinking at the prospect of having to face him.

"Was he good to you?" Connor asks, his lips barely moving.

I meet his eyes, feeling the hurt from my past starting to surface as I remember how things ended with Mitch. I don't feel the need to say anything as Connor searches my face for the answer. I'm not one to throw people under the bus, and I know Connor can read me well enough.

"Alright," he says decisively. "If he tries to talk to you, I'm here, okay?"

I nod, attempting to peer around Connor again.

"Ella Mae."

I have to tilt my head up to meet Connor's gaze. He looks even taller than usual, towering over me protectively with his big hand still wrapping around my arm.

He glides his fingertips down the underside of my forearm. Then he tucks my hand into his, threading his fingers through mine until our palms are flush together.

"Let me be your date," he says, determination on his face.

"Connor—"

"Don't argue with me about this, Ella Mae," he says firmly. "For the rest of the night, I'm your date, okay?"

"But—"

Before I can finish my sentence, Mitch appears from behind Connor's shoulder, wearing a smile that I'd love to smack right off his smug face.

My eyes dart up to Connor's, and I'm shocked to see that he looks like he wants to punch Mitch just as much as I do.

Chapter 19

Connor

"Ella Mae," Mitch Allen drawls in his thick Alabama accent. "Long time no see."

He's left his blonde companion back at the bar, seeking Ella Mae out alone. Judging by the expression on his face, I don't think he anticipated encountering me in the process. He looks thwarted.

I glance down, noticing that Ella Mae's visibly shrinking. Encountering this man is making her withdraw into herself, something I've never seen her do before.

The effect that Mitch Allen has on me is just the opposite. I find myself drawing up to my full height, filling out and shifting towards him to make it clear that he's not going anywhere near Ella Mae.

"Mitch," she says with a tense smile.

I'm still holding her hand, and I give it a reassuring squeeze, tugging her a little bit closer to my body. She brings her other hand up to the inside of my elbow.

"Connor Cane," Mitch says, acknowledging me now that he sees we're clearly together. "How've you been, man?"

We've crossed paths a few times at award shows and on red carpets, but I wouldn't count Mitch as anything more than an acquaintance. He's garnered quite the reputation since his breakout song a couple years back, allowing fame to go to his head.

I've heard it said that wealth and success just makes you more of what you already are. Mitch's success has done a beautiful job at bringing out his true nature as a first class jerk.

"I've been good," I say.

I look pointedly at Ella Mae and give her a reassuring smile. Her eyes widen a bit as she looks up at me.

"I didn't realize the two of you knew each other," Mitch says.

"Yeah," I say. "We go way back."

Mitch gives me a dark smile. "That's funny. So do we." He turns his lazy gaze on Ella Mae again. "How's the songwriting going? I'm assuming that's what you're still doing since you're here."

She doesn't answer him.

"We've got a duet coming out on my record, actually," I say with a tilt of my head. "Ella Mae's really something."

Mitch gives a derisive little laugh that makes my hands twitch. "Yeah. She sure is."

His eyes dart down to our joined hands, seeming to accept the fact that if he wants to speak to Ella Mae, he's going to have to go through me. Which means this conversation is about to come to a swift end.

"Don't let us keep you from enjoying your evening." I say. The threat is there in my voice, I make sure of it. He'd better take the hint and get out of my sight.

I'd love nothing more than to grab Mitch by his shirt and shove him up against the wall. Whatever he did to Ella Mae, he's clearly not remorseful at all.

Unfortunately, my opportunity to exact revenge on her behalf doesn't come. He takes a step back, narrowing his eyes at me.

"Y'all have a good night."

"You, too," I say flatly.

He turns his back on us and swaggers back to the bar, running a hand through his long hair.

I hear Ella Mae exhale from beside me, feeling the pressure of her fingertips on my arm lessen.

"Hey," I say. "Do you want to stay? We can grab a drink and say hi to a few more people. Or we can leave right now."

She blinks up at me rapidly, looking like the wind has been knocked out of her sails. She shoots a nervous glance at the bar where Mitch has taken up his post again. "Maybe we should just go."

"Done," I say. I tug her hand gently, and we start weaving our way through the crowd together. She's got a death grip on my hand, but I don't even mind. Like a good bodyguard, Paul is there in an instant, hustling us efficiently out the door.

I glance down at her once we're outside, noting that her gaze is firmly fixed on the ground. Is she holding back tears? So help me. Anyone who makes Ella Mae cry deserves a thorough beating. I tug at my shirt collar, my body hot and ready to do some damage after our encounter with Mitch.

"Thanks, man," I say to Paul. He gives me a swift nod, leaving us to ourselves once we reach my truck. I help Ella Mae into the passenger seat and then climb in myself.

"Mind if we drive a bit?" I ask her once we're out of the parking lot.

"Not at all," she says with a sigh.

Without much thought, I find myself driving on the familiar back roads that lead to Mooreville Road and the fields I'm beginning to think of as *ours*.

Ella Mae is quiet for most of the drive, except for an angry accosting of the radio when one of Mitch Allen's songs starts playing. I've never seen anybody move so fast to change the station.

Once we're parked out on Mooreville Road, away from the houses and lights and people, she finally seems to relax. She settles back into her seat, staring straight ahead out the windshield.

I don't want to press her, but my pulse is still running hot under my suit. I want to know what Mitch Allen did to affect her so much. I *need* to know.

I attempt to remove my jacket, but I'm way too big to effectively take it off seated inside the truck. I'm struggling, twisting my arms around awkwardly in an effort to remove it.

"Wanna sit out back?" I say with a sigh. "I've gotta get this thing off."

We hop out of the truck, and I lower the tailgate. Once my jacket is off and tossed into the truck bed, I start unbuttoning the top two buttons of my shirt in an effort to get some air.

I glance up and catch Ella Mae watching me.

"What?" I ask.

"Don't stop on my account," she says with a slanted smile. "Please continue."

I narrow my eyes. "Why bother taking my shirt off for you? You've already seen it all." I gesture to my torso. "You've got my poster on your bedroom wall, remember?"

"It's not the same." She says matter-of-factly. "That picture of you is probably highly edited. No way all those–" She clears her throat, her gaze dropping down to my stomach and then back up to meet mine. "–muscles–" she says the word quickly like she'd rather not have me hear it. "–were real."

"Oh," I say with a smirk. "They're real."

She doesn't look away, doesn't blush or giggle. Just continues to stare at me. Her focused attention makes my skin prickle. My neck is growing warm under my collar again, so I clear my throat and take a step towards her.

"Want me to help you up?"

She glances down at her fitted dress. A masterpiece if you ask me. I'd thought so when I'd seen her in it at Hunter and Chloe's wedding, and I couldn't stop staring when I'd picked her up tonight.

"Yeah."

She kicks off her heels and drops her bare feet into the dirt, angling towards me so I can lift her up onto the tailgate. I place my hands on her waist, bending my knees slightly as I pick her up. I feel the curves of her waistline under my hands, smell her perfume as her hair swings forward over her shoulders. Once she's safely seated, I loosen my grip on her waist, but I don't let go right away.

We're in a very intimate position. Her knees are pressing gently into my abdomen, her face level with mine. She meets my eyes, and a shot of adrenaline pours through my veins.

I could tug her towards me right now. Let my hands wander up her back and into her hair. Close the gap between my lips and hers.

Ella Mae reaches up, slipping a strand of her hair back behind one ear. "Thank you." Her voice is soft. "Not just for this," she says, gesturing to the truck bed. "But for tonight. With Mitch."

I reluctantly remove my hands from her hips. "Of course." I hoist myself up backwards so I'm seated beside her on the tailgate. "I can get along just fine with most people," I say. "But something about him makes me so..."

"Angry?" she scoffs. "Yeah, tell me about it."

"He's got one of those faces," I say with a squint as Mitch's smug expression comes to mind. "The kind you just wanna deck."

"He didn't used to be like that," she says. "He was a nice guy at first." I don't say anything, hoping she'll elaborate.

"We met at a co-write," Ella Mae explains. "One of my first when I moved out here to Nashville. He has a knack for clever lyrics. Turning phrases. We got along really well, so when he asked me out, it was easy for me to say yes."

She presses her hands into the edge of the tailgate, her shoulders drawing up to her ears. "We wrote a lot of great songs together when we were dating. And for a while, I really cared about him, you know? I tried to make things work."

"And he didn't?"

"He did at first," she says thoughtfully. "But then he got a couple radio hits, and the checks started coming in. He became critical of my writing. Really full of himself." She gives a bitter laugh. "Then he decided he was too good for little ol' me. He wanted to pursue his own career as a solo artist. I was bringing him down. Killing his vibe."

I swallow. Her story makes my chest grow tight.

"But that was a long time ago, right?" I ask. "So why does he still hold power over you? I saw the way you acted when he came over. Like you wanted to hide."

"I'm not a coward, Connor."

"I know that."

She draws her lower lip under her teeth for a second. "As much as I hate to admit it, Mitch still scares me. He did something really awful. Something only my family and close friends know about."

I clench my jaw and feel my hands itching to close into fists again.

"What did he do to you?" I say, and I've got no chill. My voice is all gravelly and dark and menacing. Ella Mae senses this because she looks at me with wide eyes.

"Connor, if I tell you what happened, you can't get mad. There's nothing anybody can do about it. Okay? It's in the past."

"Fine," I ground out.

"Don't get me wrong," she says, one side of her lips lifting into a smile. "I'm loving the whole vigilante vibe you've got going for you tonight. But you can't do anything to fix this. Trust me, I've tried."

I sigh. "Alright. Tell me. Please."

She gathers herself, lacing her hands together on her lap.

"We wrote a song together. A really good song," she explains. "He recorded a demo in a key that suited his voice and then sent it off to his publisher. I thought nothing ever came of it."

She shifts in her seat. "But then, one day after we'd broken up I was listening to the radio, and a very familiar song came on."

Oh no.

"He recorded and released it as one of his first singles. I had no idea he'd decided to use the song for himself."

"What did you do?"

"I called him," she says frankly. "Called him out. Asked him why he'd recorded the song we'd written without involving me."

"What did he say?"

"Not much. Made excuses. I told him I deserved a cut of the royalties since we'd written it together. He told me he'd have someone on his team get back to me."

"So a couple weeks go by, and the song is blowing up on country radio. And I finally get a call from his lawyer."

I shake my head, knowing where this story is going.

"The lawyer threatened to take me to court if I tried to claim rights to the song," she said. "Said I had no proof, no grounds to qualify for a cut of the royalties."

"Was that true?"

She nods. "Sadly, yes. Mitch recorded the demo by himself, remember? So I dropped it. I didn't have money to fight him in court. His popularity was growing and the song was doing well. They would have buried me if I'd tried to fight back. It wasn't worth it."

I give her a sympathetic look.

"Ella Mae, I'm so sorry. What he did to you was so wrong. If I had known–" I scrub a hand over my mouth. "Let's just say I wouldn't have let him leave that party without messing him up."

She gives me the courtesy of a smile. "I believe you. That's why I don't tell anyone about it."

Anger rolls through my chest. "I know you said you didn't want to fix things, but we could try," I say. "My team could get involved. Claire is one of the best lawyers—"

"No," she says decisively. "I've tried to move on. I don't want to dredge things up from the past."

I grumble and shake my head.

"You know what you can do for me, though?"

"Cut off his hair in his sleep?"

She leans in conspiratorially "Boycott his songs."

"Easy," I say. "They're second rate, anyway."

She snorts. I see a shiver course through her. I want to wrap my arm around her, pull her into me to let her know that everything is alright. She's safe with me.

"You cold?" I say instead.

"A little bit."

I reach back, grabbing my jacket and situating it around her shoulders. If it can't be my arm, then I'll settle for something that belongs to me. It swallows her up, somehow making her look even cuter. What I wouldn't give to see the girl in one of my t-shirts.

Her lips turn up into a soft smile. "Thank you, Connor."

"Of course."

She tugs my jacket tightly around her.

"Let me guess," I say. "Mitch Allen is the reason for your rule."

She clicks her tongue and points at me. "Correct."

"That sucker," I mutter. "One bad apple doesn't spoil the whole batch, you know. Not all of us musicians are like him."

She's quiet for a breath, her face turned up to the sky. "I know. That's why I made an exception for you tonight."

"Doesn't count," I say. "This wasn't a real date."

"That's right," she lets out a little laugh. "I almost forgot." She swings her legs back and forth, gaze down. Her next words come out quiet, almost as if she's saying them to herself. "It sort of felt like it."

I swallow, taking in the length of her lashes. The soft waves of her long, blonde hair falling around her face.

I feel my pulse quicken under my skin. She's so beautiful. I'd love nothing more than to twine my fingers into her hair and pull her towards me right now.

"If this was a real date," I say slowly, waiting for her to look at me. "I would have kissed you by now."

She lets out a little gasp. "Connor Cane, you can't say things like that to me."

Even in the dark, I can see the blush on her cheeks, and it gives me a rush of pleasure.

She looks away, smiling. "I guess you still could, if you wanted to."

"What?"

She turns to face me again. There's a challenge in her green eyes. One I'm ready to rise to. Consider me suited up for battle.

"Kiss me."

The air stills around us at her words. All I can hear are the crickets singing in the fields, the sound of tall grasses brushing together. My heartbeat pulsing inside my ears.

"Rules are meant to be broken, right?" She asks, arching an eyebrow. "But you don't strike me as a rule breaker."

"You're right," I say, my throat thick. "I'm not."

I can see the rise and fall of her chest as she angles her body towards mine, crossing one leg over the other and leaning back on the tailgate on one hand. She brings her other hand up slowly, brushing a piece of my hair back near my forehead with her fingertips.

My breath hitches at her gentle touch.

I shouldn't want this. For anything serious to happen between us. We both know we shouldn't cross over from teasing and flirting into this territory–this place where things start to feel real.

Mallory warned me that getting involved with Ella Mae could spell disaster for her. My fans and the media might tear her apart. Crush her confidence. I saw what Mitch did to her tonight. The way he dimmed her light. I would hate for that to happen to her because of something I did. If I choose to do this, to break her rule and kiss her, things will never be the same between us.

And yet...

She's irresistible.

She lets out a little laugh, letting her hand fall from my hair. "I need you to be honest with me about something, Connor."

I hold my breath, waiting for her to spell out her request. Is she going to ask me how I feel about her? I'm not sure I'm ready to have that conversation.

"Do you–" she leans forward. "–or do you not...dye your hair?"

I jut out my chin and let out a laugh, partly in relief.

"For the last time," I say. "I do *not* dye my hair."

Ella Mae squints at me. "You're telling the truth?"

I give her a withering look.

She's undeterred, scooting her body so our hips and legs are touching. Her thigh is warm and firm against mine, sending my pulse racing. She drops her head back onto my chest, and I respond by wrapping my arm around her shoulders and laying my cheek on top of her hair. She places her hand on my knee, rubbing back and forth with her thumb. We sit there in the quiet, not speaking, just holding each other.

Chapter 20

Ella Mae

I want to kiss Connor Cane, and it's all Frank's fault.

I don't know how it happens, but one minute I've got my head resting on Connor's chest, his arms wrapped around me. We're comfortably taking in the night sky above us, chatting about music and movies and who knows what else.

Then, as the night grows colder, Connor conjures a thick blanket from somewhere inside Frank, spreading it out behind us in the truck bed.

And now we're lying here together. Side by side. Our chins lifted up to the stars, shoulders touching.

My heart is pounding so hard I swear Connor can hear it.

Goosebumps prickle across my bare legs as a cool breeze plays over my skin. I want nothing more than to roll over into Connor to absorb some of his warmth. I can feel it, radiating between the small spaces where we're not touching, inviting me nearer. But as much as I want to, I don't move. Can't move. It's like neither one of us wants to be the one to fold and take things any further.

I'm an old-fashioned kind of girl. I want a guy to open my door and hold my hand before he tries to kiss me.

But shoot. Connor has already checked both of those off my list of gentlemanly gestures tonight. If he tried to kiss me right now, I would let him.

No questions asked.

I even gave him verbal permission, but he's not making any moves. Just breathing softly next to me in the open country air, one muscular arm tucked behind his head. Shirt collar open. The smell of his skin is making my head spin. I'm cocooned in his jacket, inches away from his big, warm body.

I slowly turn my face toward his, visually tracing his profile. He's so familiar to me, someone I feel like I've known forever. And yet there's so much more to him that I want to discover. So much more I want to know.

"You okay?"

He blinks twice. Swallows. Keeps his eyes fixed on the heavens. "Not really."

I shift my arm so my hands are pressed together, resting behind my head. He finally turns to look at me. His eyes drop slowly, his gaze coming to rest at my mouth, and every part of my face burns.

His hand moves, finding my hip. His long fingers span my waist, thumb pressing gently into my hip bone. My breath catches in my throat at his touch. He slowly moves his fingertips up the length of my body, sliding behind the curtain of my hair to hold the back of my neck.

"I shouldn't do this," he says, a raspy edge to his voice, rumbling from his chest into mine.

My eyes are already closing. With every inhale, I'm breathing him in, surrendering. Every exhale brings us closer.

"Then don't," I say softly, opening my eyes to look at him.

He clenches his jaw, and I feel his thumb skate across the side of my neck. I close my eyes again.

"What will your brother say?" he murmurs against my neck. Tingles spread all the way down to the base of my spine.

"We're not going to tell him."

Connor laughs, the rough stubble from his cheek brushing against my skin. Then he shifts his body so we're even closer. Knees touching. His chest pressing against mine.

Then he slants his head sideways, blocking out my view of the night sky. The tip of his nose traces across my jawline, then nudges my cheek. I fist his shirt in my hands, pressing my knuckles against his chest. I literally stop breathing as I feel his bottom lip against mine. I can feel my heartbeat everywhere as I wait for him to go in for it, to kiss me.

But he doesn't. At least not right away.

I feel the warmth of his lips land on the corner of my mouth, his hand firmly holding the back of my neck. Then he drags a few slow kisses across my jawline. I'm burning through, all thoughts of being cold long gone.

When Connor's lips finally find my mouth, I melt. Liquefy. He holds me gently, coaxing, his lips cautiously exploring mine.

I've been kissed before, but not by someone who had exercised this kind of intentional restraint. He's not forcing himself on me. It's just the opposite. He's barely giving me anything, inviting me to respond, to pull him closer. To show him just how much I *want* him to kiss me.

I slip one of my hands behind his neck, feeling his short hair underneath his shirt collar. I gently brush my bottom lip against his, feeling his mouth open in response as I tilt my head.

He must get the memo that I'm giving him the green light. Because then he *kisses* me.

He's all heat and wild wanting, easily persuaded into following my lead. We're one breath, one racing heartbeat. He's everywhere. He's everything. I'm learning him with his hands and lips on me like this, our breath mingling together in the cold.

I don't even know how long we lie there in the truck bed, kissing each other like the world is ending. There's an urgency in it. Like we need each other deeply but somehow understand nothing is guaranteed after tonight.

Just the *thought* of never getting to be kissed by Connor Cane again breaks my heart. No one else can have him. I'm staking my claim right now.

He's mine.

He's the good man that I wasn't sure existed for me. I'm sure of it here in this quiet, peaceful moment, being held in his arms. He's kissing me like he's been waiting his whole life to do it.

Like it was always supposed to happen. Like it was always meant to be *us*.

As our kisses start to slow, he tenderly presses his forehead against mine, brushing a thumb over my cheek. I can sense his contentment and feel it sweeping through me, head to toe, too. I keep my eyes closed, relaxing into his warmth, the safety of his arms encircling my body and holding me close. Connor buries his nose in the little corner between my shoulder and neck. I can feel his breathing begin to slow, his arm across my stomach growing heavy.

It takes me a few minutes to realize that he's fallen asleep, holding me tightly to him.

Being in his arms feels just like that first hug he gave me back at Chloe and Hunter's wedding. Strap us together and toss us out of an airplane right now, and we'd make it to the ground in one piece. I'm entirely safe right here.

Frank and I are going to have a stern chat when morning breaks. But for now, I settle into Connor and allow myself to drift off to the sound of his breathing, the steady beating of his heart inside his broad chest.

———

The sound of a distant engine awakens me in the early hours of the morning. The sky is cotton-candy pink and blue, the air around us dewy. I can feel the mist on my clothes and skin, and there's a faded slice of the moon still visible overhead.

Last night felt like I'd been swept away to a different planet in the universe. One where Connor and I were the only two people in existence. And now I'm coming back to Earth.

I sigh, registering that Connor is still here with me. My head is resting atop the underside of his arm. His face is inches from mine, smooth and peaceful in sleep. I admire him in the soft morning light. His strong nose. Defined brows. The curve of his lips.

I can't help but smile as I remember last night, how sweetly he'd kissed me. The easy way we'd fallen asleep together.

And that's all we'd done. Fall asleep.

The rumbling engine in the distance sounds like it's getting closer. As reluctant as I am to awaken the prince from his peaceful slumber, it must be done.

I lift my head from his arm, slowly bringing myself to a seated position. He inhales deeply, squinting as he rolls away from me onto his back. He brings his hands to his face, scrubbing his palms down his cheeks before meeting my eyes. I smile.

"Morning," he says gruffly.

"Morning."

He sits up beside me, and I twist around, searching for the source of the sound that woke me. I can see a tractor making its way toward us down Mooreville Road in the distance.

"Ahoy," I say. "Farmer on the horizon."

Connor snorts, scooting off the edge of the tailgate. He rolls his shoulders back, then his neck back and forth in a stretch. "We'd better get out of here."

He helps me down off the tailgate, his hand enclosing mine safely in his while I locate my shoes in the grass. We hop into the truck, and Connor turns the engine on.

He eyes me warily as he drives. "I'm sorry I kept you out all night. That wasn't my plan."

"You sure?" I say, faking skepticism. "I couldn't have escaped if I tried. You were out cold."

Connor laughs, then his expression grows serious. "I haven't slept like that in years."

We exchange a look, and he gives me a shy smile that makes me want to snuggle up to him all over again right here in the truck. "I actually struggle with insomnia. It used to be really bad, but I've been sleeping better ever since..."

His voice trails off. I swallow.

The sweetness that envelops me at his admission is consuming. Validating. He feels what I'm feeling. That sense of safety and security that allows you to be completely yourself with someone. Or to fall asleep in their arms.

He reaches across the console and places his hand on my knee as he drives. It's a simple gesture, but it brightens me from the inside out. Makes the morning sun shining through the truck window feel closer and more real.

I lay my hand on top of his, dropping my fingers in the spaces between his own.

"I've got another question for you," I say as he pulls onto the main road.

He gives my knee a little squeeze. "If you say one more thing about my hair, Ella Mae, I swear—"

"Not a hair question," I say. "A music-related question."

His blue eyes are brilliant in the morning sunlight, catching mine from across the truck cab. "Hit me."

"What are your thoughts on Jesse McCartney?"

"Jesse McCartney?" He pinches his eyebrows together in amusement. "I mean... He's got a couple good songs, I guess."

"A couple good songs?" I gasp incredulously.

Connor laughs. "Clearly, you have some thoughts on this subject."

"In fact, I do."

"I'd love to hear them."

My smile widens. There's a fondness in his voice. He cares about the little things. It doesn't matter what I'm about to say, whatever it is matters to him because it's coming from me.

"Well, for starters..." I smooth my dress. "He was my first love."

I see Connor's smile crawl up one cheek, but he keeps his eyes focused straight ahead on the road. "Really?" he says with mock intrigue.

"My first celebrity crush," I sigh. "I had this binder in middle school—you know the kind with the pocket in the front?" He nods. "I made a collage of Jesse McCartney pictures and put it in the front of my binder. It was my most-prized possession."

"Sounds like you still have feelings for him." He's trying his best to remain composed, but I hear the laughter in his voice.

"Of course I do. One never forgets their first love."

"True."

"But not only is he a beautiful soul..." I say. Connor coughs. "He wrote a few songs that made me want to become a songwriter."

"Which songs?"

"The whole *Beautiful Soul* record," I say reverently. "I used to pretend he was singing it to me when his music videos would come on TV. Then when I was a little older, I heard "Right Where You Want Me" on the radio and just about *died*."

"Why is that?"

"It was a little edgier than his previous songs. But not as spicy as 'Body Language.'"

"Pause. I like the sound of that one," Connor says. "Can you play it for me?"

"He's an icon," I say wistfully, ignoring his request. "My forever celebrity crush." I smile to myself. "Sometimes you remind me of him."

He snorts. "How so?"

I keep my mouth shut, realizing I've backed myself into a corner.

"Ella Mae Stewart," he says, delighted. "Are you *finally* admitting to having a crush on me?"

"I never said that."

"But it was implied." He grins, triumphant. "I'm your next-gen Jesse McCartney. *Forever celebrity crush—*"

I scowl. "That's Jesse's title and his alone."

"Are you going to make a binder with my face on it?"

"Of course not." I pause. "Maybe."

"You're ridiculous. Why can't you just admit it?" he says. "You like me."

I feel the tips of my ears tingle. *Truer words have never been spoken.*

"Why can't you just admit that you like *me*?" I counter.

Connor gives me a flirty look of frustration. "Is that not what I spent all last night doing?"

Memories of his lips on mine surface under my skin.

"Alright, fine." I sigh impatiently. "I like you, Connor Cane."

He looks more than pleased at my admission.

"In fact," I say, "I'd say I am well on my way to becoming a top-tier Martha."

He snorts.

"Whoever your most passionate Martha is, she'd better hold onto her crown and sleep with one eye open. I may just de-throne her soon. Stage a coup."

"Based on how *passionately* you kissed me last night, I'd say you already have."

A hot blush climbs up my neck and onto my cheeks.

He takes his hand off my knee, using both hands to make a sharp turn onto the highway, heading toward Franklin. "Wanna get some breakfast?"

I look down at my rumpled dress, my limp hair. I give him my best remorseful look. "I would love to, but I have a standing yoga date with my besties every Saturday morning."

"No worries. I've got rehearsal at ten anyway."

"Tour rehearsal?"

"Yeah," he says, then he's quiet for a minute. When I glance over at him, he's wearing a frown. "I leave in two weeks."

Two weeks.

The reality that Connor will be heading out on the road for an extended period of time hits me right in the gut. I think his thoughts are tangling with mine in the space above our heads, full of unknowns and questions about the future.

Our future.

But I'm not one prone to worry, so I give him a bright smile. "As your newly crowned Queen Martha, I'd say that I'm entitled to attend a rehearsal."

Connor's smile returns to his face. "Give us a few days to work out the kinks, and I'll have you come by."

And there it is. The guarantee that I will get to at least spend some more time with him before he leaves.

But no guarantee that he's ever going to kiss me again.

Chapter 21

Ella Mae

I could butter a biscuit with the amount of judgment Lainey's got in her eyes when I greet her in the kitchen once I'm home.

She's already dressed in her matching yoga set, a cup of coffee raised to her lips. She slowly lowers the mug, revealing a sassy smirk.

"Sleep well last night?" she asks.

I set my clutch on the kitchen counter, tugging my dress down at my thighs. "I slept great, thank you."

Lainey places her hands on the counter and leans toward me, looking far too satisfied for her own good.

"I don't need to know the details," she says. "But I do need to know whether or not you had to put that dress back on this morning or whether—"

I hold up a hand to stop her. "No, ma'am. This dress remained on my body the entire evening."

Lainey arches one eyebrow masterfully.

"Lainey Helms. What kind of a girl do you take me for? We fell asleep, alright? That's all."

"Uh-huh." Lainey takes another sip from her mug. "And how good of a *sleeper* was Connor Cane?"

"You're the worst."

"What else am I supposed to think?" she says. "I tell you to *live a little*, to have a good time, but instead, you don't come home *at all*? No texts, no calls..."

"Pipe down, Mother Goose," I chide. "And where were *you* last night? No texts, no calls." I cross my arms over my chest.

"With my soon-to-be mother-in-law."

"And?"

"My sexy fiancé."

We grin at each other.

"But I, unlike you, came home last night," she says, setting her mug down on the kitchen island. "Late last night. But still. I was here."

I sigh, taking a seat on one of the stools across from her.

"You look..." She waves a hand around, searching for the right words. "Invigorated. Refreshed."

I saw myself in the mirror on my way to the kitchen and had honestly been shocked that I didn't look like a half-dead racoon after spending the night outside in a field. My eyes were clear, my cheeks flushed where Connor had given me a soft kiss before I'd hopped out of his truck.

I'm not any worse for wear.

"I'm telling you, Lainey," I explain. "I slept like a baby."

"Was his bed one of those fancy—"

"Lainey!" I laugh. "I was not in Connor Cane's bed!"

"Then *where were you*?"

"We fell asleep in his truck...bed," I say slowly. "The *truck* bed."

"Ahh, yes." She narrows her hazel eyes at me. "The *truck* bed. Thank you for making that important distinction for me, although you still used the word *bed*, so TEN POINTS FOR GRYFFINDOR!"

I steal her coffee mug from her and bring it to my own lips.

"Ella Mae," she says, rapping her fingers on the countertop impatiently. "I won't press you, but if you'd care to share anything else about your evening, I'm all ears."

"I'd better go get dressed," I say. "Don't want to be late to roomie yoga."

"Did he kiss you first?" she says. "Or did you grab him and"—she grits her teeth and mimes shaking someone by the lapels—"let him have it?"

I laugh. "He kissed *me*."

She screams. "How long has it been since you've kissed someone?"

I run my thumb down the mug handle. "A long time."

"And?" she asks. "How was it? How was he?"

I sigh, blinking up at the pendant lights hanging above my head. "Perfect."

"I'd expect nothing less."

I take another sip of her coffee. "So now what?" she asks, leaning on her elbows. "What happens next?"

I give her a one-shoulder shrug.

"Did he tell you he likes you?"

"He did." I have to bite back a smile. "He told me I was his favorite."

She squeals. "Oh, Ella Mae!" She comes around the counter and wraps me in a tight hug. "I'm so happy for you."

I laugh into her hair. "Lainey, nothing official has happened."

She pulls back. "What do you mean? You're his *favorite*!"

"Yeah, but..." I lean back, and she releases me. "He's leaving for tour in two weeks."

"A lot can happen in two weeks," she says matter-of-factly. "Luke and I were all in just a few weeks after we met."

"I know," I say, feeling unsettled. "But there are a lot of things we haven't talked about. I don't even know if he's looking for a relationship right now. Or if *I'm* looking for a relationship right now."

Lainey gawks at me. "Ella Mae! Connor *freaking* Cane just kissed you and held you in his arms under a silver moon and a blanket of stars in his truck bed. Of course he wants a relationship. And he wants it with *you*!"

I shift in my seat. "I appreciate your support, Lainey, but there's still so much I don't know."

"That's how relationships work," she says. "You have to have faith and move forward if you feel like it's the right thing to do. There's always the risk that things won't work out, but there's also the chance that they *will*."

I smile at her. "Thank you, Lainey."

"He'd better not screw things up," she says, her expression darkening. "You deserve the absolute best."

We give each other a sisterly pouty smile, and she hugs me again. I hear her gasp into my ear.

"Oh, no!" she cries, drawing back from me. "What will Trent say when he finds out?"

My stomach knots uncomfortably at the thought of having to explain to my protective older brother that I kissed his best friend. I broke both of my rules last night, and though I don't regret it, I'm not looking forward to having that conversation.

"I don't want to tell him," I say. "At least not yet."

Trent hadn't exactly been the nicest big brother to me when I was young, and he had been equally as disenchanted with Lainey simply because she was my best friend. He thought we were both annoying little brats for most of our childhood, and then suddenly stepped into the role of protective older brother to both of us once we entered high school.

"I wouldn't either," she says, wincing. "He's scary when he's mad."

I glance over at the clock on the wall. "Oh, goodness me. We really are going to be late if I don't change right now."

"Get your booty downstairs, then!" Lainey says, spanking me as I dart past her to the door to my basement apartment. "I'm leaving in five minutes with or without you!"

Lainey is true to her word. I barely make it into the passenger seat of her moving car as she pulls out of the driveway.

"Are we still planning on visiting that apartment Luke owns today?" I ask on our way to the yoga studio.

"Yes, ma'am."

I keep my eyes out the window, watching the trees whiz by. I've been dreading this—the reality that my best friend is getting married in a matter of weeks, and I'm going to be a lone ranger in my very own big-girl apartment. No one to steal coffee from. No one to watch trashy reality television with.

Ella Mae Stewart has been in denial.

"How are you feeling about marri-*ahge*?" I ask.

Lainey sighs. "We've nailed down all of the big things, so now it's just a matter of waiting for the big day to come around."

"That must feel good," I say. "Is there anything else that you need my help with?"

"Hmm..." Lainey purses her lips. She plans events for a living, so her organizational skills are top notch. "I have my final dress fitting in a week, so you can come to that if you want."

"Absolutely."

"And I need to put together the wedding favors as we get closer. But that's pretty much it. Luke's big on efficiency, so we hired out almost everything so we can just enjoy the day as much as possible."

"You guys make a great team," I say, and I mean it. "You complement each other so well."

"You're sweet," Lainey says with a warm smile. "Sometimes it shocks me how similar our minds are, too. We think alike."

"Hmm," I say thoughtfully.

"What about you and Connor?" she asks. "Do you guys have a lot in common?"

I pull the sleeves of my crewneck down over my hands, bunching them around my fists. "We do, actually. We share a lot of the same interests, and it helps that we work in the same industry. And he's funny."

"You're funny, too. I hope he appreciates your sense of humor."

I smirk. "I do enjoy making him laugh."

"You forgot to mention the fact that you both have gorgeous blonde hair," Lainey says. "You'll make the most beautiful little golden babies."

I snort. "I swore on my life that he dyes his hair, but he insists it's natural."

Lainey laughs.

"We share a few of the same fears, too, I think," I say quietly. "We're afraid of ruining our friendship and jeopardizing Connor and Trent's relationship. And as much as it pains me to admit it, I think we're both a little bit afraid of commitment."

Lainey pulls into a parking spot in front of the yoga studio. "That's understandable. He's a rising country star. I can see how he'd be hesitant to put down roots right now." Lainey cuts the engine and turns to look at me, puzzled. "But you? I didn't think you had commitment issues."

"Hello. Mitch Allen, remember?" I say. "He's made it hard for me to want to get back in the ring."

"That's understandable," Lainey says gently. "Anybody would be hesitant to do so after going through what you did."

"He was at the party last night," I say.

Lainey's eyes widen. "He was? Did he try to talk to you?"

"He did, but it was a brief conversation." I meet Lainey's eyes. "Connor stepped in."

Lainey gasps, her hand flying to her mouth.

"He grabbed my hand and went all alpha on Mitch."

"What I wouldn't give to have seen that."

"It was sweet."

"So Connor knows about what happened with Mitch?"

"He does now," I say. "It's weird. I want to tell him things like that. Things nobody else knows. I want him to tell me things, too. But it's hard for either of us to open up. I think we're both afraid to let each other in."

Lainey gives me a look of understanding. "Your fears are valid. But..." She tilts her head, forcing me to meet her eyes. "Ella Mae, you can't let fear lead when it comes to Connor. He isn't Mitch. You can't project your past experience with that jerk onto him. It's not fair to either of you."

"You're right," I say. "But even if I can get over those fears, he's Trent's closest friend. If either of us messes this up, it will affect their relationship."

"Then you need to tell Trent," Lainey says, her eyes concerned. "If you care about Connor, you've got to be honest with your brother."

"I know." I grimace.

We watch Chloe and Ava pass in front of Lainey's car before entering the studio.

"You can do it, Ella Mae," Lainey says, pointing at me. "You can be brave. Connor might just be worth the risk. But you'll never know if you don't have the courage to be honest with yourself and with Trent."

As we enter the studio and roll out our respective mats, I feel my heart swell with gratitude for my friends—the women I look up to and admire most. They're my support system, my sisters. I know I can turn to them with any problem, and they'll come in clutch with advice and wisdom.

As I flow through my yoga practice, focusing on my breath, the length of my inhales and exhales, I feel my chest begin to expand. My heart starts to open.

I can give myself grace. I can be patient with my heart and with Connor's.

I don't have to have it all figured out right now, but I know Lainey is right. At some point, I'll have to tell Trent.

But you'd better believe I will wait as long as humanly possible to do so.

We're slurping smoothies and spooning up acai bowls at the juice bar next door after class when Lainey throws me under the proverbial bus.

"Hey, Ava," she says. "Do you notice how well Ella Mae is looking this morning?"

Ava tilts her head and scans my face. "You are looking *quite* well, Ella Mae."

"Chloe, can't you see how absolutely *adored* she looks?" Lainey grins wickedly. "Just look at the way the light is shining out of her eyes, and how perfectly kissed her lips—"

"Alright," I say, slamming my cup down on the table. "Enough out of you, ma'am."

But she's already got Ava and Chloe on the edges of their seats.

"Perfectly *kissed*?"

"By WHOM?"

Ava gasps, nearly choking on her smoothie. "You KISSED him, Ella Mae?"

Chloe's jaw drops, looking at me with her wide, doe-like brown eyes. "No. Way."

"I knew it," Ava says in a low voice. "I knew it from the moment I saw the two of you at Chloe's wedding."

"You make a beautiful couple," Chloe says.

"Won't they have the most gorgeous babies?" Lainey says. "Little blond cherubs."

"Alright, alright." I wave a hand in the air to silence them, giving Lainey a stern look. "Connor and I kissed, okay? But that's it. There's nothing else to unpack here."

Chloe snorts. "That's what I thought after Hunter kissed me for the first time. But boy, was I in for it."

Ava nods emphatically. "When Finn and I kissed for the first time, it turned my whole world upside down." She turns to her sister. "What about you Lainey? What happened after you and Luke kissed?"

"Everything," she says solemnly. "Once you've kissed the right man, you can't go back."

"Who says he's the right man?" I scoff.

"*People Magazine*," Ava says. "We all saw the article."

"The polls don't lie, sister," Lainey says, scraping up the rest of her acai bowl and spooning it into her mouth. "That man is marriage material."

"Well, this escalated quickly," I mutter.

Chloe gives me a sympathetic look. "Sorry, Ella Mae. We're just giving you a hard time because we're happy for you. He's a really good guy."

"I, for one, am eager for you to officially join the merry wives of Franklin," Ava says. "Speaking of which, Lainey...Chloe and I have been meaning to talk to you about a few things."

"Ooooh," Lainey says with a gasp. "What sorts of things?"

"*Wedding night* things."

It's my turn to choke on my smoothie. "Right now? Can't this conversation wait?"

"She's already faithfully waited her whole life," Ava points out.

"True," I concede. We're all old-fashioned when it comes to these kinds of things.

"The least we can do is give you girls a few tips," Ava says.

Chloe nods. "You can ask us anything."

I glance around uncomfortably, making sure nobody else in the little juice bar is listening in on what will surely be a very frank conversation about marital *relations*.

"I think," I say, moving to stand up, "I suddenly need to make a few phone calls."

"What?" Ava says. "Ella Mae, this advice applies to you, too." She tugs me back down to my seat.

I sigh, resigned to listening in on a conversation between those of us who have or will soon have husbands, which entirely excludes me.

"Okay," Lainey says, rubbing her hands together. "I've always wanted to know... Do I need to—"

"Oh, dear," Chloe suddenly says, her brows knitting together. "Maybe I shouldn't have ordered that green smoothie." She squints up at the menu. "What was in it?"

"You okay?" I ask, placing a hand on her shoulder. "You're looking a little peaked."

"I don't feel great." She moves to stand up. "I might step outside for a minute. Ella Mae, wanna come with me?"

"Of course."

Chloe's still frowning when we get outside.

"What's going on?" I say, gently rubbing her shoulder.

"I don't know," she says with a sigh. "Probably just low blood sugar or something. I should have eaten breakfast before the class this morning."

I nod. "Sorry you're not feeling well."

She gives me a strained smile. "All good. Plus I figured you didn't want to sit and listen to us talk about...you know."

I shrug. "It's fine, really."

She purses her lips together. "No, it's not. We weren't being very sensitive to you. I'm sorry."

"It's okay, Chlo," I insist. "There's nothing to apologize for."

"Are you happy?" she asks, crossing her arms over her stomach. "With Connor?"

"Yeah," I say. "He's wonderful. I just don't know if anything's going to happen between us. I know you're all pulling for me to hitch myself to somebody so I can be a part of the *Merry Wives of Franklin*, but..." my voice trails off.

"There's no rush, you know," Chloe says gently.

I meet her eyes.

"When you find the right person, it will be worth the wait," she says. "So take your time."

"I think I need to," I say. "Finding a husband has not been at the top of my list of priorities."

"And that's okay!" Chloe says emphatically. "You've got to be a whole person in order to contribute to a healthy relationship. I had a steady career that I loved and didn't date anyone seriously for a long time until Hunter pulled his head out of his—"

I laugh.

"We're here to support and love you right where you are," she says, placing a hand on my arm. "If you're not ready to commit to a serious relationship, then don't. Take your time. Enjoy your life. It will only make it easier for you to go all-in when the right person comes. You'll know when it's right for the both of you."

Lainey and Ava exit the juice bar, heads close together, evidently still deep in their sisterly marriage-advice chat.

"Thank you, Chloe," I say, wrapping my arm around her petite frame and giving her a hug.

She swallows. "Goodness. I'm really not feeling great. I think I should head home and rest."

"Do it. Let Hunter dote on you," I say.

We exchange our goodbyes, getting into our respective vehicles.

"You ready to go see that apartment?" Lainey asks as I buckle my seatbelt.

"Let's do it."

Chapter 22

Connor

The boys and I are running through the tour set list Monday afternoon when Mallory comes marching in, looking grim.

Usually, if she has something to run by me, she'll give me a call. The somber look on her face tells me she's got news and that it's nothing good.

"How's rehearsal going, gents?" she asks, slinging her purse up on her shoulder.

The band greets her with half-hearted waves—everyone but my drummer, who I call Fox. The aptly named forty-something bachelor gives Mallory a bright smile and a meaningful head nod. I pretend like I don't see the way she gives him an extra second of her attention before turning her gaze back on me.

It's only a matter of time before Fox works up the courage to ask Mallory on a date. The rest of us are betting it'll happen soon. If the time they'll be spending on the upcoming tour together doesn't expedite things, I don't know what will.

"Can I talk to you for a second?" she asks. "I hope I'm not interrupting."

"No, not at all," I say. "Just nailing down the set list."

I follow her back toward the doors, away from the band. When she spins around again to look at me, I'm concerned by the serious lines between her eyebrows.

"Is everything okay?"

"Remember that conversation we had a few days ago?"

"Which one?"

"About..." She lowers her voice. "Ella Mae."

I shouldn't get all fired up hearing her name again, but I do.

"Yeah, I remember," I say, dragging a hand through my hair nervously. "Is she okay? Did something happen?"

"Why didn't you tell me you were going to that party together?"

I feel a knot grow in my stomach. "I didn't think I needed to."

She gives me a sympathetic look and hands me her phone. I reluctantly take it.

"Another article," she says. "But this time from a bigger news outlet. And there's a photo."

My heart drops as I quickly scan through the article.

Connor Cane...songwriter...duet...rumored to be dating...seen getting cozy together at a local songwriter event...

Then I see the picture.

It had been taken at the songwriter soiree. A moment where Ella Mae and I were together, our hands intertwined, our bodies far too close for us to be *just friends*. It had been taken from close range, around the time we'd encountered Mitch Allen.

My stomach roils with anger as I continue scrolling through the article.

"They're essentially painting her as a social climber, saying she's using you to gain status and to boost her opportunities.

They talked to some anonymous source who said she'll do anything to get to the top."

I grind my teeth together as anger spreads through my chest.

"Who wrote this article?" I say hotly.

"A journalist. Katrina something," Mallory says with a tired sigh. "We've already contacted the site, requesting that they remove the article and the photo, but nobody's gotten back to us yet."

I scroll down to the bottom of the article to find the journalist's name. And it's there alright, in italicized font:

Katrina Devon.

And right next to her name is a photo. I zoom in, my jaw clenching as I recognize her.

The woman from the bar. The plastic blonde who'd been with Mitch Allen at the songwriter soiree.

"This is a calculated move," I say, handing Mallory her phone. "This Katrina woman...she was with Mitch Allen at the party."

"Mitch?" Mallory says, distaste evident in her expression.

"It gets worse," I say. "Ella Mae dated Mitch a few years ago. Things didn't end well."

"Ahh," Mallory says with a slow nod. "The anonymous source."

"So it would seem."

We stand in charged silence for a minute. My mind is racing with all the ways I'd like to make Mitch pay for the things he said about Ella Mae in that article. The things he'd done to her.

"Connor," Mallory says gently. "I know you care about Ella Mae. But this is just the start of the games the media will play with you two. There have been several other articles posted after this one went live. She's already becoming a target, and the record isn't even out yet."

I cross my arms over my chest, looking away. Whatever Mallory has got to say, I don't want to hear it.

"If you truly care about this girl," Mallory says carefully, "you need to think very deeply about how your involvement with her is going to impact her life."

"I *have* been thinking about it, Mallory. Non-stop." I glance back at the band to ensure nobody can hear us. "She's important to me."

Mallory gives me a kind smile. "I know that. She's been good for you. And I know this may be hard for you to hear, but you need to decide whether or not *you* are good for *her* right now. This isn't going to stop. The lies. The loss of her privacy. It's a high price for anyone to pay."

"Believe me," I grumble. "I know."

"If the timing was better," Mallory says, "things would be different. But all eyes are on you with the release of this record. And Ella Mae will already be under scrutiny simply because she's featured on it. There's naturally going to be speculation about the two of you after people hear the song."

I meet her eyes, and she rests a hand on my arm. "You need to have a frank conversation with Ella Mae before things get crazy. And if you want to keep her out of the spotlight, you need to leave her be. No more parties. No more PDA—"

"That wasn't even real PDA," I say. "I was just trying to get Mitch off her case."

Mallory's lips flatten, and she lets out a long breath through her nose. "I should have known he'd have something to do with this. I'm going to call his manager."

"No," I say flatly. "Don't do that. Ella Mae wants nothing to do with him."

She nods reluctantly. "Fine. I'll respect that," she sighs. "I'll let you get back to it. But promise me you'll talk to Ella Mae. You need to show her these articles and comments. Show her what she's up against. What you're both up against."

I level Mallory with a stare. "I don't want to hurt her."

"I know," she says. "That's why we're having this conversation, Connor. I'm gonna head out. I've got to get your tour manager up to speed."

"You guys sound great!" she calls out to the band, who isn't actually playing their instruments. Fox gives her a salute, and she responds with a little finger wave back.

The door swings shut after Mallory, and I take a deep breath in and slowly let it out.

Time to do what I do best. Perform. Fake it. Plaster on a smile and make sure nobody can see what's really going on beneath the surface.

I straighten my shoulders and turn back to the band with a grin on my face. "Workin' hard or hardly workin'?"

We all move into our positions, and I shove my in-ear monitors back in, losing myself in the music for the rest of the evening, trying to numb the discomfort that's eating its way through my ribcage.

I'd been looking forward to having Ella Mae come to a rehearsal. But just like everything else I would enjoy doing in my life, it would appear that's been taken from me, too.

The first thing I see after I walk back into my apartment is that stupid bird painting. Mocking me from my kitchen counter.

I knew as soon as my lips had found Ella Mae's that I would never be the same. There had been so much build-up to that first kiss we'd shared, and it changed me. Altered my chemical makeup.

It's been three days, and my lips still tingle every time I remember how it felt to have her mouth on mine...

I've been sleeping better than I have in a long time. Crashing hard. Even though we haven't seen each other since Friday night, that sense of security and peace I felt with her in my arms has stayed with me.

Until tonight. I'm stressed as all get out, filled with burning anger.

Thankfully, I have coping mechanisms. And I'm going to need all of them tonight. First, a workout. Then a good meal and some time with my guitar. There's no better way for me to process my feelings than through writing.

I tug my shirt off and change into workout clothes, grabbing my water bottle on my way into the makeshift home gym I've got in the spare bedroom. I used to love going to the gym or going for a run on the trail behind my last house. But those were luxuries the old Connor enjoyed. Connor 2.0 has to work out alone. At home. Indoors.

Fifteen minutes into my weight-lifting routine, I start to feel better. The endorphins are flowing, blood pumping throughout my body. Cooling my anger. Clearing my head.

An hour later, I'm dripping sweat after finishing things off with a ride on my stationary bike. I'm mopping my face with a towel, pulling out a microwavable container from my tower of macro-friendly meals I've had delivered. When the timer on the microwave goes off, so does my phone. I pick it up off the counter to see who's calling.

Stewie.

And he's trying to FaceTime me, for goodness' sake. When does the man ever video chat? I'm surprised he even knows how to do it.

Did Ella Mae already talk to him? Does he know?

I swear under my breath, then reluctantly answer his call.

"Stewie, my man!" I say.

"Hey," Trent says gruffly, propping up the phone on his table and sliding his dinner plate into the frame. "Mind if I eat while we chat?"

"Not at all." I hold up my meal container. "We can have a little dinner date."

He snorts, digging into his food with his fork.

I take a seat on a barstool at the kitchen counter. He doesn't look ready to murder me—at least not yet.

"How're things going up yonder?" I ask, hoping he can't hear the nerves in my voice.

Trent shrugs, taking a mouthful of his food. "Busy."

"Are you still trying to manage everything by yourself?"

Trent swallows, shaking his head. "I'm actually looking to hire someone else to help me out." He points his fork at me. "You looking for a job?"

I let out a cynical laugh. "Maybe."

A few years ago, Trent bought a couple of cabins out in Washington with the intent to build out the property. He'd asked me if I wanted to tag along to help him build and run the place. I'd considered making the move at first, but I'd been so close to signing a record deal, and ultimately decided to stay the course.

While I don't regret my choice, the simplicity of a life like Trent's suddenly sounds very appealing to me.

"You know I'm always willing to help out, but I don't know if I could keep up with you. The only callouses I've got these days are the permanent ones on my fingertips from playing my guitar."

Trent takes another bite. "Pitiful."

"You're telling me."

He points his fork at the screen. "So."

I start chewing my food at record speed, anxiety coursing through my body. Here it comes. The throw-down. All rational thought leaves my mind. I will say as little as possible in an effort to not put my foot in my mouth.

I wait for him to continue, but instead, he takes another bite of food and stares me down. It's slightly intimidating, even though we're conversing virtually.

"I got a call the other day," he finally says.

I assume he's talking about Ella Mae. He has to be. I slowly lay down my fork.

"Yeah?"

"An interesting call."

I swear, scrubbing a hand over my mouth.

"Trent," I say slowly. "I didn't plan for anything to happen. I hope you know that."

He stares.

"She invited me to go as her friend, but as I'm sure she told you, things may have gotten a little more than...friendly."

One of his eyebrows raises a fraction.

"If you want to fire me as your best friend, I completely understand."

He slides his plate aside, leaning forward with his massive arms crossed on the table.

"I'm sorry, I don't think I understand what you're talking about," he says.

I cringe. "Do you really want me to spell it out for you?"

"Yeah," he says, shifting back and forth. "Yeah, I do."

I sigh and close my eyes.

"I kissed her," I say finally, opening my eyes a fraction. "I kissed your sister."

Trent doesn't react. Doesn't move or even blink. He simply stares at me through the screen until the silence is so uncomfortable my skin starts to itch.

"Well?" I say. "Let me have it."

One corner of his mouth hitches up infinitesimally.

Trent clears his throat. "Uh..." He tilts his head, raising his eyebrows and then lowering them again. "I got a call this week...from your mom."

My eyes slowly close again, embarrassment heating my face.

"My mom," I say with understanding. "About the Knoxville show. She told me she was going to try to convince you to come." I squint at Trent hesitantly. "That's what you were calling me about."

He simply nods, arms still crossed. Shoulders rounded over.

"I'm an idiot."

"You're an idiot."

I sigh, scrubbing a hand over my mouth.

"Tell me more about this," he says, amused—shockingly not angry. "You and Ella Mae."

"I thought that's why you were calling me," I explain. "I thought she must have told you."

He shakes his head.

I sit back on the barstool. "Well, as I'm sure you know, we've been working together."

"And by working together, clearly you mean *working* together," he says, the shadow of a smile on his lips.

"Stop it," I say. "We wrote a song together. We started seeing each other more after that."

"Great song," he says gruffly.

I know Trent doesn't dole out compliments lightly, so I take his approval of our duet to heart.

"Thanks, man." I pause. "Your sister and I...we've been casually hanging out. But last weekend..." I swallow. "We went to this party together. It wasn't a date, but I'd be lying if I said I didn't try to make it feel like one."

Trent rubs his nose with the back of his hand and sniffs.

"Finally," he says.

I frown. *Finally?*

"What do you mean?" I ask hesitantly.

"You're an idiot."

"We've established this."

"No, man," he says. "I can't believe it's taken you all these years to take my sister out on a date."

"What?" I bark out a confused laugh. "She's your *sister*. I never saw her that way..."

"But you do now?" He raises an eyebrow at me.

"Yeah. Yeah, I do."

He leans back in his chair, looking toward the ceiling thoughtfully. "You got her to break her rule. That's a big deal."

"So I've learned," I grumble. "Mitch was at the party."

Fire flashes in Trent's eyes. The dude is fearsome when he's angry. "I hope you told him to keep his distance." I can hear the protectiveness in his voice, that same urge I feel to protect her from harm. From the media. From the crazy fans. The desire to hide her away from the world and to preserve her sweetness. To keep her just the way she is right now.

"I did."

"Good." Trent grunts.

"So you're not upset?"

Trent shrugs. "Why would I be upset? You're two grown adults. You can take care of yourselves."

I let out a long exhale. "I thought you'd immediately book a ticket out here to mess me up once you found out."

"I would never do that," he says, then tilts his head in consideration. "Unless you screwed things up. Then I definitely would."

"That's the thing," I say slowly. "I really care about her. But I don't know if I'm good for her, you know? I'm always on the road. My schedule is insane. My album is about to drop, then I'm leaving for tour—"

"On second thought," Trent says with a snort. "You're right. You should probably leave her alone."

I pause, sitting back in my chair. "I know. The odds seem to be stacked against us."

"Then beat the odds," he says with a shrug.

After my conversation with Mallory, I thought the right thing to do would be to set my feelings aside and focus on my work. To let Ella Mae be. But Trent's frank advice brings clarity to my mind.

Ella Mae matters to me.

"You know your sister better than anyone," I say. "What do you think I should do? What should I say?"

Trent's quiet for a moment, contemplating.

"Lay it all out for her," he finally says. "Let her decide. And if she says she never wants to see your sorry face again, you can move out here and work for me."

I laugh. "Deal."

My eyes land on the bird painting again, and my mouth hitches up in a smile.

Chapter 23

Ella Mae

I'm off to a writing session in East Nashville at someone's home—a rare invitation. A group of us writers have banded together to crank out a bunch of songs over the course of a few days with an older country artist trying to make a comeback.

Shannon, the songwriter Connor and I ran into at the soiree, calls me just as I'm about to leave the house.

"Do you have any extra guitar strings?" she asks. "Randy broke one a minute ago, and I told him I'd ask you first before he goes out to buy a replacement."

"Yes, ma'am, I do," I say, hefting my guitar case into one hand and shifting the phone between my ear and shoulder as I open the front door. "I'll see you guys soon."

I lower my phone and shove it into my bag, turning to lock up before I head out. I haven't checked the time since coming upstairs and running around like a madwoman to collect my things, but I'm certain I'm running late.

Because of this, I almost don't notice the dark-blue sedan parked on the street right outside our house.

Almost.

I squint at the unfamiliar vehicle as I walk to Wanda and load up all my stuff. Parking restrictions are insanely strict here at

Carriage Court. Just ask Lainey. One night after we'd moved in, she forgot to pull her car into the driveway and earned herself a parking ticket, which Luke somehow got her out of. If this blue car had been parked on the street overnight, it would certainly have a boot and a ticket tucked into the windshield wipers.

I watch as the window rolls down, and an unfamiliar man pokes his head out.

"Morning," I say with a friendly wave before pulling my own car door open. Maybe he's a friend or a relative of one of the neighbors. Maybe he's lost.

He doesn't reply immediately, just continues smiling at me. I turn, about to hop inside my car, when I hear him speak.

"Good morning, Ella Mae," he replies.

I freeze.

A chill travels the length of me, and my heart starts racing.

I've never seen this man before in my life. How does he know my name? I turn back and squint at him.

"Connor Cane coming around today?" he asks and sticks a camera out the window. I hear the distinct click of the button as he takes a photo.

Of me.

I quickly whirl back around, ducking my head as I lower myself into the driver's seat and slam the door shut.

What in the world? Who is this man, and how did he find me?

And how does he know about me and Connor Cane?

My hands are shaking as I insert the key and Wanda sputters to life. I throw my sunglasses on and quickly reverse out of the driveway. But his car is facing mine as I pull out onto the street, and he's still got that stupid camera trained on me.

I frown as I speed away, my heart pumping in my chest as I turn out of the neighborhood.

Why was he at our house? How long had he been there? Why was he taking *pictures of me?*

I've never felt unsafe here in Franklin, but as I make my way to my songwriting session, I'm beyond paranoid, obsessively checking in my rearview mirror to make sure I'm not being followed.

I dial Lainey's number as I'm driving. I know she's at work and might not answer right away, but I feel a sweet sense of relief when she finally does.

"Hey, girl," she says. "Everything okay?"

"Ummm..." I do a shoulder check and change lanes, still scanning the roads for that blue sedan. "Not really."

"What's going on?" she says, concerned.

"Did you see a car parked outside our house this morning when you left for work?"

"Hmm," she says. "I don't think so."

"Well..." I let out a nervous laugh. "There was a man parked outside when I left the house. He knew my name. He had a camera, and he was taking pictures—"

"Pictures of what?" Lainey asks, her tone serious. "The house?"

"No." I swallow. "Of me. He asked me if Connor Cane was coming by."

I hear her intake of breath. She's quiet for a minute.

"Is it okay if I tell Luke what's going on?" she says.

"I don't want to interrupt anything," I say, knowing they're both at the office just starting their workday. "But if he doesn't mind, I'd love to talk to both of you."

"Oh, he won't mind. This is important," Lainey says, and it sounds like she's walking somewhere, and fast. I hear a door close and then a brief muffled exchange.

"Hey, Ella Mae," Luke's voice comes through my phone speaker.

Lainey repeats what I just told her to Luke. "What the heck?" Luke says, and I can hear the worry in his voice. "Was he paparazzi or something?"

"Maybe," I say, feeling uncomfortable. I've never encountered paparazzi out here in Tennessee. You'd think they'd stick to haunting Hollywood, but this man knew who I was and had an agenda.

"Where are you now?" Luke asks.

"On my way to a writing session."

"Did he follow you?"

I glance beside me and in my rearview mirror again. "I don't think so."

"This is scary," Lainey says. "I'm so glad you called."

"Have you told Connor?" Luke asks.

"You guys are the first to hear about this," I say. "I don't know if I should bother him."

"You need to tell him," Luke says firmly. "He's going to want to know. I think he has his own security team. Maybe they can help us figure out what to do next."

Connor and I have exchanged a few casual texts but haven't really spoken since last week when we kissed. As much as I wish I could spend more time in his company, I know he's busy getting ready for tour. I haven't wanted to be a distraction.

"I don't want to make you nervous," Luke says slowly, "but if this guy was able to find you at home, alone, there will be others."

"Call Connor," Lainey reiterates. "Then call us back."

I glance down at my maps app. I'm five minutes away from the house. "Okay. I'm almost at the session, and I'll be there for the whole afternoon. But I'll call him as soon as I'm done."

"Sounds good," Luke says.

"We love you, Ella Mae," Lainey says. "I'm going to check the security cameras at the house and see if they picked anything up."

I hang up the phone as I reach my destination.

I'm definitely not on my game during the writing session. All fluttery and uncharacteristically quiet.

It's not often that I feel genuine fear, but I'm feeling it now. The need I feel to talk to Connor and to get some reassurance grows exponentially as the morning fades into the afternoon.

I pull over on a random side street after the writing session, take a deep breath, and dial Connor's number.

I wish that I was calling him for a different reason. A light-hearted conversation where I could flirt and laugh with him. But I'm carrying a weight on my chest, and I know I have to share it with him.

"Well, well, well," he says as he answers the phone, the warmth of his voice immediately sending a wave of calm over me. "Look who decided to finally call me."

"Hey," I say, trying to keep my tone casual. "Do you have a minute?"

"Yeah," he says, sounding like he's in motion. "Just give me a second..."

I can hear some shuffling and movement, and then a door closing. "Sorry about that. I'm at Back Road, looking through tour merch, and had to find an empty room."

"Oh, nice," I say, my voice lacking enthusiasm. "That's fun."

"Are you alright?" he says.

I take a deep breath. "I need to talk to you about something."

"Okay," he says slowly.

"This morning," I say. "There was a man outside my house."

I then explain what happened. The photos the man took. How he called me by name. Connor listens, not interjecting or offering any verbal sign that he's listening.

"Luke told me to call you," I say. "He thought you should know."

He's still silent on the other end of the line. Quiet for a long, pregnant pause. I feel tears pooling at the edges of my eyes and fight to hold them back.

I do not want to cry on the phone with Connor Cane. Connor Cane is for teasing, and kissing, and feel-good time together. He's not mine to seek out for consolation, for understanding and comfort.

But it pains me just how badly I *want* him to be all that for me. The person I can turn to in times like this.

My safe place.

"You still there?" I say, my voice sounding timid.

I hear him exhale into the phone.

"Where are you?" His voice comes out strong, hot with anger. There's that same protectiveness in his tone that I heard when we ran into Mitch. Relief sweeps through me as I recognize it, as I identify his concern for me.

He cares.

"I just finished a session in East Nashville."

"Okay," he says. "You're close to Belfair. Can you meet me at my apartment? Paul can get there sooner and let you in."

"You sure?" I say. "I don't want to inconvenience anyone."

"It's not an inconvenience. I'm not letting you out of my sight for the rest of the night," he says gruffly. "You'll be safe with me."

Those words flood my body with emotion, with warmth. A burning ember that starts to flicker in my heart space.

You'll be safe with me.

"I'm texting you the address right now."

I swallow down the emotion knotting in my throat. "Thank you, Connor."

"I'll see you soon," he says. "Everything will be okay."

He hangs up the phone, and I sit back in my seat.

Everything will be okay.

I'm not typically a nosy person. I'm really not.

But when a security guard lets you into Connor Cane's apartment and then takes your keys to re-park your car, you start to feel real awkward waiting there in the entryway.

The place lives up to its name: Belfair Luxury Apartments. Emphasis on the word *luxury*. The apartment Luke had shown me a few weeks back wasn't nearly as nice as this one. I slip off my heeled boots, not wanting to accidentally scuff up the pristine floors as I move farther into Connor's place.

There are massive windows on the far wall of the main living area, but Connor's got all the white shades drawn. They're filtering the evening light as the sun sets outside, casting a diffused golden glow.

I scan the room, taking in a modular, expensive-looking white couch, empty black coffee table, and a modern lamp arched over one arm of the couch. As I move toward the kitchen, something catches my eye.

Birds. Colorful birds captured in a painting.

He's got it propped up on the countertop to the left of the stovetop, the only piece of color in the kitchen.

I smile.

I knew he said he was only here temporarily, but it literally looks like nobody's living here. This is telling. Connor must be here to eat and sleep and that's about it.

Something in my stomach twists as I think about Connor here...alone. Alone eating his meals. Alone in the quiet of the morning and the silence of the night.

I've never had to live alone before. I cross my arms over my chest and swallow as the realization hits me.

This is going to be my life soon.

What I have to look forward to when Lainey gets married and I'm in my own place.

Quiet.

Lifeless quiet.

I'm incredibly uncomfortable with it already.

This isn't what I want. I don't want a practically empty apartment. I want laughter. Music. Someone to talk to when I come home. Color. Warmth and light.

Maybe I'll get a dog so I have someone to keep me company.

I turn my head back toward the entryway, listening for any sounds of Paul's return, not wanting to be caught in the depths of Connor's apartment when he comes back. When I hear nothing, I wander down the hallway off the right side of the kitchen.

The first room on my right is dark, so I flick on a light switch. It's massive, essentially empty on one side, while the other side has been turned into a gym. Weight rack. Stationary bike. Treadmill.

I turn the light back off, shuffling in my socks to the final room at the end of the hall.

The door to Connor's bedroom is wide open. The shades are drawn on the windows in this room, too, but it's still bright. A shaft of light settles across Connor's wide bed.

It's simple, white on white on white, but at least the bedspread has some texture. He's got a guitar rack in the corner, a nightstand with a lamp, and a little catch-all dish filled with guitar picks.

My eyes travel toward the walk-in closet and stop as they land on two big hard-top suitcases, tags still wrapped around the handles from his last flight. My heart lurches in my chest.

Connor Cane. Country superstar. Celebrity.

Always going, going, going. Working too hard to ever truly be home. About to head out on the road again. I'm sure he'll get a break sometime, but if the record does as well as I think it will, he's going to be on tour for years.

I walk swiftly out of the room and back into the living area, settling down onto his couch and letting out a long exhale.

Something has been nagging at me for months now, ever since I realized that my best friend was getting married, and I'd be left to figure things out on my own. It's difficult for me to acknowledge, but being here is bringing my emotions to the surface.

I'm not entirely okay with moving out and being alone.

I can put on a front and act like writing songs and my career fills every single crack in my life, but it's a lie.

Because what I want, what I truly want, is a place to call home and a person to share it with.

And sitting here in Connor Cane's apartment is making me feel like he can't be that person for me. He's not here. He's *never* going to be here.

I don't want to be left behind, puttering around an apartment like this all by myself while he's out living his dreams on the road. And that knowledge hurts more than I thought it would, eclipsing the fear I've been carrying ever since my encounter with the paparazzi this afternoon.

I'd be lying if I said I hadn't been entertaining the idea of him. Of us. He's so much of what I want, what I need. But he's a moving target, one I'm not sure I could hit even if I tried.

I don't know how long it's going to be before Connor gets here, but I'm not about to sit here in this painful silence until he arrives.

So I do the one thing that always brings me peace. Settles my soul.

I pull out my guitar. And I write.

Chapter 24

Connor

I know she's here as soon as I open the door to my apartment.

The smell of her perfume hits me. Subtle and sweet. Her boots are placed neatly next to the welcome mat.

But it's her voice that makes my ribs constrict. It's filling the entire apartment, carried into the corners of the ceiling. I slowly follow the sound like it's a siren call.

She's sitting on my couch with her guitar on her lap and her notebook open on the cushion beside her. The contents of her bag are emptied out on my coffee table. She stops mid-phrase as I walk into the room, clutching her guitar and looking up at me with wide eyes.

I can't help but smile with relief.

She's here. She's safe.

A beautiful splash of color in my monochromatic apartment. Lush blonde hair held back by a knotted headband. Green eyes and rosy lips.

"Don't mind me," she says quietly. "Just making myself at home."

My heart surges at her words. There's nothing I would like more than for her to make herself right at home here. With me.

"Don't let me interrupt," I say, raising my hands up.

She closes her notebook and places it on the coffee table, setting her guitar aside. "It can wait."

I cross the room as she stands, no longer able to resist the urge I have to be near her. In three strides, I'm there, tugging her to me with both hands and pressing my cheek against her hair. She doesn't hug me back right away, but when she does, it's with a fierceness. She buries her face in my chest and wraps her arms around my waist, locking her hands together behind my back.

"I'm so sorry," I say into her hair.

She sighs, squeezing me in tighter. We stand there, holding each other and not speaking for a moment.

"Me, too."

What she's apologizing for, I'm not sure.

She starts to pull away, but I'm not ready to let her go yet. I cradle the back of her head in my hand, nuzzling my nose into her shoulder. She snickers.

"Connor Cane," she says into my ear. "You're such a hugger."

This time, when she pulls away, I reluctantly let her go. She looks up at me earnestly, her pink lips flattened into a firm line.

I take her hand and lead her back to the couch where we both sit, our legs touching. I don't care what Mallory advised me to do, there's no way I'm giving Ella Mae any sort of space tonight, unless she specifically asks me to.

"Thank you for helping me out," she says. I give her hand a squeeze, drawing our joined hands over until they're resting on my knee.

I scowl. "Believe me, there's a lot more I'd like to do. Starting with tracking down that guy who—" I break off with a shake of my head. "I'm so sorry, Ella Mae. This is all my fault."

She looks at me, frowning. "Don't say that."

"If I hadn't persuaded you to sing on the record..." I say. "If I hadn't invited you up to sing with me at the listening party, or agreed to be your date to the soiree, this wouldn't have happened."

"You can't blame yourself, Connor. I *wanted* to do those things."

"Yeah, but there are inevitable consequences when someone gets involved with me."

"Like what?"

"I know you're not on social media much, and you don't read the news, right?" I ask. When she nods, I continue speaking. "There has been some...backlash."

I look down at her hand in mine and run my thumb over her smooth skin.

"What kind of backlash?" she asks, frowning.

I sigh.

"I don't want to worry you with things like this," I say. "It's ridiculous, and I wish I could make it all disappear. But there's been a few articles written about us. About you."

"What did they say?" she asks.

"A bunch of crap," I say. "Lies."

Her frown deepens. "I see."

"This is stuff that I deal with every day," I say slowly. "Trolls. Hate. Constant speculation about who I'm dating, who I'm writing songs about, who I'm seen with." I give her a pointed look. "I'm good at tuning out the incessant chatter. But you..." I swallow. "You're so untarnished. It's because of me that people are saying these things about you. It's my fault you're becoming famous by association and not for the reasons you deserve to be."

Ella Mae stills beside me.

"And now paparazzi are camping out in front of your house, making you unsafe." I give a bitter laugh. "That's on me, too."

She stares out at the coffee table for a full minute, and I let my eyes wander over her face. The slope of her cheekbones. Delicate jawline. The arc of her bottom lip. What I wouldn't give to gently tug her lip between my teeth again like I did that night in the truck.

"I'm not fragile, you know," she finally says. "I may be optimistic about the world and the people in it, but I'm not naive."

She gives my hand a squeeze, finally meeting my eyes. "I appreciate all that you've done to try and protect me, but I don't need to be sheltered from reality, Connor. I need to know the truth. I always tell you the truth."

"I know that," I say. "But you deserve better than this, Ella Mae."

Her eyes cut to me sharply. "Better than what?"

My jaw clenches, my gaze fixing on a coffee stain on the table from this morning where I'd spilled. "All of this crap that comes along with being with someone like me."

She lets out a long breath from her nose. "That's all I've been thinking about, sitting here in your apartment."

I suddenly feel self-conscious, unsure of what she's going to say next.

"Do you have paparazzi following you around?" she asks.

"Sometimes," I say honestly. "But that's why I hired Paul. He never lets anybody get too close to me. I could help arrange security for you, too, if you wanted it."

She nods, her eyes downcast.

"Is there something else?"

She gives me a hesitant look. "Connor..."

"Say it, Ella Mae," I say. "I can take it."

She sighs. "You live here," she says softly. "But it's so...empty." Her eyes wander around the room. "You're so dedicated to your work that you're never here, are you? You're too busy to make it feel like home."

I feel a defensiveness rising in my chest.

"The past few months have helped me to realize that I want more than just a successful career like you. I'm ready to pursue more..."—she pauses—"personal ambitions."

"Like what?" I ask. "What do you want?"

"What I really want," she says delicately, "is to have a *home*."

Cold seeps into my limbs as I hear what she's saying and everything she's implying.

"My best friend is moving out soon. I have to find a place to live." She swallows. "Alone. Like..." She looks at me. Finishing her sentence is unnecessary.

"Like me?" I say.

She's silent.

"It's hard for me, you know," I say. "Living out of a suitcase. Being on the road. You think I enjoy it?"

"You do, Connor," she says matter-of-factly. "It's clearly what you want right now. That's what you're choosing every day. Your career is your top priority." She places her other hand on my knee. "And there's nothing wrong with that. I've done the same thing for years. But recently, my desires, my dreams...they're changing."

"But I understand you. I understand you completely. Your career is part of your calling in life. It fulfills your soul. Just like writing songs does for me."

It's as if I'm physically growing weaker the longer she speaks. Her honest words are undoing me, burning away all the walls

I've protectively crafted around myself to prevent having to face the reality of my life.

My lonely, solitary life.

I release her hand, standing up abruptly.

"When I asked you if I was your only friend," she says, "I kind of meant it. Who do you spend time with, Connor? When was the last time you saw your family?"

"Why are you bringing them into this?" I ask angrily. "This is about us."

She steels me with a look that feels like ice washing over every inch of me.

"Exactly." She stands up, moving toward me cautiously. "I don't want paparazzi waiting for me outside of my house. I don't want to constantly smile and perform for people like you do. I value my privacy. My relationships."

"And I don't?" I say hotly. It's like everything I've bottled up and shoved down over the past two years is surfacing, and I have to let it out.

"You think I knew what I was getting into when I signed my record deal? I was hungry. Eager to prove myself. I didn't know that there would be so many trade-offs."

I stalk closer to her until we're less than a foot apart, but she doesn't flinch.

"I can't go anywhere without people recognizing me," I say. "I've lost so much of my freedom, Ella Mae. I spend most of my days indoors. Or on a bus. Music is everything to me because it's all I have left now. Everything else I used to love has been taken from me. Until—"

Her expression shifts as I catch myself, and I see tears forming in the corners of her eyes. But I can't stop now. She's unknowingly opened the floodgates to the stress I've carried for years.

"I used to have other dreams. I still do," I say, my voice cracking. "But I can't have everything I want all at once. I know that now. If I don't take advantage of these opportunities I've worked so hard for, I will regret it for the rest of my life."

Her eyes dart between mine, and I watch a tear fall down her cheek. "I know." She quickly swipes it away.

"I didn't want this to happen," she says. "I wanted things to stay surface level between us. But then you had to go and win me over," she says, giving me a censuring look. "And now look what's happened, Connor Cane."

She reaches up, placing a soft palm on my cheek. Her thumb grazes over my jawline, and her eyes drop to my mouth.

"We're getting to the good stuff," she says quietly. "I think that means we have to make some decisions."

I lean into her touch, closing my eyes and bringing my hand up to cover hers.

"What do we do now?" she asks.

I shift her hand, gently pressing my lips to her palm and then her wrist. She takes a tiny step toward me, placing her other hand on my chest over my heart.

"I don't know," I sigh.

I lower my forehead to hers, and she responds by wrapping her hand around the base of my neck.

"I don't care what people have to say about me," she says. "I never will. But the paparazzi today...that scared me."

"Me, too." I slide my hand behind her neck. "I'm so sorry. I know what it feels like to have your privacy violated. Have you found a place to live yet?"

"I think so."

"I can help you move out. If you want security, I can get you security."

"And then what?" she breathes against my lips. It's taking every ounce of self-restraint to not just kiss her right now. "I'm supposed to live like...like you now?" her voice breaks. "I'm not sure if I want that."

I take a deep breath, feeling pained all over again at her honesty.

"What do you want?"

"I don't know."

"That's a lie." I drag my thumb across the smooth skin of her neck. "You seem to know exactly what you want. And if it's not me, just say the word, and all of this will stop. Things can go back to the way they were before."

She lifts her head from mine, capturing my gaze.

"No," she says stubbornly. "I don't want that either."

"You can't have everything, Ella Mae," I say. "You know how this works. You have to give some things up in order to get what you really want." My eyes flick between hers. "You need to figure out if I'm worth it."

She strokes my jaw with her thumb. "Are you?"

Her question is so direct, so honest, it catches me off guard.

Am I worth it?

"That's not for me to decide," I say. "It all depends on what you want."

Her eyes find mine and there's a flicker there, that tell-tale shimmer.

"I want you," she says breathlessly.

The last thread of my resolve snaps at her words, and I drop my head, catching her lips with mine. She pulls me to her, parting her lips and allowing me to deepen the kiss. There's an emotional undercurrent guiding our movements. A pure, deeply personal way for us to communicate our feelings without saying anything. My pulse spikes as she frames my face between her hands, pressing a slow, lingering kiss to my lips. She holds me tightly, like the clock is ticking and we both have full awareness that this moment is temporary when we so desperately want it to be infinite.

We breathe together, the space between our kisses lengthening as we regain our footing, and the world rights itself.

She drops her head to my chest, wrapping her arms around my torso. I hold her close, burying my lips in her hair.

I may not know how I'm going to convince her that I'm worth it, worth everything that comes along with my crazy life, but I want to. I want it more than I've ever wanted anything.

Chapter 25

Ella Mae

Kissing Connor Cane is nothing short of soulful. Whole-hearted. The man does nothing halfway. I'm attempting to sort myself out in the guest bathroom after our kiss in the kitchen. My headband is askew, my lips swollen and pink. My eyes are heavy from holding back tears. And so is my heart.

I called Lainey a few minutes ago, and she informed me that no suspicious cars had been parked out front when she returned home from work. Luke was there, waiting at the townhome for me to come home, and would be staying the night on our couch to give us some peace of mind.

To that, Connor had simply said, "Good."

After deeming myself presentable, I exit the bathroom and find Connor seated on his couch. The interior lights are off, and he's opened the shades, giving us a spectacular view of the city at sunset.

I take a seat next to him, and he turns toward me. His expression is drawn, eyes worried. But there's also a confidence in his gaze, an assurance that makes my belly swirl.

"Mallory told me that I should stay away from you," he says. "But I can't, Ella Mae. Especially now that I know you *want me*."

I give him a weak smile. "I do, Connor Cane. But if staying away is what's best for you right now, then I want to respect that."

"It's not what I want," he says earnestly. "I hope you know that."

"I do."

I take his hand in mine, gently tracing over his knuckles with my thumb. "Maybe we give ourselves some time to figure things out. You're leaving soon, and I can keep myself busy."

He scowls. "I hope that doesn't mean with other men."

"You know me," I say. "Can't keep the boys off my doorstep. There's practically a line down the street."

My words were supposed to land as a joke, but given the events of today, it falls a little flat. Connor rubs a hand over his mouth.

"Hmm."

"I know how much this record means to you," I say gently. "And this tour. This is your chance to share the songs you've poured your heart into."

He simply nods, staring back out the window.

"Ask me what *I* want," he says finally. He meets my gaze, brilliant blue eyes golden around the pupils in the fading light.

"What do you want, Connor Cane?"

He locks me down with his gaze. "I want you," he says, his voice quiet. "I want to stay here with you. To have a real home together."

My chest aches at his words. Everything I want to hear.

But there's more at play here, and we both know it.

"That's not true," I say firmly. "You need to focus on what's ahead. You have to go. It's who you are. The world needs you,

Connor. They need your songs. They need your shows. You can't give all of that up for me. It wouldn't be fair."

"I meant it when I said that I have other dreams," Connor says. "Other things I want to do, too."

"That may be true, but even in the pursuit of those dreams, you'll always be creating *something*. A creative person like you can't simply turn off your inspiration, Connor. You can't clock out," I say. "I get it because I'm the same way. I could never give up writing songs."

Connor and I are the same in this respect, ingrained with a deep need to create. And because we have this in common, I completely understand his heart—or at least the part of it that will forever come alive through acts of creation unique to him. He can't betray his own heart, alter his path or his destiny for me.

If he's what I really want, I just have to somehow learn to be okay with his path looking a little different than mine.

He gives me a long, intense look, setting my face aflame with the clear wanting in his eyes.

"You know me better than anyone, Ella Mae," he says. "How can that be possible when we haven't spent nearly enough time together?"

"You forget yourself, Connor Cane. I'm Queen Martha," I say, giving his hand a squeeze. "And you'll do well to remember it."

He pulls me to him then, wrapping me up and pressing me to his chest. I don't cry, can't cry. I breathe steadily, holding onto him with both hands, hoping I can convey my feelings properly in this critical moment without verbalizing anything at all.

I want to leave him with a bit of light from me. An ember he can plant in a little corner of his heart and carry with him while we're apart. I squeeze my eyes shut, steeling myself for the goodbye that neither of us want.

But it has to happen.

And I have faith that if things are meant to work out between us, somehow Connor Cane will come back to me.

As soon as Luke shuffles me in through the front door, Lainey pulls me into her arms with a sniffle.

"Oh, Ella Mae," she says. "I'm so sorry."

I sink into her and allow the tears I've been holding back to finally fall. When her shoulder is thoroughly soaked, we make our way to the living room. Luke's already got a makeshift bed set up and ready to go.

"Don't feel like you have to do this, Luke," I say, swiping at my cheeks. "That couch won't be nearly as comfortable as your bed at home."

He gives me a determined frown. "I'm staying."

"You're family to us," Lainey says, gently giving my arm a squeeze. "It's what we do."

"I love you guys," I say. And I mean it.

"We're here for you," Luke says, reaching for Lainey's hand. "Especially once he's gone."

I nod, uncharacteristically somber.

"What are you going to do when Connor leaves?" Lainey asks cautiously. "Did you guys talk about it?"

I take a deep breath, standing a bit taller and brushing the back of my hand across my nose. "We'll each do our own thing, I guess. What else are we supposed to do?"

Lainey gives me a shrug. "I don't know, leave your life behind to go on tour with him?"

I let out a laugh. "Don't be too disappointed, Lainey. I didn't get the invite."

"Would you have accepted it if you had?" Luke asks.

I sniff. "I don't think I would have." I gesture to the two of them and to the room around us. "I'm right where I need to be. And he is, too."

"You're both being very mature about this," Lainey says, taken aback. "I'd be following Luke to every city, sitting front row at every show, whether he liked it or not."

Luke snorts. "Cute."

"I would!" she insists.

Luke grins at his fiancée and then turns back to me, his face growing sober again. "We're going to get you moved out as soon as possible."

I nod in gratitude. "Thank you, Luke."

"Considering the circumstances," Lainey says, "we thought we could help you move out and take my stuff over to Luke's while we're at it. Then I could come stay with you at your new place until the wedding, if you'd be okay with that."

My heart lifts at her words. "Really?"

Luke nods. "That way we could get renters moved in here sooner, and I'd sleep better at night knowing both of you were safe."

"You guys are the best," I say. "Truly. What am I going to do without you?"

Lainey tilts her head. "What do you mean? We're not going anywhere."

I shrug. "Yeah, but...you'll be married. I'm being replaced as your roommate," I say with a laugh that borders on cynical.

Lainey gives me a loving smile. "Nobody could ever replace you, Ella Mae. You're my best friend, and I'll still need you, *especially* once I'm married."

Hearing those words brings warmth to my heart. I've been so worried about myself, my own circumstances and impending loneliness that I hadn't truly considered Lainey's feelings. She may be gaining a husband, but she'd still need her sisters.

She still needs me.

Luke nods in agreement. "As much as I enjoyed donning leggings and a tank top to match Lainey for yoga, that was a one-time thing."

"Bummer," Lainey mutters.

"You sure?" I say. "I heard you were quite the stunner."

"Never say never," Luke concedes.

"Are you hungry?" Lainey asks, pulling me into the kitchen. "We picked up some takeout for you."

"Thanks, Mom and Dad."

"We've got you," Lainey says with a kind smile.

We sit together at the kitchen counter as I eat, the weight in my chest easing as I tell them everything. The articles written about me and Mitch Allen's part in them. The speculation about Connor and me on social media. His manager's advice that we give each other some space.

Luke and Lainey are the perfect audience, jumping to my defense and listening intently at the appropriate times. I feel better, steadier than I have all day. We chat and even laugh about things together.

"Your life is like a movie." Lainey sighs. "It's all so romantic."

"Which part?" Luke quips. "The paparazzi or the internet trolls?"

She rolls her eyes. "You know what I mean. The forbidden love. The intimate connection they have through music. Their insane chemistry that's making every Connor Cane fan jealous."

"Marthas," I correct. "I call them Marthas."

When I recount my story and explain the origin of the term, Lainey tosses her head back with laughter.

"Oh, Ella Mae," she says. "You always handle things with such humor. You're going to be just fine."

Chapter 26

Connor

I may not be free to spend time with Ella Mae right now, but I can text her as often as I'd like to.

And I do. Every chance I get.

Thankfully, she doesn't allow our circumstances to impact our ever-flowing dialogue. Her sense of humor continues to reign supreme.

I find myself with a constant smile on my face, even though I'm not physically with her. She's my sunshine state of mind. The place I can go when things start to feel overwhelming or stressful. Ella Mae's light simply can't be dimmed.

Two days before I leave on tour, we shoot the music video for "Ghost of Me."

It's poetic justice, really.

The whole concept of the video is isolation, minimalism, stark contrast. Harsh lines. The dark side of my life.

Everything I've had to battle alone up until now. Somehow, this project feels like closure. An acknowledgement of what I've lost and had to give up. But also permission to look ahead to what I want my life to look like in the future.

I show up early, and Chloe's already set up to do my hair and makeup. Since no one else will be featured in the video, she doesn't have to rush to get me ready.

"I'm going to try this new product out," she warns me. "I tested it on Hunter this morning, and he loved it. I'm hoping it will work for you, too."

She's gentle and thorough as she styles my hair.

"How's married life?" I ask.

"Close your eyes for me," Chloe instructs, barraging me with hairspray. "Being married is the best. We have way too much fun together."

"Really?" I ask. "It's not as hard as everyone makes it out to be?"

"Of course we argue and disagree. Things can be challenging," she says. "Every married couple you talk to will say the same thing. But it's worth it to have somebody in your corner."

I nod, thinking of the only person I'd like to have in my corner. What it would be like to have her by my side at every turn. To not have to do anything alone. The thought brings a smile to my lips.

"Does that look alright?" she asks, holding up a mirror for me to look into.

"Looks great."

"You sure? I know how particular you are about your hair."

"Come on now," I say with a frown. "I am not."

She arches an eyebrow at me.

"Is there anything that's surprised you about marriage?" I ask.

Chloe steps back, playing with the front section of my hair with a tilt of her head. "Oh, so many things."

"Like what?" I cough as she spritzes me with more product. "If you don't mind me asking."

"I've been surprised at how much we still have to learn about each other," she says. "Even though we've known each other since we were fifteen, we never seem to run out of things to talk about."

"Dang," I say. "I didn't realize you'd been friends so long."

"Since high school," Chloe says, her cheeks growing pink. "He was my first real crush."

"You'd better be talking about me," Hunter says, clapping a hand on my shoulder before coming to stand next to his wife.

"Of course," Chloe says. "Who else would I be talking about?"

"I don't know," he says with an impish grin. "Charlie with the frosted tips?"

She snorts, picking up powder and a brush to dust over my skin before I step in front of the cameras. "I never liked him like that, Hunter."

"That's right, darlin'." He turns to me. "Don't worry," Hunter says reassuringly. "He's her chiropractor now. Strictly professional."

Chloe rolls her eyes.

"How's it coming? What did I miss?" Hunter asks.

"Connor and I were just discussing the wonders of married life," Chloe says.

Hunter raises his eyebrows in interest. "Were you now?"

"She was just telling me all of your secrets," I say.

Hunter leans in closer. "I'll let you in on my biggest secret. The key to marital bliss."

I snort.

"You can't let the sparks die just because you're married. Gotta keep 'em burning, you know what I mean?"

"I'm not sure I do."

"Like, for example..." Hunter says, clearing his throat. Chloe gives him a cutting look.

"What on earth are you about to divulge?" she asks, bringing her brush to my face.

"The other night," he says. "I got home before she did."

Chloe gasps, her cheeks turning crimson. "Hunter Ward! You *cannot* tell him about this!"

Hunter holds up his hands in innocence.

"I'm not listening," Chloe says with a shake of her head.

"All the lights in the house are off, and I leave a note on the table by the front door," Hunter says. "Next to a Nerf gun."

"I like where this is going," I say. "What did the note say?"

"*Don't you dare…*" Chloe breathes.

"It said," Hunter says ceremoniously, "*Wifey…*" —he pantomimes writing a note on his palm—"*I'm hiding somewhere in this house with a second Nerf gun. Naked.*"

I throw my head back and laugh, forcing Chloe to pause her makeup application.

"*Bring your weapon, and come find me—if you dare,*" Hunter says in a theatrical deep voice.

I laugh.

"Connor, I'd like to apologize for my husband's lack of filter," Chloe says. "He can't be stopped."

"You married a keeper," I say, my shoulders still shaking.

Hunter spreads his arms wide. "It's brilliant. She'll never divorce me now."

"Says the man who pelted me with Nerf darts in the dark." Chloe attempts to give him a censuring look, but I can see the laughter in her eyes. "That's enough, Hunter. Leave us alone, would you? Don't you have a shoot to set up for?"

"We're ready to roll," he says, clapping his hands together. "Just waiting on you, darlin'."

"I'm almost done," Chloe says, messing with my hair again.

"I was talking to Connor."

"Be right there, sweetheart," I say with a smile.

Hunter darts off with his PA, Jax, when he announces that the donuts he'd requested had arrived.

"Alright, good sir," Chloe says, taking a step back to look me over. "I think you're good to go."

I slide out of the chair and adjust my denim jacket I've got on over a plain white t-shirt. "Thank you, Chloe."

"Oh!" she says suddenly. "I almost forgot!" She grabs her purse and fishes around for a second. "Here." She hands me a white envelope. "For you."

I flip it over. My name is scrawled across the front.

"You shouldn't have," I say, sliding my finger under the seam.

"Oh, it's not from me," Chloe says with a small smile. She gives my arm a little squeeze before leaving me to it.

I flip open the floral card, my chest pinching as I read.

Do you like me? Check yes or yes.

There are two empty check boxes next to my identical options. The note is signed with a loopy, feminine signature, gorgeous enough to adorn vinyl covers and posters.

Ella Mae.

The dumbest smile breaks out across my face.

She remembered.

My first heartbreak. The girl I wrote my first song about who'd checked 'no' on the note I'd given her.

I find a pen, check both boxes, take a picture, and send it to Ella Mae.

Then I pocket the note to keep.

I take a seat in a chair at the center of the cavernous white room, and Hunter comes to talk me through the first shot.

I've opted to sing without my guitar in this video, which is completely out of my comfort zone.

"What do I do with my hands?" I ask, half serious.

"Whatever feels natural," Hunter says. "You ready?"

I nod, and he retreats to his chair behind the line of cameras and monitors set up in front of me.

As we start rolling and I sing along to "Ghost of Me," I channel my frustration. My dissatisfaction. All the things that weigh on me.

It's all surprisingly cathartic to get it all out. By the end of the day, I feel cleansed. Renewed. Ready to head out on the road and start this next chapter of my career and my life.

Chapter 27

Ella Mae

H^{*ear ye, hear ye.*}

Hear ye, hear ye.

If you're looking for Ella Mae Stewart, you'll most likely find her at Back Road Records, making herself at home in Studio B as often as she is able. Especially now that Connor Cane is on the road.

Call me a studio hog. I'll own it.

The Back Road label execs made good on their promise to get me into writing sessions with more of their artists, which has resulted in me spending lots of time in Connor's territory. It's impossible for me to be here in this room and not feel connected to him. The memories of our sessions here are sweet, laced with tension, magnetic chemistry, and our voices twining together in the spaces between us.

It's been three weeks since Connor left on tour, and I have thoroughly tried to live up to my status as Queen Martha by liking every single one of his Instagram posts. I've refrained from commenting so as to not draw undue attention to myself, but you'd better believe I'm filling his DMs with more fire emojis than what is deemed appropriate. His phone is positively stuffed with texts from me on the daily—memes, and astute observations, and five-minute-long voice memos detailing the happenings of my day.

I *live* for his replies.

He is sometimes slow to respond, which naturally I forgive, considering the schedule he has to keep on tour. But when he does, I'm transformed into my teenage, brace-faced, Hollister-low-rise-jeans-wearing self. Sprawled out on the couch, kicking my feet and giggling away. He's my real-life celebrity crush.

You know what really does it for me these days? When he *calls* me. A good ol' fashioned telephone conversation.

PHEW.

Hearing his voice on the phone makes the depths of my stomach ache with desire for him, for us. The wanting remains for hours after we say goodbye, and it takes everything in me not to book a flight to wherever he is so I can wrap my arms around his neck and show him just how much I miss him.

Lainey's not helping my attempts to give him the space I know we both need. She's constantly sending me flight deals or offering to drive me to whatever state he's in.

"Distance makes the heart grow fonder," I remind her.

To which she says, "Well, *distance* can stuff it. Chase the man down and kiss him, for crying out loud."

Connor hasn't invited me out to one of his shows yet. I know he's trying to be respectful, to give me space to figure out if I want to be the *someone* who would fly out to see his shows. Or if I'd rather date someone more stable. Someone less busy. Someone with a lived-in home and a steady nine-to-five job who would help me learn to be on time to things.

Blech. The more I think about it, the more I think I'd do it. I'd fly anywhere if it meant I'd get to be with Connor. And I hope he'd do the same for me.

The tour kicked off in Iowa, then he played his way through the Midwest before hitting New York and Connecticut. This week he started out in Mississippi and will be playing his second show in Louisiana tonight.

I've just wrapped a writing session with Harper Jackson at Back Road. After walking her back out to the lobby, I return to Studio B to gather up my things.

Drew has a different session pulled up, and a catchy song is flowing out through the speakers. I'd know that voice anywhere. I hear it in my head on repeat all day, every day.

"Oooh," I say, eagerly sliding in next to him at the mixing chair. "What have we here? Contraband Connor Cane content?"

Drew smiles. "He's been sending me stuff from the bus to mix. A new song every couple of days."

"Really?" I say, my heart dropping an inch in my chest. Connor had mentioned he'd been writing but didn't offer up anything for me to listen to. I suddenly feel miffed, wondering why he chose not to share any of these new ideas with me.

Then again, I've been writing like a madwoman the past few weeks, too. And I wouldn't send any of these new songs to Connor because...well...

They're pretty much all written about him.

Curiosity seizes me. I scoot my chair up to the mixing board. "Mind if I stay and listen in?"

"I mean, sure, if you want to," he says, pausing the song as he uses a plugin to add some sparkle to the acoustic guitar track. "Connor gave me a song to reference for the production."

"Which song?"

He clears his throat, adjusting the reverb on the guitar. "You remember Jesse McCartney?"

I bark out a laugh. "*Remember?* Remembering would imply that I had forgotten. I can assure you, dearest Drew, I have not forgotten my beloved Jesse."

"Beloved?" He gives me an amused look. "You're a fan." It's not a question.

"*Huge* fan."

"Interesting." Drew raises an eyebrow at the screen. "Coincidence?"

I smile with pleasure, flushed with satisfaction at this new piece of knowledge. A glimpse into the heart and mind of Connor Cane.

He's referencing Jesse McCartney for his songs?

"I think I can take full credit for this."

"I think you're right," Drew says. "Connor has been hit with an insane amount of inspiration. He hasn't written this many good songs in a long time." He gives me a sidelong glance.

"Hmmm," I say, unable to keep the smile off my face. "Can I hear it?"

Drew shifts in his chair. "I don't know if I should play it for you now that you know it's about—" he cuts off.

"Why?" I ask. "Is it going to break my heart?"

He laughs. "Uh...no." He pushes play on the track and continues to adjust and mix as we listen in.

I close my eyes, reveling in the early 2000s vibe of the production. Layers of shimmering acoustic guitars. Pop-inspired kick and clapback beat. Synth bassline. I'm swept back to burning CDs for my friends and making mixed albums to play in my car. Buying physical albums on release day at my local Target. Painting my nails with my cheap headphones on while the CD spins in my Walkman.

Oh, yeah. Connor has nailed this Jesse McCartney thing.

Then his voice comes in, and I hear the lyrics he's written.

A hot blush starts to spread from the top of my head all the way down to my toes. Suddenly, the room feels too small, too warm. My heart is pounding. I'm breakin' a sweat.

Connor Cane didn't just write me a Jesse McCartney-inspired bop. He had to go and make it *sexy*.

He delivers the verse in that low end of his voice, all smooth and sultry. It takes everything in me not to fan myself when the song reaches the chorus.

So many promises and implications of what he'd like to do with...to...me? I guess it's about me.

I'm undone.

The song ends, and I sit, speechless, staring at the session on the screen.

"Drew," I say, my voice almost a whisper. "I'm sorry. I didn't know."

"Well, I did," he says. "I just have to try not to think about you and him—"

"Stop!" I squeak out with a laugh. "Let's not talk about it."

"Clearly he doesn't want to talk about anything," he says with a snort. "He's just gonna use his hands and—"

"*Drew.*"

"Okay, okay," he relents. "It's good, though, right?"

"Good?" I say incredulously. "It's incredible." I swallow. "There are more like this?"

"Oh, yeah."

"Like, how many more?"

"A lot."

"And they're all about..." I shake my head. "No, they can't be. That's so presumptuous of me."

"Presume away. You're his muse," Drew says with a smile. "Honestly, I'm grateful. His well was running dry there for a minute. Now he's a flood of"—he waves a hand through the air—"this."

I sit there, aghast.

Me. The songwriter. The best friend's little sister. Connor Robin Cane's muse?

It's too much.

"Have you been out to see one of his shows yet?" Drew asks.

"Not yet," I say. "But I hope I can soon."

"He's playing here in Nashville on release day," he says. "May 28th."

I sigh. "I know. My best friend is also getting married that day."

Drew grimaces. "Ooh. Tough one."

"Don't remind me." I purse my lips together. "Do you think it's possible to be in two places at once?"

"Mentally? Absolutely," he says. "I'm sure you guys can figure something out," he says with a reassuring pat on the armrest of my chair.

"I should leave you to your work," I say. "Thanks for letting me hang for a bit."

"For sure."

As I exit Back Road Records, I feel like I'm carrying a sparkling little secret in my pocket.

Connor Cane is writing songs about *me*.

I walk into the new apartment I moved into a week ago and drop my keys on the entryway table—one of the only pieces of furniture I've purchased thus far. Lainey gave me the gray couch she had in the townhome, along with her barstools for the kitchen island. She and Luke have been slowly furnishing his loft in Franklin for months, so I was the benefactor of a few pieces of furniture she wasn't planning on taking with her.

Finding a place within my meager budget in such a short amount of time was no easy feat, but somehow Luke pulled it off. The owners were embarking on a year-long sabbatical abroad, so they were eager to get someone moved in before they left town. I fit the bill: single, good credit, no pets.

This place is a little dated and absolutely tiny, but it's in a very safe, family-friendly part of Franklin. And it's mine—and Lainey's, I guess, until the wedding next month. She has temporarily set up camp in the living room, and we're currently sharing one itty-bitty bathroom.

I'm grateful to have her here. I'm not looking forward to the day I'll come home to this empty apartment once she's wedded.

Despite the fact that I've been here for a week, all my recording gear is still in boxes. But thankfully, guitars are portable and take up very little space. Mine has been my second-best friend these past few weeks since Connor left, keeping me company when the sun refuses to shine or after we finally hang up the phone late at night.

I've never been more grateful for these songs, these heart-ramblings I'm able to get out onto paper. They're how I make sense of my feelings. How I process emotions and moments and cautiously held hopes. The way I capture the stories that make up the life of Ella Mae Stewart.

I can always count on my dearest baby Taylor to be there for me when I need her. She's always got my back.

I open the window over the kitchen sink, inviting the cool evening air inside as the setting sun begins to color the sky. After warming up some leftovers from the night before, I settle in at the kitchen island to eat, checking my phone for updates from Connor.

Connor: Baton Rouge meet-and-greet was wild tonight. A girl asked me to sign a part of her body that I had absolutely no desire to see, let alone sign.

Connor: You'll be happy to know I respectfully declined.

I snort, typing out my reply.

Ella Mae: You mean that's not included in the VIP package?

Ella Mae: I want a refund.

As soon as I send my reply, a series of texts from my brother come through.

Trent: Hey, are you still good to pick me up on May 26th?

Trent: My flight gets in at midnight.

Trent: Midnight, as in 12 a.m.

Trent: I'll remind you fifteen more times so you won't be late.

Trent: Probably should have lied and said 11.

I squinch my eyes shut, closing my mouth around my fork so it's dangling in the air.

Eesh.

Trent, along with the rest of my family, are coming into town for Lainey and Luke's wedding next month. I still haven't told him about Connor and me.

I squirm in my seat, setting my fork down so I can hold my phone with both hands.

Ella Mae: I'll be there. 3 a.m. on the dot.

Ella Mae: Do you still want to stay with me that weekend? You're far too big for the couch but we could commandeer an air mattress.

Ella Mae: And we'll have to share a bathroom.

Ella Mae: I'm really selling this, aren't I?

Ella Mae: Would love to have you, dearest.

Trent: Connor said I could stay at his place. He's got space.

I inhale through my teeth. Oh, dear. Not only will Trent be here in town, but he'll be staying at Connor's?

The plot thickens.

I know I've got to tell him the truth soon. Definitely before I see him in person. Can't have my confession ruining a perfectly good wedding and reunion with his best friend.

I set my phone down and finish my dinner. The longer I think about it, the clearer it becomes that I need to tell Trent as soon as possible to avoid any altercations. If I tell him now, he has a month to process and accept things before he gets here.

Maybe it will lower the risk of him punching Connor's lights out when he sees him, or trashing his house in an act of mountain-man rage.

I retreat to my bedroom, settling with my back on the headboard. I take a deep breath and call him before I can chicken out.

Chapter 28

Ella Mae

I'm secretly hoping Trent is occupied with work and won't answer immediately.

But after just a couple rings, he picks up.

"Hey," he says gruffly.

"Well, hello there, sunshine."

"Give me a second."

I hear a muffled conversation on the other side of the line followed by some shuffling.

"Sorry about that," he says. "Just helping some folks check in."

"You okay?" I joke, knowing how much my introverted brother loves human interaction.

He snorts. "Yeah."

"Don't most rental places have, like, a lockbox? Why are you helping people check-in?"

Trent sighs. "There was a lockbox, but I think a bear or a racoon got into it. The buttons are all mangled."

I gasp. "Wildwood is being ravaged by beasts? You need a reality TV show, Trent, starring you and your collection of flannels."

Trent snorts.

"Aside from avoiding rabies and key-eating wildlife, how are things up in the great wild wilderness?"

"Good," he says. "Busy."

"Surprise, surprise," I say, fiddling with the edge of the quilt on my bed. "Are you still trying to do everything yourself?"

"I wish I could," he says. "But I'm having a hard time keeping up."

"Why don't you hire some help?"

"I'm trying," he says. "Haven't found the right person yet."

"You need someone personable," I say. "Someone who can interact with your guests and deal with in-person issues so you can concentrate on what you do best."

"Which is...?"

"Being an axe-wielding hermit."

Trent laughs, and I feel slightly eased by the sound of it. His laughter is not freely given. It has to be earned.

"How have you been?"

I swallow, gearing up for *The Admission*. "Good," I say brightly. "You know me. Always plugging away."

"Write any new songs lately?"

Yes. Twenty-five of them. Did I mention that they're all about your best friend?

"Yeah, actually," I say, omitting any details. "I've been feeling pretty inspired."

I gather my courage and sit forward on my bed, crossing my legs. "So you're staying with Connor when you come?"

"Is that okay?" he asks. "Sounds like your new place is...cozy."

"That's a nice way to put it," I laugh. "I don't blame you for not wanting to bunk up with me. You'll be much more comfortable at his place. It's nice."

There's a pause on the other end of the line. "Have you seen it?" Trent asks.

This is it. My segway.

"I have, actually," I say slowly. "I also saw Connor quite a bit before he left on tour."

"Did you?" Trent says, his tone unreadable.

"Yes," I say, taking a deep breath. "Trent, I've been wanting to tell you for a while now but haven't had the guts to do it."

He stays silent.

"Trent, my dearest, most darling-est older brother," I plead. "Please don't kill him."

He lets out a grunt. "Ella Mae—"

"No," I say. "I'm serious. Trent, Connor and I are..." I bite my lip. "Well, I don't know exactly what we are. But we're something."

"Something?"

"Something good," I say finally. "He's good to me, Trent."

He's quiet for a minute. Then he lets out a long sigh.

I squeeze my eyes shut and brace for impact.

"I know," he finally says.

My senses sharpen at his words, and I frown in surprise. "What do you mean *you know*?"

"I know about you and Connor," he says. "He told me."

The nerves bouncing around in my stomach start to settle as I process his words. "What did he tell you?"

"Not a lot," he says. "But he did mention that you'd..." He clears his throat and grates out the next words like it pains him to do so. "Kissed."

"*What?*" I let out a surprised laugh. "And Connor Cane is still walking around *alive*?"

"I don't know why you both are so afraid of me," he grumbles, and I can hear a smile in his voice. "You give me no credit."

"He's your best friend, Trent," I say emphatically. "I'm your little sister. This whole thing isn't supposed to happen."

"Why?" he says. "You're an adult. He's a good dude. We wouldn't be friends if he wasn't."

I sit back against the headboard, my lips parting in shock. "I can't believe how well you're taking this."

"Come on, Ella Mae," he says. "I'm not a monster."

"Only when the moon is full."

Trent snorts.

"You're not worried about what could happen if things don't work out?" I ask. "Won't it be awkward?"

"For whom?" he asks. "I rarely see you guys as it is."

I close my eyes again, this time in relief. A smile stretches across my lips. "Trent, if I were there right now, I'd be giving you the biggest hug and never letting go."

"Good thing you're far, far away," he says.

I roll my eyes. "I can't tell you how relieved I am to know that you're on board."

"Why wouldn't I be?" he asks, like it's the most obvious thing in the world. "You're my sister. You deserve somebody who will appreciate you, and it sounds like he does."

My heart warms at his words. "I appreciate him, too."

"Is that what they're calling it nowadays?"

"Calling what?"

"Being smitten."

"I am *not* smitten," I insist, feeling a blush climb my neck.

"Well, you may not be, but he sure is," he says. "Go easy on him."

Of course my brother would be the one worried that *I'm* going to break Connor Cane's heart. Not the other way around.

Knowing that Connor has already talked to him and explained things, and that Trent was supportive of us, fills me with a deep sense of calm. I appreciate that Connor didn't interfere with my relationship with my brother. He allowed me to confide in him myself when I felt ready to do so.

Connor and I may still have obstacles to overcome, but this was a big one.

"Have you been alright since he left?" Trent says, his voice muffled like he doesn't want anyone to hear him. He'd be risking revealing the fact that underneath his gruff exterior, he's as cuddly as a teddy bear. One who cares about his little sister's feelings.

"Yeah," I say. "It's hard, for sure, but I've kept myself busy. And we talk pretty much every day."

"Glad to hear it," he says.

"I've been stressing about May 28th, though," I confess. "The wedding and his Nashville show are on the same day." I sigh. "How can we support everybody?" I ask myself mostly. "How do I prioritize?"

"Hmm…" Trent rumbles. "He's got a couple days off after that, so even if we can't make it to the show, I'm sure you'll be able to see each other."

He tells me that Connor's mom was trying to arrange a get-together with our two families, agreeing to keep me in the loop as plans are made. I can tell he's reaching his capacity for socialization as his answers to my questions grow shorter.

"Hey, I'll let you go," I say. "But thank you. You're a good one, Trent."

"No worries," he says. "I'll talk to you soon."

"Sounds good. Love you."

He mumbles out a, *"Love you, too,"* before hanging up.

I feel like dancing, waltzing around my room with an imaginary partner. I can't keep the smile off my face as I pull my guitar onto my lap and flip open to a blank page in my notebook.

These sweet feelings are bubbling over, easily spilling out through my fingers onto my guitar strings. A song flows out effortlessly. It's one of those that feels like pure inspiration. Like this song already exists in the stratosphere, and I'm just the vessel through which it flows into existence.

At the top of the page, I carefully write in bright-green gel pen: *For Connor Robin Cane.*

Chapter 29

Connor

It's her body, body, body language...

I recently added a handful of Jesse McCartney songs to my tour workout playlist. My excuse is that he's informing much of my writing style these days. Not to mention I can't resist imagining Ella Mae dancing around to his songs.

Especially this one.

I look around the tiny hotel gym warily, ensuring once again that my music is still playing in my headphones and not blasting out loud. I may be well on my way to becoming a Jesse fan, but nobody else needs to know that.

I have to stay disciplined with my daily workouts while on tour, or I find myself with far too much time to think and pent-up energy to burn. My trainer created some HIIT and weight-lifting circuits I can do anywhere, and I relish this time I get to myself. A chance to raise my heart rate and boost my mood before the madness of the day begins.

Every other tour before this one, I was the opening act. This is my first go-around as the headlining artist. I've leveled up my game in every way. Some nights, if the venues are close together, we're able to stay in a hotel. I never appreciate having access to a hot shower and a real bed as much as I do when I'm on the road.

Mallory strategically worked with my booking agent to book mid-sized venues and theaters across the country, many of which are in college towns. We've sold out a few shows, and the rest have been pretty packed.

"It's better to play smaller venues and sell them out than to play empty arenas," she'd said, and now that I've experienced it myself, I completely agree.

There's no way to possibly describe what it's like to play a sold-out show. The crowd makes or breaks the experience for us. The more stoked they are, the better we play. When the crowd is going buck wild, their palpable energy feeds us. It's a high that's hard to replicate. One that keeps you coming back night after night.

It's only once you're back on the bus, lying in your bunk, that you start to slip back into reality. The hum of the bus engine and laughter from your bandmates are the only sounds to keep you company. It's then you start to think about what life on tour can't give you.

Sure, it's an incredible experience—one I wouldn't trade for anything. But the difference now is that there are things that feel more important than hearing fans sing the lyrics I wrote back to me. Or having a number one song on country radio, or a viral video or streaming hit.

I'm missing someone to share it all with.

I finish up my workout, wrap a towel around my neck, and take a long drag from my water bottle. It's hot as Hades in Kentucky this morning, the humidity outside pressing and thick. The A/C unit in this little gym is on the fritz, leaving me with a good, slick sweat. I head back to my hotel room to shower before going to a local radio station for an interview and to play a few acoustic songs.

On show days like today, nearly every hour is booked out. Live acoustic sets and interviews at radio and local news stations, occasional visits to high schools or middle schools to surprise younger crowds. The days are long, but I'm okay with that, all things considered.

Since I'm simultaneously doing promo for my album on this tour, I've had to make most of the press and radio stops on my own. Sometimes I feel envious of my bandmates who get to sleep in or explore the city before they have to show up for soundcheck. The crew, on the other hand, get even less down-time than I do. I appreciate the amount of sleep and free time they sacrifice to make sure our show runs smoothly and try to express that as much as I can.

Soundcheck at each venue is pretty standard. Our monitor tech offstage ensures everyone's individual ear monitor mixes are adjusted to our liking. The house sound engineer perfects the mix from his booth at the back of the venue. We run through a few songs, switching things up each day to keep things fresh.

But soundcheck is not until 2 p.m. I've got a full day's worth of work ahead of me before then.

After showering and packing up my duffel bag, I exit the hotel lobby and hop into the black SUV my tour manager, Austin, brought on tour. He follows behind the bus as part of our caravan. His wife and our merch seller, Jenni, drives another van that carries all our merch, instruments, and gear. We've all clocked an insane number of miles, and we're only a little over halfway done with this leg of the tour.

"Morning," Austin says with a smile as I slide into the backseat. Jenni is sitting shotgun, making me feel like they're my parents chaperoning me on this tour.

"How nice was that hotel last night?" I say, accepting the coffee Jenni passes back to me. "Thank you."

"Amazing," Austin says, slapping the steering wheel. "I blacked out as soon as my head hit the pillow."

"You sleep okay?" Jenni asks. She's motherly, always checking in on me like I'm one of her own.

"Slept great."

"Did you do your vocal warmups already?" she asks. "The radio station is only ten minutes away."

"Not yet," I say, setting my coffee in the cup holder beside me. "Thanks for the warning."

I start doing my routine of annoying lip buzzes and tongue trills up and down the scale. Austin joins in with me as the notes get into my higher range, his voice cracking repeatedly.

"I'm gonna get it one of these days," he says with determination.

"You're almost there, man." I grin.

As we pull into the parking lot adjacent to the radio station, my phone starts buzzing in my pocket. I slide it out, and I bite back a smile as I read the name on the screen.

Stewie Two.

"Sorry," I say, opening the door before Austin has even put the SUV in park. "Gotta take this call."

Jenni gives me a knowing look. She's covered for me more times than I can count on this tour so I can sneak in conversations with Ella Mae. Everybody probably thinks I've got some serious digestive issues or family drama, but I don't care.

"Hey," I say, pressing my phone to my ear and walking around to the back of the SUV.

"Good mornin', sunshine." The sound of her voice is the sweetest indulgence. The perfect way to gear myself up for a busy day. "How are you?"

"Doing great and getting better," I say, reaching a hand out to pop the trunk. Austin waves me away, insisting on doing it himself. As he drags my guitar out, he points at me with his index finger. "You've got ten minutes," he says in a hoarse whisper. I give him a thumbs up.

"Aren't you chipper," Ella Mae says with a low chuckle.

"It's good to hear your voice," I say softly, checking over my shoulder that Austin and Jenni aren't nearby. "I've missed it."

"I've missed yours, too." The way she says it makes something tug inside my chest.

"Is that all you've missed?" I say in that same intimate way she speaks to me. Like we're not hundreds of miles apart, but face to face.

"I've also missed those impeccably natural blond locks of yours. I'm sure they're shimmering like gold in that Kentucky sunshine."

I snort. "Oh, they are. Absolutely radiant."

"Lustrous."

"Incandescent," I counter.

"Incandescent?" she says incredulously. "Is someone reading books in their spare time?"

What spare time?

"You know me," I laugh. "Closet bookworm."

"Ooh, I like that, Connor Cane," she says.

"Oh, you do?" I say, shoving my other hand in my pocket. "What else do you like?"

"I'm a simple girl," she says. "I love a hearty meal. A drive out in the country in a nice truck."

I groan. "You're killing me. Why'd you have to bring Frank into this?"

"I wasn't finished," she says. "I also love a good truck-bed rendezvous."

"Do you?" I grin. "What exactly does that entail?"

"Oh, you know," she says. "A little cuddling and snuggling."

"No kissing?" I say, pressing my tongue against the back of my teeth. "That's too bad."

"There might be some kissing involved, but only if my date behaves himself."

"Your date?"

"Yeah. If he wants to kiss me, he's gotta take me on a proper date."

"Guess I'd better make a dinner reservation for when I'm back in town then. And order a whole bushel of flowers."

She giggles, and the sound of it makes my face split into a stupid grin.

"Only if you want to kiss me again, Connor Cane."

I squint up into the morning blue sky. "There's nothing I want more."

"Good," she says, satisfied.

There's a beat of silence in which I know we're both thinking about kissing each other. She has no idea what this time away from her has done to my level of desire for her. My appreciation of everything she is and does.

We've always flirted effortlessly, but things have been dialed up since we've been apart. I love the playfulness and teasing. The anticipation of how things will feel once we're together again. But it always makes my blood run hot and my mind run to places it probably shouldn't go when we're so far apart.

"Two reasons why I called this morning," she says, all business.

"Hit me."

"Reason number one," she begins. "I talked to Trent last night."

I grimace, hoping their sibling conversation went something like ours had. "How did that go?"

"Surprisingly really well," she says, and I can hear the relief in her voice. "I didn't know that you'd already spoken to him about us."

"I had to," I say, relieved. "I didn't intend on telling him when I did, but it happened."

"Well, I'm glad you did." she says.

"Now we don't have to worry about getting murdered in our sleep."

She laughs. "What a relief."

I exhale a long breath. "It is, actually. One thing down."

"A million to go," she says.

"Have you reconsidered my offer?" I ask.

"About having a security guard?" Ella Mae asks. "I told you. Nobody is going to find me here, Connor. I'm practically living in the sticks."

I laugh. "I'm serious," I press. "Any sign of anyone following you or hanging out outside your house, and Paul can have a guy there within the hour."

"Thank you," she says softly. "That's really reassuring. But like I've told you before, I feel safe here. Things might change when you come back, but we can cross that bridge when we get to it."

We may not have a perfect idea of how things are going to work once we're reunited, but with each long-distance conversation, we're slowly talking through Ella Mae's concerns and getting a plan into place. "Okay," I say. "I'm looking forward to getting the grand tour of your apartment."

She snorts. "You'd better curb your excitement. Even Trent wasn't eager to bunk up with me. He told me he'll be staying at your place when you get back in town."

"Yeah," I say, rubbing a hand across the back of my neck. "Sorry for offering without talking to you first."

"I get it. It's but a humble dwelling. Not fit for massive men such as yourselves."

"That's not why I asked him to stay with me," I admit. "It was mostly an attempt to protect myself."

"What?" she laughs. "Is Trent taking Paul's place as your bodyguard?"

"No," I say with a low, awkward laugh. "I just don't trust myself to be alone at home once I'm reunited with a certain someone I'm missing a whole lot right now."

"Hmm," she says, and I can hear the pleasure in her voice. "You don't want to be alone with me?"

I exhale again. "Ella Mae, trust me when I say it's better if we have someone else around. If we didn't, I'd keep you all to myself until my next show. We wouldn't leave the house."

"Connor Cane spending time in his own home? Shocking," she teases. "Maybe if you hunkered down with me for a couple of days, it would finally look lived in. I'd be happy to help you muss up your pillows and leave a few dishes in your sink. Give the place some life."

I laugh. "Don't tempt me."

My phone buzzes in my ear with a text from Austin. The clock is winding down.

"What's the second reason you called?" I ask.

"Oh," she says, "I was at Back Road the other day for a writing session, and Drew played me a song he was working on."

I start walking toward the building as she talks.

"One of yours. He told me it was inspired by a certain musical artist you may have heard of," she says. "Jesse McCartney?"

"Oh, no." Heat floods my body. "He played you that one?"

"It took a little coercing, but he caved."

I should feel embarrassed. I really should. That song was the result of post-show hype and a whole lot of pent-up wanting for the girl I left behind in Tennessee.

"What did you think?"

"Honestly?" she says. "I'd say based on that little song of yours, you wouldn't mind being alone with me one bit."

"I think you're right," I laugh.

"But with Trent acting as our chaperone," she says, lowering her voice, "I doubt we'll be able to make good on any of those promises you made me in that song."

I groan. "I'm trying to be a gentleman, Ella Mae. Stop making it difficult."

"Difficult? Me?" she says incredulously. "Get me alone. See what happens. I promise I won't compromise your honor, Connor Cane."

"It's not my honor I'm worried about," I mutter. "It's yours."

We're both silent for a beat.

"I miss you," she says, and I can hear the smile in her voice.

"I miss you, too." I glance down at the time on my phone. "I've gotta get inside," I say reluctantly. "Got a radio station to play."

"Call or text me later when you have time," she says. "Go kill this set and enjoy every second of tonight's show for me."

"I will," I say. "I'll talk to you tonight."

"Sounds good, honey."

Honey, honey, honey. She's as Southern and sweet as it gets. Probably calls everybody honey. But it sticks to me like she means it.

It's show time.

The house music and lights go down in the venue. The crowd responds with a roar of anticipation. It sends a rush of chills down the back of my neck and spine. I grin at my bandmates, slapping their shoulders as they pass by.

They take the stage first, and while they're getting into position, I press my in-ear monitors into my ears. This blocks out the sound of the crowd, allowing me a moment to take a deep breath and wait for the band to start playing.

I stare down at my shoes, bringing my palms together at my nose. I commit to play my best and to enjoy this show, to keep my promise to Ella Mae. As much as I miss her, I can't waste this opportunity. It wouldn't be fair to either of us.

Fox's steady kick drum hits my ears first, followed by the rest of my bandmates as they join in the intro to the song. I wait sixteen bars. Hop up and down a few times to hype myself up. Our guitar tech hands me my guitar, and I sling it over my shoulder.

Then I walk out onto the stage, the bright-white lights hot on my face as I find my microphone.

The chords come to my left hand easily, my right hand strumming along to Fox's rhythm on the drums. I've played these songs hundreds of times and know them well enough that I can play them with my eyes closed. It's muscle memory.

I breathe in, then allow the opening line of the song to flow out on my exhale.

For me, singing is so much more than just using my voice. It's a chance to connect to the meaning of the lyrics. To try to convey an emotion, a feeling, or a moment to the listeners.

Even through my monitors, I can hear the audience screaming and singing along. Some crowds politely listen, while others scream at the top of their lungs. I can tell this is not a listening crowd.

I lose myself in the music, in the groove of the song. There's nothing quite like this feeling of playing onstage with a full band. You can feel the vibration of the bassline moving through your body, the deep pounding of the drums inside your chest. You physically embody the music while you play it. I live for this feeling.

We play through three songs until I take a moment to switch out my guitar and greet the crowd.

"How we doin' tonight, Lexington?" I say into the mic. I'm met with wild screams. "Mind if we play a few more songs for you?"

I look out at the crowd, unable to keep a grin from breaking out across my face. It's euphoric, playing songs I wrote live with some of the most talented musicians I've ever worked with.

But at the same time, I feel a twinge in my stomach. A pressure building in my chest.

Night after night, I get high off this feeling. And night after night, I look out at all the pretty girls in the crowd and somehow feel unsatisfied.

Chapter 30

Ella Mae

The weeks leading up to the wedding are a tornado of last-minute preparations. I accompany Lainey to her final dress fitting, meetings with her chef of a sister, Ava, and brother-in-law, Finn, who are heading up the catering, and walk-throughs at Old Cedar Farm, the venue.

In true Ella Mae form, I'm the last of the bridesmaids to find a dress. I think I nearly made Lainey regret her decision to let each of us choose our own dresses within her color scheme of ivory and various shades of green. But I'm glad she was patient, though, because the dress that found me is one of the most beautiful things I have ever put on my body. A flutter-sleeved sage-green sheer dress with a silky satin underlay. Understated, yet classy.

I've learned to live with Lainey's intensely organized personality, but that doesn't mean she's rubbing off on me at all. I nearly threw up when she showed me her spreadsheet with color-coded cells. The sharp edges of her scheduling down to the minute make my little free-spirited heart splinter.

"Put your phone down," I say to her one night in my apartment a week before the wedding. We're side by side on the couch, getting our dose of reality TV in together. "Just relax,

Lainey. There's nothing you could possibly get done right now. It's ten o'clock at night."

"I'm confirming details for tomorrow with Ava!" she says defensively.

I snatch her phone out of her hand and shove it under my leg. "That's *her* job, Lainey. Let your sister throw your bachelorette party without you meddling in her plans!"

She huffs out a breath, crossing her arms over her chest.

"We've all got your back," I say, throwing my arms around her. "Let us each play our part and do what we do best. All you need to worry about is getting ready to marry the man of your dreams."

She snorts. "I've been ready to marry Luke since he proposed last year. Take note, sister. When you find the right man, make sure your engagement is *very* short."

We laugh together, my arms around her shoulders, our heads pressed together affectionately.

"I can't wait," I say, feeling a little flutter in my stomach as I envision the magic and beauty Lainey's wedding day will hold for all of us.

"Me neither," she says, giving me a smile. "Have you spoken to Connor today?"

"Mhhm," I say, returning to my spot on the couch. "He's in Alabama tonight."

"When does he play in North Carolina?" she asks, sitting up suddenly.

"He's playing two shows, actually," I say. "Charlotte and Raleigh."

"Those are the shows we ought to be at."

"We?" I scoff. "Lainey soon-to-be Ward, need I remind you that you will soon be on your honeymoon?"

She looks genuinely disappointed at the realization. "Dang it."

I raise an eyebrow at her. "Says the woman who told me, not two minutes ago, that her engagement has been far too long."

She laughs. "You're right."

"Has he told you where he's taking you yet?"

She shakes her head. "It's killing me."

"I'm sure he's got something perfect planned," I say. "I can't wait to find out where you're going."

"You're sneaky." She narrows her eyes at me. "Changing the subject on me."

I give her an innocent look.

"Are you excited to see Connor?" she asks. "Only one more week."

My heart feels like someone is squeezing it inside my chest. We've been apart for almost two whole months, and though we talk every day, everything has been building up to our reunion next week. It's hard to progress in a relationship from a distance. We need longer and deeper conversations. Time together.

If things go as well as I hope they will when we see each other next week, then I'd love to be at the show in my hometown, invite my parents to come along.

"Honestly," I say with a sigh. "I've been counting down since the day he left on tour."

"We both have such wonderful things to look forward to," Lainey sighs. "How romantic."

"Happy Album Release Day!" I say to Connor at midnight on May 28th. We've been on the phone, awaiting the moment his album officially goes live online. I've got him on speaker and can hear the cheers and hollers of his bandmates on the bus in the background. It's going to be a full day of celebrating, and clearly, they're getting an early start.

I'm alone in my apartment, packing up my things in advance at Lainey's behest so I'll be ready to head to the wedding venue first thing. She's spent the past few nights in her sister, Ava's, guest room. I assured her that I'd be safe and that she needed a good night's sleep in a real bed before her wedding.

"Thank you," Connor laughs. "Can't believe it's finally here."

"You should be so proud," I say. "I'd give you a raving review, but I"—I give a pointed *ahem*—"haven't heard the record yet."

"I sent you a few songs," Connor protests. "You've heard more of it than anyone else has."

"I want to listen to the whole thing," I say. "Start to finish. The old-fashioned way."

"I think I can remedy that," he says. "Go check outside your door."

I whirl around, looking at my open bedroom door. "What?"

"Check outside," he repeats. "There should be something waiting for you."

I hop up, carrying my phone with me as I make my way to the apartment entrance. My apartment is upstairs, and I've got my own little deck off the front door.

"Connor Crow," I chide. "What did you do?" I unlock my front door.

"I wanted you to be able to hear the record tonight. I pulled a few strings and had something dropped off at your place earlier."

I glance down, and there it is, right in the middle of the welcome mat. A square wrapped in brown paper with a twine bow. There's a card and a single white rose tucked beneath the string.

I gasp. "Connor! What is this?"

"Open it," he instructs. "But save the note for later."

I take my package inside and obediently set aside the envelope. I peel off the ribbon and the paper, and there he is. Connor Cane: The Album in its sepia-toned glory.

"A vinyl?" I say, swallowing the emotion gathering in my throat.

"Now you can listen to it properly," he says. "I hope you like it."

I flip it over and see that he's got our duet—track five—double-underlined in Sharpie. He's signed his name to the right of the track and even added a tiny—albeit masculine—heart.

The thoughtfulness of his gesture presses into me, and I find myself on the verge of tears.

"Thank you," I say. "This is incredibly sweet."

"You're welcome, Stewie Two," he says affectionately. "Are you ready for tomorrow? Or...today, I guess."

"I think so." I sniffle.

"Which song did you decide to sing?" he asks.

I smile. "'Always You.' It's Lainey's request."

"Man," Connor sighs. "I wish I could be there to hear you."

"Tell you what," I say, swiping at my wet cheeks with my sleeve. "I'll give you your own private concert next time I see you."

"I like the sound of that."

We talk for a few more minutes before Connor is wrangled into celebrating with his band and crew. After I hang up the phone, I gently place the vinyl on my turntable. I flip the switch, raise and lower the needle, and listen to the Connor Cane album from start to finish. I close my eyes, resting my chin on my fist, imagining Connor singing these songs to me, and only me. They're brilliant. Poignant lyrics. Catchy hooks. Gorgeous production.

When I reach track five, I press my fist to my lips, feeling my face warm at my own voice crackling on the record. If I close my eyes, I can pretend he's really here. It's almost as good as the real thing.

Almost.

Dear Ella Mae,

Thank you for writing the song that saved this record. To me, it will always be our song. This album is my best work, and I have you to thank for making it complete.

Can't wait to see you soon.

Always,

Connor

P.S. Still waiting for my hunting song. Get to work.

Chapter 31

Ella Mae

"I'm not going to lie," Chloe says with a pleased smile. "I'm so proud of how this look turned out on you."

We've spent the morning together in the bridal suite at Old Cedar Farms, taking turns in Chloe's makeup chair set up near the window so she can work in natural light.

"Here," she says, handing me a mirror. I gasp as I take in my reflection. She has styled my hair in glam waves, with one side slicked back behind my ear and held by a pearly vintage clip. A thick-winged liner accentuates the edges of my eyes, making me look like I've stepped straight out of an old Hollywood film.

"Chloe!" I say. "You've outdone yourself."

She smiles. "You look absolutely gorgeous."

"Everyone does, thanks to you," I say. "Now please, sit down. You need a break." I vacate my seat and allow her to take my place.

"Thank you," she says as she sits, taking a sip of her sweet tea. "Feels good to get off my feet for a minute."

I frown. She's looking a little pale, not quite herself. "Are you feeling alright?" I ask quietly.

She looks up at me and sighs, letting her exhaustion show in a private glance. "I know this is Lainey's day, and I don't want to steal anyone's thunder..."

"Steal away," I encourage.

She gives me a pleading look. "Please don't tell anyone."

I put a hand on her arm. "What is it?"

"I'm so tired," she says with a dry laugh. "The room is spinning. I could throw up without warning at any second because I'm..." She gives me a frantic grimace, pulling me toward her so she can whisper in my ear, "*I'm pregnant.*"

I gasp.

"Chloe!" I whisper back. She shushes me, glancing around to ensure nobody can overhear our conversation. "Are you serious?"

She nods, giving my hand a squeeze. "Somebody needs to know in case I get sick during the ceremony or something. Will you cover for me?"

"Of course," I say, in awe of the miraculous news she's shared with me. "Do any of the other girls know?"

Chloe shakes her head. "I'd like to keep it that way, if you don't mind."

"My lips are sealed," I say, doing a little happy dance with her hand still in mine. "I couldn't be happier for you."

Chloe smiles weakly. "Thank you, Ella Mae."

The room is sparkling with light and happy energy, and not just because the sun is streaming in brilliantly through the windows. Chloe is having a baby. It's Lainey and Luke's wedding day. I can't help but feel like my heart is going to burst with happiness for my friends. There's a peaceful sense of rightness to things today. Knowing that we get to be a part of this mile marker in Luke and Lainey's love story.

It's a new beginning, in many ways. But also a continuation of their journey that began when they unexpectedly met in her driveway a year ago.

Lainey is radiant, her skin luminous and glowing. Her long red hair is swept back into an intricate braid, dressed with tiny glittering pins that look like luminescent flowers in the sunlight. She's seated on the couch next to her mom and sister, still dressed in a silk robe. I can't seem to take my eyes off her. You can feel her contentment, a sense of steady assurance that she's making the right decision in marrying Luke Ward.

She's never looked more beautiful.

A knock sounds on the door, and in comes Luke's mother, Maggie.

"Oh!" she gasps when she sees Lainey, moving toward her with her arms extended. Lainey rises off the couch and embraces her soon-to-be mother-in-law. "My goodness," Maggie says, and I can hear her sniffle into Lainey's shoulder. "You are absolutely stunning, my dear."

"Thank you," Lainey says, her voice breaking.

Maggie seems to be at a loss for words, simply pressing Lainey's hands tightly with her own and looking her over for a moment. It's an emotional thing to witness, and I find myself growing misty, too.

"Glad it's not just me," Chloe says, and I see her swiping a tear away.

"Chloe Ward!" I say in surprise. She's a sweetheart, but tough as nails and definitely not a crier. I grab her a tissue from the box near her makeup kit.

"I'd blame it on the hormones," she laughs, "but this just takes me back to my own wedding day," she says with a soft smile. And I see it there, too, in the smile lines around her eyes.

The way she holds her chin with confidence. The set of her shoulders. That same pure happiness that Lainey is radiating today.

It's a good look for all of them.

I can't help but wonder how marriage would look on me.

For the first time in my life, I can see myself in their shoes. It would require a bit of growing up for little ol' Ella Mae Stewart, but if there's one thing I know about myself, it's that if I want something, I will work as hard and as long as I need to, to get it.

I'm learning that I can hold two things to be true at once. That I can be myself, independent and whole, embodying my femininity and unique personality with confidence. But at the same time, I can also be vulnerable enough to tie my destiny to someone else's. To acknowledge that, together, we could become more than we would alone.

My friends weren't trying to "fix" something in themselves by getting married. It's just the opposite. They are becoming their true, most naturally radiant selves by choosing to be vulnerable enough to love someone else forever.

It may be too soon to say, and I might be jumping the proverbial gun, as it were, but there's only one man I can imagine growing through life with. He comes with some inconvenient circumstances, things that I wasn't sure I'd be willing to take on, but our time apart has made it clear to me that choosing to love someone always requires sacrifice.

And getting to love and be loved by Connor Cane might just be worth sacrificing a few things, if it means I get to have my own version of *this*.

I sniffle a tear away, and Chloe hands me a tissue. "Thank you," I say.

"Suck it up, Ella Mae," she teases. "That eyeliner won't survive the day if you start crying now."

Lainey notices me watching her and motions for me to come closer.

"Oh, Ella Mae," she says approvingly. "You are stunning."

"So are you," I say as we embrace.

Ava suddenly stands, holding up her phone to show us the time. "Lainey! We've got to get you into your dress."

"Oh!" Lainey exclaims, fanning her eyes to keep the tears at bay. "Okay, okay, okay. Everybody relax."

We laugh together, helping her change into her gown. Sisters and friends. Mothers and mother figures. Connected by the threads of love.

It's impossible to attend a wedding without thinking about your own.

From my position in the wedding party, I can see my mom, stepdad, and Trent in the second row. Lainey hasn't even walked down the aisle yet, and my mom is already crying. Mark looks over at her with the most tender expression in his eyes and gives her a kiss on her temple. I'm certain they're remembering their own wedding day, and the memory sweeps over me in turn.

I can still remember that swelling happiness I'd felt as a nine-year-old girl as I watched my mom take her vows. Knowing she wouldn't have to do life alone anymore brought a sense of sweet relief to our whole family. Mark is a good man. My true father by all accounts.

When I'd sent my parents "Always You," they'd sent me a video in response. Both had gotten misty and had deemed it to forever be *their song*.

I catch Trent's eye, and he gives me a half-smile. He looks handsome in his gray suit, and I told him as much when he walked into the venue before the ceremony had started.

"I love this look on you," I said, straightening his tie. "You're a master class in rugged charm."

He swatted my hand away and grumbled something about being too hot in the suit. I geared up to tease him further but thought better of it when he rebelliously loosened his tie at his neck. A handful of girls nearby eyed him appreciatively, thinking they were about to witness my mountain of a brother undress himself right then and there. But being the good sister that I am, I put an end to their fantasies and promptly yanked that tie back up tight. He glared down at me wordlessly.

"It's one night," I reassured him. "You can do it, big guy."

More grunting and grumbling ensued, but thankfully, he complied.

I turn around and find Chloe in the bridesmaid lineup to make sure she's okay. She gives me a little nod and a smile, looking steady on her feet despite the nausea she's fighting.

Ava lets out a gasp from her position in front of me, pulling me from my thoughts. "It's time!"

I lean around Ava, and Luke comes into view. He's got his hands clasped in front of his body, eyes fixed at the back of the venue where Lainey will soon be walking toward him. His twin brother, Hunter, clasps him on the shoulder as the instrumental music starts playing, signaling Lainey's entrance.

The wedding guests stand collectively, all eyes turning to the back of the room. My throat grows thick as I see my best friend come around the corner on the arm of her father.

She's a fairy, lithe and ethereal in her white gown, her long red braid flowing down her back. We all get to witness the moment she and Luke make eye contact. The smile they share brings a burning warmth to my heart.

Luke comes off as a stoic, no-nonsense kind of guy, but I'm unsurprised to see his chin wobble as he presses his lips together. How could he hold it together when the woman he loves is looking at him like that?

Lainey makes her way toward us down the aisle. Once they reach the end, her dad gives her a gentle kiss on her cheek before handing her off to Luke.

My eyes once again find Mark and my mom amongst the guests. The tightness in my chest eases as I realize that when it's my turn to walk down the aisle, I can have my stepdad by my side.

The pastor begins the ceremony, and I get to witness Luke and Lainey make promises of love and fidelity to each other. Their words are both beautiful and rich, soul-satisfying and humorous. When they are pronounced man and wife, Luke wastes no time pulling his bride in for a deeply touching kiss.

I feel it again. That swelling happiness. It leaks out into my smile, into my hands as I clap and cheer for the newlyweds. Golden and sweet.

Chapter 32

Ella Mae

Dinner is served. Toasts and speeches are given. Then, once the bride and groom have eaten their fill, I make my way to the corner of the dance floor where the mic stands are set up and ready. My guitar is waiting for me, resting patiently on a stand. I quickly sling it over my shoulder and tune the strings, feeling my heart thumping in my chest.

Connor's advice sounds in my ears. I have to pretend I'm singing to just one person—or in this case, two people. I need to remember why I'm doing this. It's the only way I'm going to make it through this song without choking up or bursting into tears.

I love Luke and Lainey. This is for them. No one will even be looking at me. I'm honored that I get to be the one to provide the music for their first dance. This is a once-in-a-lifetime opportunity, and I intend to enjoy it.

"You ready?" Lainey's dad, Andy, who's been acting as emcee, asks me.

"Yes, sir," I say with a smile, trying not to let the horde of butterflies swirling around in my stomach show in my face.

"Thank you again for doing this," he says, giving me a pat on my shoulder. "It means so much to have you sing tonight."

"Well, you and I both know I'm a starving artist," I say. "There's not much else I could do for them."

Andy booms out a laugh and gives me another pat on my back before turning his microphone over to power it on.

But before he can speak, a flurry of squeals and screeches erupts from the back of the room. I lift my chin to see what the commotion is about. Maybe someone dropped a glass, or perhaps one of Lainey's inebriated relatives started a food fight. Wouldn't that be a riot?

I glance over at Lainey from her seat at the head table so I can be ready to start playing as soon as they make their way to the dance floor, and she fixes me with a look that says, *I told you so.*

What is she being so smug about? I glance back toward the commotion, and my eyes catch movement at the back of the room. Someone is walking toward the dance floor, weaving between tables and eliciting gasps from each party he passes.

I feel my heart in my throat as he draws nearer. His electric-blue eyes meet mine from across the room, and I nearly lose my grip on my guitar.

Connor Cane.

He's stalking toward me like I summoned him from the crowd. His gaze is locked on mine, and my grip slips on my guitar.

He gives me a blinding smile as he nears, his strides even and confident.

"Hey," he says as he reaches my corner of the dance floor. He towers over me, reaching out to grab my mic stand.

I'd envisioned our reunion hundreds of times, and in every scenario I'd imagined, we were alone. Not front and center at a wedding, being watched by a room filled with family, friends, and strangers. I don't know what to do with myself. My throat is dry, devoid of words as I watch him quickly adjust the mic stand and raise it up slightly.

"Connor," I manage to eke out, hungrily taking him in. He's somehow grown even more handsome in our time apart. His hair is a bit shorter, his face clean-shaven. He looks immaculate in his suit and black skinny tie. "What in the world are you doing here?"

He turns to me, and every part of my body hums in response to the look in his eyes. He wraps an arm around my shoulders, angling me away from the microphone. I blink, savoring the warmth of his palm against my skin.

His lips find my ear. "I couldn't let you sing our song alone."

"You don't have time for this," I say, still feeling like I'm in shock. "It's your album release day! You shouldn't be here right now."

"Yes, I should," he says firmly, giving my arm a little squeeze before he lets go. "But I've only got a few minutes. I've gotta get back to the venue to play the show."

"This your day," I say before swallowing. "Your night."

"I know that. But it's yours, too," he says earnestly. "I needed to be here for you."

I feel tears pricking at the edges of my eyes and blink them away, not wanting to cry before having to sing.

"Hey." His eyes roam over my face. "We've got this."

I nod, still gripping my guitar like it's going to run away from me.

"There's only one mic," I whisper as we turn back toward the dance floor.

Connor's smile widens. "Guess we'll have to share."

Happiness floods through me. He's here. He made the effort to be here for me when I needed him, without me having to ask. I can't possibly articulate what that means to me.

The room has gone quiet now, every eye fixed on us. So much for fading into the background. How am I supposed to do that now with Connor Robin Cane commanding the room next to me?

Connor nods to Lainey's dad, who lifts his microphone.

"It will now be my pleasure to invite Luke and Lainey to the dance floor to share their first dance as husband and wife."

I glance up at Connor and gesture to my guitar. "You sure you don't wanna play?"

He shakes his head. "I'm just here to support you, Ella Mae."

His words nearly make me shed tears again. On the most important day of his career, he's choosing to make time for me. To put this personal performance of mine first before all the other things he could be doing right now. The knowledge fills me with a sweeping warmth that sets me ablaze from my head down to my toes.

This has to be what love feels like.

I love him. I love Connor Cane for doing this for me. And I'm going to pour that love into every word of this song, let it drip off every note so that he knows it.

We watch as Luke takes Lainey's hand and slowly leads her to the center of the dance floor. I take a steadying breath and start to pick the intro of the song out on my guitar.

Luke pulls Lainey to him, and they become lost in each other as they sway back and forth in time to the music I'm creating. Connor leans forward, clasping his hands in front of his body as he begins to sing.

We've sung together several times now, but never have I been this close to him while doing so. I can see the curl of his eyelashes, the movement of his lips as he shapes each word of the song against the microphone. My heart is tripping as the smooth sound of his voice fills the room, but by some miracle, I'm able to keep my fingers steady on my guitar.

Connor looks over at me every so often as he sings the first verse, and I can feel his intention in his phrasing, the gentle way he's delivering the lines to match my delicate playing.

"Like the morning sun on the rise
I didn't see you
'Til the soft light opened my eyes
Warming me right through

I remember when you noticed me
For a moment then I couldn't breathe"

He shifts to the left, making room for me to lean in and join him at the microphone for the chorus. Our cheeks are nearly brushing together, and the awareness of our proximity burns through me.

"I knew then and I know now
You were all I wanted
Couldn't say it out loud
Didn't wanna lose this
Gold light, your eyes
Summertime feeling
There is nothing more true
It was always you"

Our eyes meet on the last line, and I feel a tingling warmth spread across the surface of my heart. Like the moment you step from the shade into the sunlight.

I know he feels it, too, because he gives me the most brilliant smile as he steps away from the mic so I can take the second verse. I watch Luke and Lainey dance together as I sing, feeling a smile of gratitude rise on my lips. I can't believe I get to be a part of such a beautiful moment.

"I could see you ten years from now
Holding my hand tight
As we walked down this same winding road
Under the streetlights

I remember when you looked at me
For a moment then I couldn't breathe"

Without rehearsing things at all, Connor and I somehow instinctively know when to raise our volume and when to exercise restraint. Our vocal dynamics are entirely in sync as we harmonize through the second chorus together. We're the same note, different octaves.

"When we're standing face to face
Everything falls into place"

I increase the force of my fingers on the guitar strings as our voices rise together on the bridge. On the last line, our eyes meet again, and I follow his lead, dropping the guitar out and holding out the last word with him until his voice fades out.

He takes a breath and sings the down chorus with a tenderness in his voice. I swear I hear sniffles arising from various places around the room. I'm not the only one affected by his performance.

"I knew then and I know now
You were all I wanted
Couldn't say it out loud
Didn't wanna lose this"

I join back in for the rest of the chorus, our eyes locked on each other. It's like there's nobody else here. Only us and this song.

"Gold light, your eyes
Summertime feeling
There is nothing more true
It was always you
It was always you"

We both lean away from the mic on the last word of the song, letting our voices echo and hang in the air until they fade out. We watch as Luke ducks his head, pulling Lainey to him for a kiss. She frames his face with her hands, laughing with her forehead pressed against his as they break apart, and I can't help but laugh along. Her bliss is palpable and precious. Applause breaks out, and Connor and I join in, my eyes cutting to his.

He leans down, gently pulling my hair back behind my shoulder before brushing a soft kiss across my cheek. That simple act of affection turns me completely inside out. I've missed him more than he knows, and my body is a sparking live wire at his long-anticipated touch.

I turn my face toward his, and the tips of our noses brush. The moment is so charged, so electric, that I nearly grab him by the lapels and bring his lips to mine.

But Connor is conscious of the eyes on us. I can see in the rise and fall of his chest that he would love nothing more than to kiss me right now, too, it's not our moment.

Lainey and Luke walk hand in hand to where we're standing, followed by her Dad.

"Thank you," Luke says as he reaches us, his smile and eyes bright. "That was incredible."

"It's an honor to be a part of your special day," Connor says, extending a hand to shake Luke's.

"We'll never forget it," Lainey says, pulling me toward her for a hug. She presses a watery kiss to my cheek. "I'm so proud of you, Ella Mae."

The tears start to flow at her kind words. I'm barely able to find my voice, overcome with emotion. "Thank you," I whisper as she pulls away.

"Are you able to stay?" Luke asks Connor. "There's still plenty of food left, and we're going to open up the dance floor soon."

"I wish I could," he says with a gracious smile.

"It's album release day for this guy," I say, pressing a hand to Connor's abdomen in a familiar gesture that feels nothing but right. "He's got a big show to play tonight."

"We're honored to have you here," Lainey says, swiping tears from underneath her eyes. "It means the world to us."

"There's nowhere else I'd rather be," Connor says, his eyes fixed on me.

"Congrats on the album," Luke says.

"I wish we could be there to support you," Lainey says. "Next time we get married, we'll time things better."

Connor laughs. "Thank you. Congratulations to you both."

Lainey turns to her dad. "You ready for our dance, Daddy?"

"I guess so. I've only been practicing for a whole month," Andy says, straightening his suit jacket.

As Andy and Lainey make their way back to the dance floor, I slip my guitar off and place it back on its stand.

"I don't want to leave," Connor says in a low voice, taking my hand in his. "But I'd better go. The opening act is already on."

His hand swallows mine, and I feel the rough calluses on his fingertips brush over my knuckles. I squeeze back with all the strength I can muster. "Let me walk you out."

We make our way around the perimeter to the back of the room. Despite the slow sustain of whispers that follow us from the wedding guests, I'm grateful nobody blocks our way. We make it to where Trent is waiting with a man I don't recognize just outside the door.

Connor goes in for a man hug, which Trent reluctantly allows.

"Good to see you, Stewie," he says.

"You, too." Even stoic Trent can't keep himself from smiling as he reunites with his best friend. "You guys sounded great."

"Thanks," Connor says. "Always a pleasure to sing with Ella Mae Stewart."

"We need you on tour with us," the bearded man says with a smile.

"What was your name?" I ask.

"Austin," he says, shaking my hand. "I'm Connor's tour manager."

"Ahh," I say. "Glorified babysitter."

"Exactly," Austin laughs. "I hate to take him away from you again, but we've gotta get going."

"Thank you for allowing him to sing with me," I say, swallowing the emotion in my throat as I meet Connor's intent gaze. "I know today has been a circus, but it means everything that you came tonight."

"Wouldn't miss it," Connor says, giving me a half-smile. He turns to Trent. "Did you guys get things taken care of?"

Trent nods, not bothering to fill me in. I assume it's got something to do with Trent staying at his house, so I don't ask any questions.

"Okay," Connor says with a long exhale through his nose. "I'll see you soon." He begins walking backward down the hallway. Away from me. The exact opposite direction I want him to go right now.

But he came. He sang. And now he must go.

I take a few frantic steps forward to close the gap between us, crushing myself to him in an embrace. I've waited for months to be held by him, and I need this, even if it's brief. One of his hands finds the back of my head, the other splays out across my lower back. I close my eyes and breathe him in, savoring the safety of his arms encircling me, the press of his firm chest on my cheek. Everything I've craved in the time we've spent apart.

Well, not quite everything.

"I'll see you later," he says into my hair, "Stewie Two."

I reluctantly release him, giving his hand one more squeeze. "Have the best time tonight. You deserve to celebrate."

"Believe me," he says with a smirk. "I plan to."

Warmth swirls through my stomach as he and Austin briskly make their way out the door.

I stand there watching him leave, wanting nothing more than to chase him down again.

When I finally look over at my brother, he's already watching me.

"You okay?" he asks.

I nod. "Let's go back in."

He gives my shoulder a reassuring squeeze. "We've got tickets to Connor's show, and Austin invited us to the after-party. When things wind down here, I'll drive you over to the venue. Hopefully, we can catch the end of Connor's set."

"No way," I say in disbelief. "That's what you were talking to Austin about?"

Trent nods. "Connor didn't want you to feel obligated to be there, but he wanted to give you the option. He knows how important this wedding is to you."

I give my brother a side-hug, resting my head on his shoulder for a moment. "Thank you, Trent. You're a good brother."

"Just give me the signal," he says, tugging the door to the reception open. "And I'll get you out of here."

"Done," I say, grinning. "But not before you accompany me to the dance floor."

"I don't dance," Trent says flatly.

"Don't tell that to the horde of Luke's cousins at table nine," I say, giving him a pointed look. "They'll be heartbroken."

Together, we rejoin our family in celebrating Luke and Lainey, my heart filled to bursting.

Chapter 33

Connor

Album release night is by far the best show we've played on this tour. The band was tight, my voice on lock. The sold-out crowd was stoked, giving really good energy from the moment we stepped out onstage.

Tonight's show is at Cannery Hall, located near The Gulch neighborhood in Nashville. The audience is young and wild, full of enthusiastic Marthas who somehow already know the words to most of my new songs even though they were just released today.

I'm having the time of my life, but nothing can keep my mind from wandering to what I plan to do once the show is over. I don't know how late the wedding is supposed to go, but I will play a ten-song encore if I have to. Whatever I've got to do to make sure Ella Mae can be here to hear me sing.

We're two songs away from the end of the set when I see movement side-stage near my sound tech's setup. I glance over, and a rush pulses through my body. She's here.

My mind blanks on the lyrics as Ella Mae smiles over at me. I swallow, then let out a laugh into my mic, having to find my place again. Thankfully, the band doesn't miss a beat. If anyone mentions it, I'll chalk it up to album-release-day nerves.

"Nashville," I say after the song ends, taking a swig from my water bottle. "Thank you so much for having us tonight. It has been an absolute pleasure to share these new songs with you."

The crowd cheers, and I can't help but smile offstage at the beautiful girl watching me. She's wearing the smile I've been aching to see for months, and now that she's here, it feels surreal. Like she's a mirage or a figment of my imagination. Too good to be true.

"We've got one more song for you," I say. "If you know the words, sing along."

Fox's kick drum starts up, signaling the intro to the last song of the set. I force myself back to the present moment, remembering that I only get to do this once. I've got to enjoy it.

The song is over as quickly as it begins. The band plays a killer outro as we close out the set.

"Goodnight, Nashville!" I say, raising a hand in gratitude before exiting stage left to where Ella Mae is waiting for me. I amble down the stairs with the band on my heels, high off the show I just played and the continual roar of the crowd out front. I tug my monitors out of my ears and stride toward her, not even caring that my team and bandmates are watching.

I take her face with both hands, tilting her head up toward mine and bringing my lips down over hers. I can feel her tremble under the pressure of my hands as I kiss her. I breathe her in, slowly allowing our lips to part before pressing a soft kiss to each of her cheeks and her forehead. Her skin is warm under my mouth, and all I want to do is continue to kiss her until we're both thoroughly satisfied. She's still wearing her bridesmaid's dress, and though she looks beautiful in anything, I'm awestruck by how stunning she is in this green, fitted gown.

I have to resist sweeping her up and carrying her far, far away from here, knowing that we'll have time to reunite properly when we're alone.

"You sounded amazing," she says into my ear, the only way I'm able to hear her over the chanting from the crowd. They're begging for an encore.

"I'm so glad you came," I say, cradling her face in my hands. I press another kiss to her mouth, and she smiles against my lips.

Only after she's pulled away, her cheeks flushing pink, do I bother to look around us. My bandmates are snickering and giving me loaded looks. Mallory is smiling at me like I've done something to make her proud, and Trent looks like he wants to wipe the floor with my face.

I give him a little shrug, and he shakes his head in return.

"We've got a few more songs to play," I say, dropping my hands to pull Ella Mae to my chest in a hug. "Then I'm all yours."

"Can't wait," she says, closing her eyes briefly as I hold her to me.

"ENCORE! ENCORE!" Fox yells in sync with the crowd as he walks by. "Kiss her again!"

I laugh, giving him a shove.

"You ready?" Fox says, twirling his drumsticks between his fingers.

I nod, taking my place at the base of the stairs, allowing the band to pass me. The high-pitched screaming resumes as they take the stage.

Ella Mae gives me a little thumbs-up. I've played every show before this one without her, and now that I've gotten a taste of what it would be like to have her with me, I know I'll never be able to settle for anything less.

We kill the encore, each of us hyped at a whole new level at the end of a near-perfect show.

I'm wired when we come offstage for the last time, filled with buzzing energy. I've still got to attend the after-party Mallory planned for us, but as soon as that winds down, I know just who I want to spend the rest of my evening celebrating with.

***

"Don't keep him out too late," Trent yells across the parking lot to his sister.

"Don't worry, I will," Ella Mae calls back.

I've got my arm draped around her shoulders, her body pulled tight to mine as we walk out to the tour bus. Paul trails along behind us at a distance. The rest of the band and crew are still chillin' inside the venue, but I bought Ella Mae and myself a moment alone by telling everyone I was going to show her around the bus.

"Right," Fox had said with a heavy wink. "You kids enjoy yourselves."

It's well past midnight, so the parking lot is cleared of lingering fans. We reach the tour bus, and I tug the door open, allowing Ella Mae to climb up the steep steps ahead of me. Paul stays outside, giving me a nod as I close the door behind me.

"Don't mind the smell," I say as the stiff scent of air freshener hits me like a wall. "A bunch of sweaty guys have been living here for two months."

Ella Mae laughs, and the sound makes my smile widen. I've missed her laugh. I've missed everything about her. Pictures, videos, and voicemails don't do her justice. Having her in front of me in radiant 3D and full color is a sensory overload.

"How charming," she says, gesturing to the stack of packaged cookies resting on the tiny counter next to the sink in the kitchen area. Crumbs litter the surrounding area.

"Pre-show ritual."

"You, too?" she says, turning to look at me in surprise. "I thought you were a no-sweets kind of guy."

"I have my vices," I say, blatantly lacing my words with meaning.

Ella Mae turns around to face me, continuing to walk backward down the narrow hall of wall-to-wall bunk beds.

"Such as?" She lifts her chin, revealing the smooth skin of her neck. She stops walking, both hands resting on the bunks on either side of her. I take two steps, wrapping one arm around her waist to bring my body flush with hers. Her lips ease into a smile, her eyes fixed on my mouth.

"Feisty blondes," I say, nudging her jaw upward with my nose. "Can't resist them."

"Mmm," she hums as I press a lingering kiss to her neck. She brings a hand to the back of my head, closing her eyes as I slowly mark her soft skin with my lips. I want to savor every press of my lips against hers, to leisurely explore the mouth I've waited two months to taste.

"What about you?" I breathe into her ear before gently taking her earlobe between my teeth. I grip her waist, turning us both so her back is pressed against the bunks. I hang my hands from the edge of the bunk above her head, trapping her between my arms. She looks up at me, her eyes burning into mine, lips tilted in a smile.

"Blond musicians," she sighs. "The natural variety, of course."

I laugh against her lips, teasing her with a kiss on the corner of her mouth. Ella Mae fists my shirt with both hands, bringing her mouth to mine. Gone is the restraint we've both patiently exercised tonight. She kisses me hungrily, her hands finding the edge of my t-shirt and sliding it upward. I keep my hands above my head, clasping the bunk overhead as her fingertips graze up my waist and over my stomach.

She pulls back suddenly, pressing her thumbs into my torso. She looks up at me with wide eyes. "You weren't joking."

"Told you they were real."

Ella Mae sighs into me, her lips finding mine again. My hands tangle in her long hair, coaxing her lips apart with my own.

After indulgently kissing me for several minutes, she pulls away, giving me a teasing nudge with her nose against mine. "Which bunk is yours?"

"Why?" I ask, kissing the corner of her jaw underneath her ear. "Want to see it?"

She nods. I don't hesitate, reaching down to sweep her up into my arms. She giggles, wrapping her arms around my neck as I carry her to the back of the bus.

"This is where you sleep?" she asks as I slowly lower her down on the wrap-around couch.

"During the day, my bed converts into this," I say, taking a seat next to her on the couch. "It gives us some space to hang out while we're driving."

"How nice," she says, gently brushing a thumb over my cheekbone. I grab her hand and press a kiss to her palm.

"It is," I admit, standing up to ease the door to the back section of the bus closed. "I'm the only one who can have real privacy."

"What do you need that for?" she asks with a teasing smile.

"So I can write songs about you without everyone giving me crap."

"About *me*?" She presses a hand to her chest in mock surprise.

I slide closer, laying a palm on the couch behind her. She leans back into the corner of the couch. "It's becoming annoying, actually. I just want to write you into every song."

"Hmmm." She smiles at me as I take her face in my hands. "Nobody's ever written a song for me before."

"Consider yourself warned," I say, tracing her bottom lip with my thumb. "My whole catalog from here on out is officially yours."

I move to kiss her again, but she speaks before I can do so.

"Does that mean I get a cut of the royalties?" she says, her eyes sparkling. "I'm flat broke, you know."

I pull away an inch so I can meet her eyes. Those gorgeous, green eyes that I've had in my head for months.

"How about you get me instead?" I ask. "Then you'll be rich twice over."

"How so?"

"You'll have more money than you'll know what to do with," I say. "And you'll be rich"—I try to keep the smile from my face—"in...blessings."

"Blessings?" she laughs. "What sort of blessings?"

"The usual. Happiness, health." I swallow. "Love."

Her smile flattens out, her eyes flicking back and forth between mine. Her voice comes out soft, almost a whisper. "You love me, Connor Cane?"

I let myself take in her beautiful face. The light that shines from her eyes. The way she brightens up every corner of my life. I'm certain now of how I feel about her.

And it's no fleeting, temporary feeling. It's real. And she needs to know it.

"I think I do, Ella Mae Stewart." I swallow. "I love you."

She smiles then, gripping the back of my neck with her hand. "Well, isn't that convenient," she says, her eyes glistening. "Because I love you, too."

I now know that Hunter's words were true. I may not have a home in a physical sense, but Ella Mae is it.

She's home to me.

I capture her lips with mine, sinking into another blissful kiss.

⸻

"If we decide to do this," I say. "Things might get messy for you."

We're parked just outside Ella Mae's apartment, getting ready to say goodnight. We're holding hands, our faces close as we talk quietly in the darkness of the truck cab.

"I'm asking you to give up a lot if you choose to date me," I say slowly. "Things are going to change. More paps might come after you. People will probably spread lies about you. You're going to start getting recognized in public—"

"I know," she says gently. "Believe me, I've had a lot of time to think about this with you gone."

She looks out the windshield thoughtfully.

"These past months without you have helped me realize what I'd be giving up if I let you go," she says, her eyes wide and vulnerable. "I can't do it."

"But is it worth it?" I ask quietly, finally voicing the question that has been on my mind since I left for tour. "Giving things up to be with me?"

"I think the real question is," she says finally, "are *we* worth it?"

"You know what my answer is," I say, brushing my thumb across her cheekbone. "I'd do anything for you."

She gives me a little smile. "Anything?"

"Name your price."

"Hmm," she says with a tilt of her head. "Jesse McCartney tickets. With the VIP meet-n-greet package."

I snort.

She looks at me expectantly, one eyebrow raised.

"You're serious."

"I don't play when it comes to my boy Jesse."

I give her hand a firm shake. "Done."

"I hope you know," she says, "I feel the same about you, Connor Cane. I want this. We have to try this thing out and see where it could go."

My chest inflates with relief at her words.

"Tell me your concerns," I say. "Let's talk through them."

She shifts in her seat. "You know I'm worried about my privacy. I get that it's unrealistic to think that things will stay the same, but is there anything we can do?"

"Absolutely," I say, pulling from my own experiences. "We can get you your own security guard," I suggest. "Outfit your apartment with a good security system. We'll keep our relationship off socials. Be strategic about where we go and when."

"Most grocery stores deliver nowadays," she adds. "And I guess we can get takeout."

"You wanna see a movie?" I say. "I'll rent out the theater."

She laughs. "I like it, Connor Cane. It doesn't sound impossible."

We continue our conversation, calming Ella Mae's fears and helping me feel more confident in my ability to balance the demands of my career with our relationship.

"Maybe we can get a dog," she suddenly says, almost like she doesn't want me to hear it.

"A dog?"

"For safety purposes," she clarifies.

"A small dog," I say. "One that can come on tour with us."

"Done." She yawns, trying to cover it up unsuccessfully.

"Let's get you inside," I say.

"We still have a lot to figure out," she says with her arms wrapped around my waist outside the door to her apartment. "But I feel better about things already."

"Me, too," I say, pressing a kiss to her hair. "We'll take things one step at a time."

She sighs into my chest, closing her eyes. "Preach, Jordin Sparks."

"What?"

"Never mind."

I kiss her goodnight, walking back to Frank with a thoughtful frown.

I'm going to have to call in some favors to get those dang Jesse McCartney tickets.

Chapter 34

Ella Mae

"Are you feeling alright?" Connor asks, placing a hand on my knee. "Do you need a break? This is a lot for someone like—"

I glare up at him, hand poised over my notebook where I've been scribbling away for nearly two hours.

"Like what, Connor? You wanna finish that sentence?"

"Nope," he mumbles.

"Then I will," Trent says from his perch on the couch behind us. "Take a break, Ella Mae. This is entirely out of character for you."

I look between them, holding my chin stubbornly. "Well, gentleman, this is what's required of a woman who wants to date a celebrity. *Planning.*" I spit the last word out with a shiver of revulsion.

Connor hides a grin behind his knuckles, scrolling through his calendar on his phone. We've been mapping out the last month of the tour, trying to figure out when and how we can see each other.

"I'm proud of you, Ella Mae," Mallory says from her seat to my left. "Trust me. I get it. You artist types are wired differently. That's why I'm here."

I meet Connor's eyes and arch an eyebrow. *So there.*

"This flight might work," Mallory says, turning her laptop toward me. I lean forward to see her screen. "You'd get into Charlotte around ten in the morning, so you could come straight to the venue for soundcheck."

Connor called Mallory yesterday, and we both explained our desire to pursue a relationship. Whatever it required, we were willing to put in the effort to make things work long distance.

Thankfully, she'd been more than supportive, recruiting members of Connor's team to help rearrange his schedule in the coming months to give him more time off.

Time off to spend with me.

We're both going to have to make concessions if we want to be together, with me traveling to see him for two weeks of shows, followed by him spending two weeks with me at home.

Once the tour is over, he'll have more freedom. Time to figure out the next steps in his career and personal life.

After Mallory books flights that allow us to see each other twice over the next month, she packs up her things. "I've got an appointment this afternoon."

"With Fox?" Connor asks innocently.

"What?" Mallory becomes flustered. "No, of course not. Why would you say that?"

"No reason," he says, feigning innocence as he leads her to the door. "Have fun, Mal."

Trent mutters something about getting a bite to eat and swipes Connor's truck keys from the counter.

"Careful, Trent," Connor warns. "Frank's a bit of a match-maker these days."

"Don't even try to blame all of this"—Trent gestures to Connor and me—"on a truck."

"It's true." I shrug. "Frank made me do it."

Connor grins. "Good ol' Frank."

Once we're alone again, Connor stalks toward me, tugging me into a big bear hug. I lean into him, curving my arms around his waist.

"What are your plans tomorrow?" he asks.

"You tell me," I say. "You're the one leaving. How do you want to spend your last day off?"

"With you," he says, burying into my neck. I feel his lips on my skin, and I squeeze him tighter. "I've got something special planned for us tomorrow," he mumbles against my neck.

"Really?" I say. "I'm intrigued."

"You should be," he says, lifting his head so I can see his face. "I know I don't need to say it—"

"Then don't."

"But we can't be late," he says, his expression serious.

I steel him with my gaze. "Connor Cane, I'm only going to say this once, so you'd better listen up and listen good."

He looks at me expectantly, his lip twitching as he tries to hold back a smile.

"When it comes to you," I say. "I'll always be on time."

"Can I get that in writing?"

I press a kiss to his lips, even though he doesn't deserve it.

I may be sweating from the effort and wearing mismatched socks, but it's 8:25 a.m., and I'm ready and waiting by my front door.

This is a monumental occasion. And what better way to celebrate than by spending my morning with Connor Cane?

"Morning, Frank," I say, giving him a pat on the right head-light as I pass.

"Be honest," Connor says as I take my seat in the truck. "If you had to choose between me and Frank, who would you pick?"

"Don't make me." I gasp. "I couldn't possibly choose."

He gives me a slow smile, his eyes lingering on my face for a moment before he starts driving. "I was thinking I could leave Frank here for you to drive while I'm gone, if you'd like."

I feel like I'm being played. "Is this a joke?" My lips part in surprise. "You would let *me* drive Frank?"

"That way I don't have to buy you a dog. You can feed him, take him on walks..."

"Frank is more than a pet," I say reverently. "He's family."

"I know," Connor says, reaching across the console to take my hand in his. "Would you take care of him for me?"

"I would be honored," I say, and though I smile, I'm quivering with emotion inside. It's a small gesture, but it means the world that he'd trust me with his truck. Frank holds so many happy memories for me. For us.

"Do I get a gas stipend?" I ask, patting the dash. "I love you, buddy, but you're a guzzler."

Connor laughs.

"So where are you taking me this morning?" I ask. Connor has got the windows rolled down slightly, letting the morning air swirl through the cab of the truck. Spring blossoms and dew.

"You'll see," he says, looking far too pleased about whatever secret he's keeping from me.

"Okay," he says. "You can open your eyes now."

I obey, popping one eye open, cautiously keeping the other closed in case he's taken me to a haunted house at nine in the morning. No, sir. No clowns are coming for me today.

Instead, I realize I'm standing at the entrance to a familiar building. The tall glass doors are etched with waves and dolphins. Ethereal instrumental music is leaking out from inside.

I gasp. "The aquarium?" I say in disbelief, doing a slow turn to face Connor with my jaw agape.

"I had to," he says, a delighted smile on his face. "I told you I'd help you make up for the last time you came here."

"Stop it." I glance around, noting that the aquarium is significantly less busy than the last time I'd come.

"We only have an hour before it opens to the public," he says, taking my hand in his.

"You booked out the aquarium for me?" I say, my chest growing warm.

"And," he says, leaning closer, "I made sure to wear my contacts. Just for you."

I laugh. "What a relief." I link my arm through his as we enter the building. "Thank you, Connor."

"Don't thank me yet," he says. "We're here so early all the fish might still be asleep."

Thankfully, he's wrong. As we walk from exhibit to exhibit, hand in hand, my heart feels like it's encased in a bubble of happiness.

"I could get used to this," I say as we watch the glowing jellyfish lazily float around their tank. "No hordes of children blocking my view. No teenagers occupying the shadowy corners."

"Shadowy corners?" Connor says, his lips tilting up in a grin. We make our way into a covered tunnel where the resident octopus lives. "Does this count as a shadowy corner?"

I squint around in the dark. "I'd say so."

"In that case—"

Before I can register what's happening, he's got me backed into a wall in the darkest part of the tunnel. He ducks his head, dragging his lips across my jawline.

"Connor Robin—"

"Hey," he mumbles against my mouth. "You keep my terrible middle name out of this."

"Oh, for the love," I say as he presses a kiss underneath my ear. "What makes you think I want to be kissed like a handsy teenager in a dark corner? What if a security camera picks this up?"

He snorts, ignoring my feeble protests, winding his fingers into my hair with one hand, using the other to gently nudge my chin upward to bring my lips to his.

Wholehearted. Soulful. His kiss both makes my head spin and grounds me with its sincerity. I smile against his lips, and he grins.

"You like it when I sing to you, right?"

"Maybe." I wrap my arms around his neck. "Why?"

"Mind if I sing you a little something right now?" he asks. He takes a deep breath and presses his lips to the shell of my ear.

"*Are you a trout or a minnow or an albacore—*"

His sweet serenade of my fishing song is cut short by my laughter ringing through the tunnel.

Epilogue

Ella Mae

O *ne year later...*

"How do I look?" I ask. My dress swishes against my legs as I turn to take in my reflection in the floor-length mirror.

Connor eases into the space behind me, wrapping one arm around my shoulders. His other hand lands on the swell of my growing belly. I meet his eyes in the mirror, and he presses a soft kiss to my temple.

"Stunning," he says, turning me to face him. "Gorgeous. Ravishing."

"Good," I sigh. "Because I feel like a busted can of biscuits."

Connor laughs, folding me into his arms. My six-month-pregnant belly prevents us from hugging as closely as we used to, but we sure do try.

"How are you feeling?" I ask.

"Pretty good," he says with a nervous grin. "You?"

"I'm a wreck," I say candidly. "A bundle of nerves."

"A bundle of nerves carrying our bundle of joy," Connor quips, looking far too pleased with himself.

"Didn't know I married a comedian," I mutter. "You should stick to writing country songs."

Connor tsks, pressing a hand affectionately to my middle. "Don't listen to your mother," he says in a loud whisper. "She thinks I'm hilarious." Then he leans down and presses a warm kiss to my belly. I watch him rise, admiring the gentle strength and confidence he exudes as my husband and soon-to-be father of our daughter.

After only three months of dating long distance, Connor decided he was ready to lock things down. He buttered me up with an epic Jesse McCartney concert, followed by a late-night stop at our spot on Mooreville Road where we shared our favorite chicken strips and fries.

"I got a marriage proposal the other day," Connor said, sitting next to me on Frank's tailgate. "From a woman at the car wash."

"Frank!" I scolded, giving him an affectionate pat. "Why do you have to be such a good-looking truck?"

Connor laughed.

"And? What did you say?" I asked.

"I tried to let her down gently."

"Naturally," I said. "That's good of you."

"I told her..." Connor said, taking my hand in his, "that I'd already met my wife."

My heart started thumping wildly in my chest then. His blue eyes found mine, bright and sincere. No longer joking.

"Connor," I said, my tone carrying a warning. "Are you seeing someone else?"

"What?" he laughed, looking at me in that incredulous way he does when he finds me funny.

"Someone who is marriage material?" I said as he brought my legs up to rest over his lap. "Someone who meets all of Connor Cane's lofty requirements?"

"Last I checked," Connor said, "*you* were the one with the lofty requirements."

We stared at each other for a beat.

"Ella Mae," Connor said softly, his expression softening. "I've put a lot of thought into this—"

"Wait."

He looked at me expectantly.

"You realize that once we have this conversation," I said, "you're going to be stuck with me. Forever."

"Yes," Connor said. "I know that."

"No take-backs."

He stared at me, blinking twice.

"Are you done being difficult?"

"For now," I said with narrowed eyes and a half-hidden smile.

Connor pulled me close then, grinning like I'd already given him my answer.

"Let's get married," he said affectionately, making my pulse race. "Let me be your husband. Let me make you my wife."

I couldn't joke my way out of such a heartfelt, earnest request. And so, I framed his face with my hands and pressed a slow kiss to his mouth.

Connor slipped off the tailgate, taking both my hands in his. Then he dropped one knee down in the dirt and pulled out a ring.

"Ella Mae Stewart." He looked up at me, a brilliant smile on his handsome face. "Marry me?"

I had no comebacks, no desire to tease or string him along. A simple, "Yes," fell from my lips, and from that moment on, I knew I'd never doubt again.

It had always been Connor.

Two months later, we tied the knot in front of our closest family and friends on a blazing-hot August day in the middle of an orchard. Connor took two weeks off for our honeymoon in St. Thomas.

And then we got the unexpected gift of a positive pregnancy test two months after that.

A rap sounds at the hotel room door. "The car is waiting out front," Mallory says as she enters. Her gaze sweeps over us, and she smiles in approval. "You two look fantastic." She gives me a quick hug and squeezes Connor's shoulder. "I'm so proud of you both."

Connor takes my hand in his, and we share a look of nervous excitement. While today is a big day for my husband, it's also a big day for me.

Connor's self-titled second record racked up some pretty amazing nominations at tonight's award show, including Album of the Year. Which means if this record wins out in any category, he becomes an award-winning artist. And by default, I gain the title of award-winning songwriter.

But it gets better.

A song I'd written with Harper Jackson is up against Connor's song "Cry Baby" for Song of the Year. Though we've sparred good-naturedly over this turn of events, ultimately we're pulling for each other. We're a unit now. A team in every sense of the word. His wins are my wins, too.

We're shuttled over to The Ryman, hands entwined in Connor's lap. Our driver pulls up to the artist entrance and gets us checked in.

"You ready?" Connor asks once he's out, extending a hand to help me descend from the car.

"Make way, people," I say. "Wide load coming through."

He rolls his eyes.

"You've got one job tonight," I say. "And one job only."

Connor looks at me expectantly.

"If I trip, you'd better be there to catch me."

He smiles at me then, lightly guiding me by the elbow as we begin our walk down the red carpet. "I've got you, darlin'."

This is our first time publicly stepping out as husband and wife and the first time anyone will see that I'm pregnant. I debated skipping the event altogether, but Connor convinced me that we needed to experience this monumental night side by side. It's admittedly uncomfortable for me to stand with him and smile in front of a wall of blinding lights as the press take our photos. But I remind myself that they're helping us place a bookmark in our story. Connor keeps me steady on my feet, and I tell myself that, one day, our daughter will get a kick out of looking at these photos of her mom all gussied up.

We're hustled off the red carpet and into the venue, finding our seats before the show is set to begin. I take a moment to scan the crowd, feeling more at ease as I recognize a few Back Road Records executives, Connor's bandmates, and our favorite producer, Drew, seated a few rows back.

Connor gives a little snort, and I whip back around, curious to see what it is he finds so amusing.

I follow his gaze to a couple being seated further down our row. Connor and I share a look. We don't have to say anything, but I know we're both thinking that Mitch Allen has dialed things up a notch to compensate for his recent public scandal.

Several producers and songwriters had come forward, claiming that Mitch's label and team had mismanaged their projects, shorting them on royalties and providing bogus contracts. When Connor got wind of the news, he and his lawyer quickly approached me with a plan to rectify my similar plight. I reluctantly agreed, not expecting anything to come of it. But when a check with a generous number of zeros had shown up in the mail after Mitch's lawyers had settled things, I hadn't felt a stitch of guilt cashing that thing in.

His gaudy orange suit and flashy stud earrings make him look like he belongs in a prison cell. I'm sure it's intentional—Mitch likes to walk on the edge—but the damage to his already precarious reputation has been done. He might still have the loyalty of his fans, but nobody in Nashville is going to be eager to work with him anytime soon.

One of Mitch's songs is up against ours for Song of the Year. I don't even care if neither of us takes that award home as long as Mitch walks away empty-handed tonight.

As the lights begin to dim and the cameras get into their positions, I lean over to Connor. "Whatever happens," I say in a low voice, "remember that you've worked so incredibly hard to be here. You've earned it."

"Thank you," he says with a sigh, finding my hand again.

The show is filled with scripted gags and big-budget performances. As the hosts gear up to announce Song of the Year, Connor and I are twitching with nervous energy.

Harper's photo lashes across the screens situated on either side of the stage, followed by Connor, then Mitch. There are several other artists in the mix, but my mind doesn't even register the other nominees after seeing the three of them pitted against each other in quick succession.

"The award for Song of the Year goes to..." The presenter pulls out the card to read the results, and my eyes lock on it like he's Willy Wonka holding the last golden ticket right there in his hands.

I've left my body at this point. My soul is currently floating above me in the air, my heartbeat ticking loudly in my ears as the silence stretches on.

"Harper Jackson!"

I watch a flurry of blonde curls implode in the row in front of me as Harper jumps to her feet. She's sobbing, quickly being embraced by members of her family and her team.

"Get up there!" Connor's voice brings me back to myself. "It's your song, woman!"

He stands, helping me to my feet and gently guiding me into the aisle. Connor hands me off to Drew, who gallantly takes my arm, beaming with pride. As the producer on the song, this is his win just as much as it is mine.

It's dream-like, this moment we're experiencing. I miraculously make it up the stairs, falling behind Harper as she strides forward to accept her award. I attempt to blend into the small group of Back Road execs gathered onstage behind her, but Drew nudges me to the front. I'm most definitely going to be in the shot of her acceptance speech, and there's nothing I can do about it.

I stare out at the crowd, blinded by the heat of the stage lights, suddenly feeling light-headed and a little dizzy.

"Oh my GOODNESS!" Harper cries into the microphone. "How did this happen?"

My gaze lands on Connor. He gives me a reassuring grin, compelling me to try to be present and soak in this accomplishment.

"Thank you to my team at Back Road," Harper says. "And to my brilliant co-writer, Ella Mae"—she turns and gives me a smile—"for helping me write the things my heart didn't know it needed to say."

I smile back, barely hearing the rest of her speech. When she's finished, the group as a whole shuffles down the stairs to our seats. I'm hugged by no less than seven people before I make it to my row, and my capacity for having my belly touched has nearly expired for the night.

Connor embraces me then, holding me tight as the show goes to a commercial break. "I knew you had it in you, Stewie Two." His constant confidence in me brings a wave of emotion to my chest. "But you'd better watch out next year," he says into my ear as we take our seats. "I'm coming for your title."

I snort. "Bring it on."

Connor rests his hand on my leg as the show resumes, and we have to wait for the hosts to cycle through several more categories before his second chance to win an award arrives.

When his album cover shows up on the big screen, I let out a shameless, Martha-worthy whoop. He laughs, but I can feel his nerves in the death grip he's got on my hand as we anticipate the moment we've waited for since the record came out a year ago.

"And the award for Album of the Year goes to..." The host opens her envelope and smiles as she reads her card. I rest a

hand over my belly, my breath growing shallow as we anticipate the result.

No matter what happens, we're grateful to be here. We've
worked hard. We deserve it.

The host looks into the camera, and her grin widens.

"Connor Cane!"

We look at each other, open-mouthed, frozen to our seats as
the venue breaks out into supportive applause. He tugs me up
to my feet, pulling me in for an elated hug.

"We did it," he says, and I can hear the relief in his voice. "We
both did it."

"Get up there!" I say, making room for him to pass me,
which is no easy feat considering the size of my belly.

Connor buttons up his suit jacket on his way up to the stage
to accept his award, beaming like a kid on Christmas morning.
My cheeks hurt from smiling, and I feel tears gathering in my
eyes as I watch my husband accept the award he's worked so
hard for.

"Wow," he breathes into the microphone with a disbelieving
laugh. "I'm in shock." The crowd laughs at his candor. "This
means everything to me, to be here tonight." His eyes find
mine, and I give him a teary smile.

"I'd like to thank my beautiful wife, Ella Mae..." He grins
at me, and the cameras close in to capture my reaction. "For
making this record what it is. I'm so incredibly proud of these
songs, and because of her, there will be many, many more."

He graciously thanks his team, his family, and the fans
who've supported his music. Regrettably, he does call them
fans and not Marthas on live television. I'll be sure to take this
up with him later.

When he walks back to his seat, he's got a golden glow surrounding him. It's blinding. He's a beautiful soul, that Connor Cane. And I couldn't be more proud to call him mine.

———

"I'm too pregnant for this," I grumble as Connor hoists me up awkwardly onto Frank's tailgate later that night.

He kisses both of my cheeks affectionately. "I don't think I've ever been more attracted to you." His eyes travel the length of me. "You in that dress...mmm."

I give him a reluctant smile. "You're generous."

He lays his big palms on my thighs, tilting his head. The fondness in his gaze fills my chest with sunny warmth.

"I love you," he says.

I rest a hand on his cheek. "I love you, too, you darling man."

He fits his lips to mine, kissing me soft and slow. My breath catches, still, every time.

Connor settles next to me on the tailgate, handing me the milkshake I'd ordered in the drive-through. "For you, madam."

After the long day we've had, all I want to do is snuggle up with my husband in our cozy bed at our apartment. But he insisted on keeping our tradition of a late-night fast-food run, enjoyed at our spot on Mooreville Road. I wasn't about to kill his post-win vibe, so I'm counting on this milkshake to keep me awake a little bit longer.

Our awards are carefully situated in the backseat of the truck, side-by-side evidence of the fulfillment of both of our long-held dreams.

"So," I say, swirling my straw in my cup. "What's next for the great Connor Cane?"

"I could ask you the same question." He gives a little laugh through his nose. "I don't know how we're supposed to top this."

We sit in comfortable silence, taking in the spread of twinkling stars overhead.

"I was thinking," Connor says, "that it might be good for me to take some time off once Baby Girl gets here."

"A novel idea," I say flatly.

He gives me an impatient look, taking my milkshake from my hands. "Let me explain." I gesture for him to continue as he drinks from my cup. "I've got a new project in mind for next year."

I look at him with raised eyebrows. "Oh?"

"Yeah." He runs a hand over his mouth before returning my milkshake. Then he reaches back into the truck bed. From the dark back corner, he slides out a wooden stake, sharpened on one end.

"Are we warding off vampires?" I ask, snapping my fingers in fake disappointment. "Rats. I didn't bring any garlic."

He laughs, shaking his head as he slides off the tailgate. He takes a few steps away from the truck and drives the stake into the earth.

"I was thinking the front porch would go right about..."—he pats the stake—"here."

"Front porch?" I slowly set down my milkshake, confused. "What are you going on about?" I say, moving to scoot off the tailgate. Connor strides over, assisting me to the ground. He's wearing an even bigger smile than the one I saw on his face at the award show.

His hands span my hips, and I settle my grip on his strong arms.

"I've been keeping a secret from you," he says, entirely self-satisfied.

I narrow my eyes. "I don't like secrets."

"You're going to like this one," he says, taking my hand and leading me to the stake. He takes me by the shoulders, turning me to face the field that sprawls out behind Frank.

"We're going to build a house," he says into my ear. "Right here on Mooreville Road."

My jaw drops. My heart swells. It takes me a minute for his words to sink in.

"A *house*?" I say. "But— How did you— How can we—"

"I bought as much of this property as I could."

I press my palms to my cheeks, my mouth forming an O.

"You bought this for us?"

He nods. "I had to. It's ours. It's got to be."

And right then, I feel a tiny pop of a kick from Baby Girl inside my belly.

I gasp, grabbing Connor's hand and bringing it around to my stomach so he can feel her moving, too. He rests his chin on my shoulder, his nose in my neck as we wait for her to kick again.

"Did you feel that?"

"Hey, little one," he says softly. "She knows we're here."

"This will be her home," I say.

"*Our* home."

I sniffle. Connor turns me to face him, fitting me into his arms.

"Are you happy?" he asks.

"I've never been happier," I say, sighing with contentment with my ear pressed against his heart.

"Good."

I love the way his voice rumbles from his chest through me.

"How could it get any better than this?" I ask, squeezing the man I love with every ounce of my strength, standing in the field where our future home will stand.

Connor takes my face in both of his hands and brushes the tip of his nose across mine. "I can think of a few things we could do to make tonight *even* better."

Then he slants his mouth over mine and kisses me.

And he's right. Things are looking up for Ella Mae Cane.

THE END

Enjoyed Ella Mae and Connor's story? I'd love for you to leave a review on Amazon or Goodreads!

Acknowledgments

This book was an absolute joy to write, in part because of my passion for music and songwriting, but mostly because of you lovely readers who have shown the Falling for Franklin series so much love!

Thank you to everyone who took a chance on *The Retreat*, who championed *The Make Up*, and enthusiastically shared about *The Holiduel*. Your excitement and anticipation around Connor and Ella Mae's story motivated me to write it well. I hope it was worth the wait!

To the Bookstagram community—you're the real MVP's! Thank you for tagging me in your gorgeous, aesthetic posts, sharing about my books, and for building me up and constantly making me laugh. I adore you all!

Thank you to Lenae and Amanda for critiquing an early draft of this book. You're my teammates now, whether you like it or not. I'm so grateful for your feedback, your confidence in me and for giving me ideas for the perfect epilogue.

To my wonderful friend and editor Heather, thank you for your hilarious commentary and meticulous edits, and to Jenn for once again helping to make this book shine!

I'd be remiss if I didn't thank my Heavenly Father for blessing me with the innate desire to create happy, beautiful things, and for helping me find the words when the sleep deprivation made it hard to do so.

To Cayden—my real life cinnamon roll hero, and my boys. You are my world!

And finally, to my readers—thank you for spending time in Franklin with me. More books are on their way!

About The Author

Hailey Gardiner writes cheeky, sweet romantic comedies inspired by the hilarious and awkward moments that make up her real life. While she is best known for her career as an acoustic folk singer/songwriter, Hailey has been writing stories as long as she's been writing songs. Hailey is a master at quoting movies, a dark chocolate fanatic, and lives in Utah with her husband and son.

Official Website: www.haileygardiner.com

Instagram & TikTok: @authorhaileygardiner

Made in the USA
Columbia, SC
24 October 2024

45000499R10207